'It's a riotous, tumbling, hilarious, terrible, sad, powerful, defiant, triumphant and riveting account of an astonishing story. It brings the age alive and it arouses the strongest feelings we are capable of, those feelings instinctive to us when we are young and which should never die—our deep outrage at unfairness, injustice and bullying. The defining phrase—"the bumpiest ride on the biggest ever rock'n'rollercoaster".'

STEPHEN FRY

'It's a gripping story. What rogues. Nice to read a story which shows lawyers in a good light—and is touchingly optimistic. I wish the TV show could have been ROCK BOTTOM rather than ROCK FOLLIES.'

SIR RICHARD EYRE

'A long court-case makes for gripping reading. Add a triple helping of mouthy heroines who will walk all over m'learned friends, and you have the bones of Annabel Leventon's engrossing, enchanting memoir The Real Rock Follies: a narrative fuelled by furious resentment, a justifiable desire for revenge, and a keen recollection of that muddled, flamboyant era, the 1970s.'

VALERIE GROVE

'You will never read a more gripping story; this is the Truth Behind the Lies. You laugh & cry with these magic madams. The hideous betrayal, the scumbags who do anything for money—all here—all true & written with flair & passion & humour.'

MIRIAM MARGOLYES

'This brilliant book captures the excitement and disasters of a girl singing threesome. Annabel Leventon is a natural writer.'

T0017150

'She tells the tale so well. I kept thinking of superior journalism, the way the Insight team used to tell stories, the way that Bernstein and Woodward described the Watergate shenanigans. She has a way of pinning down place and time with a few brushstrokes, whilst never letting the tension slip. At the same time it is unquestionably her story, and her thoughts, hopes, triumphs and setbacks give the story a beating heart. It has clarity of intention—and the tribulations and trial of the three girls (who all come across as very strong well-drawn characters) is what binds it all together.

The Rock Bottom trial is interesting and important in its implications and as a milestone along the rocky road of defending creative independence. And the good guys win, and immediately end up squabbling.'

MICHAEL PALIN

'A deeply personal David and Goliath story, full of blazing attitude, about three women who had their lives, identities and ideas appropriated. But against all expectation the High Court recognised that wasn't right. It has a dash of The Commitments, a pinch of Gypsy, a peppering of Rocky Horror, a splash of 9 to 5, and a smidgen of Bowie, but it's very much its own thing.

And the context—70s London glam-pop-meets-theatre culture, the rock chick, the British Girl Group—is fabulous. Rock Bottom had something new for the time. They were, and are, three flamboyant and tenacious individuals. They were flawed, they had heart, they had flair, they were different— Annabel is blonde, middle-height, middle class, tenacious, the driving force; Gaye Brown is red-headed, tall and posh, a lethal wit; Diane Langton is working class, dark-haired and as infuriatingly unreliable but easy-to-forgive as Judy Garland.

It's a terrific read.'

SAMUEL ADAMSON

THE REAL ROCK FOLLIES

The great girl band rip-off of 1976

Annabel Leventon

NW1
BOOKS

NW1Books

A CIP catalogue copy of this book is available
from the British Library.

ISBN 978-1-9997054-0-4

Typesetting by Pallas Athene (Publishers) Ltd
Printed in England

info@nw1books.co.uk

For
GB, Di-Di, Don
and Harry, who carries the musical torch

Contents

List of Illustrations

Dramatis Personae

Rock Bottom:
Annabel Leventon—Annie in the group
Gaye Brown—GB in the group
Diane Langton—Di-Di in the group
Donald Fraser—composer, arranger, pianist, manager

Peter Straker: singer in *Hair!* Shares concerts with
    Rock Bottom
Julie Covington: actress, singer. First big break—*Rock Follies*
David Toguri: assistant director on *Hair!* Stages Rock Bottom
Larry Fenton: music publisher and mentor to Don Fraser
Sandra Fraser: secretary to Larry Fenton and Don's sister
Douglas Trout: hairdresser for Rock Bottom
Petra, his wife: model, make-up artist for Rock Bottom
Michael White: theatre impresario
Jack Rosenthal: television writer and producer
Maureen Lipman, Jack's wife: actress and friend
Howard Schuman: television writer and friend
Jenne Casarotto: Howard's agent
Brian Degas: BBC Light Entertainment producer
Andrew Brown: producer of *Verité*, *Rock Follies*
Verity Lambert: Head of Drama, Thames Television
Liz Sadler: Head of Casting, Thames Television
Oscar Beuselinck: show-biz solicitor for *Hair!* and Rock
    Bottom
Nick Strauss: barrister, junior counsel for Rock Bottom

Keith Schilling: solicitor in Oscar's office, prepares the Rock
    Bottom case
John Wilmers: QC, Counsel for the Prosecution
David Hirst: High Court Judge
Gordon: Judge's Clerk
Jeremiah Herman: QC, Counsel for the Defence

Fraser et al v Thames TV [1982]

Claimants had idea for TV series concerning a female rock group. Was partly fictional and partly based on experiences of Claimants. Idea was communicated to Defendant 1 (a scriptwriter), who then communicated it to Defendant 2 (a producer). D1 D2 and D3 (Thames Television) went on to produce TV show based on idea, but using different actresses. Claimants sued for breach of confidence.

Prologue

Before she rang, I was settled. Before she rang, I hardly ever thought of her. Twenty years is long enough, even for me. Okay, I'm not good at letting things go, saying goodbye. I tend to cling to the driftwood of a failed romance, for instance, treading water, believing the boat will right itself, given time. It hardly ever does, of course. It's more practical to strike out for land, swim away before it drags you down with it. With friends, it's a different matter, I haven't lost many of those. We might drift apart from circumstance, like going to another school or off to live in Australia. But most of the time, a friend is a friend. That's that.

Settled, did I say? Yes, to my surprise, that's the right word. After a disastrous two years living in the country, I'd found a place to live in North London for me, my son Harry and Purdey the dog. I feel cast adrift anywhere else. A little maisonette on the Horton Gardens Housing Estate in Swiss Cottage. Technically Kilburn but it's closer to Swiss Cottage. I could do my weekly shop at Waitrose on the Finchley Road just as I always had. John Barnes, it was called once.

Horton Gardens Estate is on the wrong side of the Finchley Road, where the roads all take a sudden lurch downhill. I prefer to be a bit higher up. But as homes go, mine was fine. Tiny, but with a pretty, west-facing, walled garden and behind that, a little enclosed park just for residents. No-one ever went there till I moved in. A fox or two. Quite a few birds. There was no way in except through my garden gate and climb over the fence. Purdey loved it. She leapt the fence, chased the foxes, rolled in the grass. She didn't mind the thunder of the Metropolitan Line beneath. She didn't mind the green metal signs screwed into every wall: Camden Council—No Ball Games. Camden Council—No Dogs Allowed.

Dogs can't read, but I minded. What did it matter if a child kicked a ball on a deserted patch of long grass with no windows to break anywhere near? Why shouldn't my dog run round in a space no-one ever used except her and me? I snuck out one night with a screwdriver, took them all down and binned them.

I began to feel more at home once I'd done that. Most of my neighbours had lived there since the estate was built forty years before. One elderly couple told me they used to drive over to watch it going up. They served on the Residents' Committee, they said, had done for years. They were ready to step down, it was getting too much for them, but nobody new ever volunteered.

'I will,' I said. 'That'd be fun.'

They smiled.

'It's very dull, dear,' said Mildred. 'I'm not sure it'd be up your street, not with you being so busy with your acting.'

'I could have a go. There are plenty of gaps between jobs, you know. And I'd get to know more people here. I'd like that.'

Mildred looked pleased. 'I'll invite you to the next meeting, dear. We're getting on, you know, all a bit mutt'n'jeff now. You'd have to speak up a bit.'

'Speaking up is what I'm trained to do,' I said.

That's where I'd been, the evening Di rang, to a committee meeting. I was desperate to pee, trotting back to my front door, hunched over, holding on very tight, fumbling for my keys. Damn, damn. Should've gone before I left.

'Shut up, Purdey, shut up. Sssh. It's me.'

Key in lock, door half open, Purdey barking through the gap and my mobile phone ringing. I scrabble round inside my bag. It could have gone off in the meeting. I must remember to switch it off in future. 'Hello?'

A little gasp at the other end.

'Annie? Annie?'

I know that voice. It's in my bones, in my DNA. Nobody except my long-dead father calls me Annie. Except the girls. It's Di. Di from Rock Bottom. My darling ex-friend. The one I never speak to. Who never speaks to me.

'Annie? It's Di. Di Langton.'

I can no more move than fly. I sit down hard on the doorstep. Purdey pushes through the open door, snuffles at me, licking the cascade of tears.

It's Di.

Di and Gaye and me.

The three of us.

What we lost. What we won. What we were.

A Group is Born

West Kensington, 1971

What does an impecunious, provincial grammar-school girl do when she leaves Oxford, apart from becoming an actress and moving to London?

She forms a rock group, of course. At least, that's what I did, a long time ago now. In the summer of 1973, we dreamed up the first three-woman rock group in England: Gaye Brown, Diane Langton and me. Or to be more precise: Gaye, me and Di—I was always in the middle. Not because I was the lead singer—far from it. Di, deaf in one ear, stood on the far right so she could hear us, Gaye needed to be next to me so she could get my harmonies. I had to be the one in the middle. We were all as different as three girls could be—red-haired, six foot, upper-crust, (Gaye); blonde, middle-sized, middle-class, (me); dark-haired, tiny, working-class (Diane). Together we were electric—raunchy and rude and funny. We called ourselves Rock Bottom. And we nearly made it.

1973. RULES for FORMING FEMALE ROCK GROUPS

1) Don't. Wait for a manager to package you, choose your material, choose the lead singer, groom you for stardom, market you and then drop you when he's made enough money out of you.

2) Start when teenagers. You're over the hill by 30.
3) Be sisters or look as if you're sisters.
4) Be black and American, look alike, dress alike, sound alike.
5) Do as you're told. Shut up.
6) Don't write your own material. You have nothing to say. Shut up.
7) Look sexy and keep your mouth shut.
8) When your first and only brilliant idea gets stolen, accept it and move on.
9) Shut up.

Tough. We broke every single one. We didn't mean to, it's the way it worked out. It all seemed random at the time. Random and inevitable, glorious and new. Looking back now, it doesn't seem so accidental. I needed a group, for reasons I didn't then know. I never liked being a solo singer. Gaye and Di gave me strength. They were both huge personalities. On stage I felt I was being pulled apart by two horses galloping in opposite directions. But that's what a middle child does—hold things together. So I had my role.

As a child I always sang. It was natural, my mother always sang. Hummed when she was annoyed, sang full out when she was happy. I sang too. I never thought about it, certainly not as a possible career. I knew what I wanted to be—I was going to be an actress. I never thought of anything else.

Life after the war was tough, especially if you had no money. We lived outside London, we never went to musicals or pantos, we had no television. So when my aunt took me to see *Peter Pan* on stage one Christmas when I was five, and took me backstage afterwards to meet the actress playing Peter, I was awestruck. Bowled over. Hooked. Acting was what I was born to do.

I was lucky. I somehow passed the eleven-plus and went to grammar school. And when I was fourteen, something momentous happened: I fell in love. It was my first teenage party, in some-one's front room. The lights dimmed, someone put a record on and a boy asked me to dance. I no longer remember who he was, but I'll never forget what we danced to: *Dream, Dream, Dream* by The Everly Brothers. It was the very first pop song I'd ever heard. I fell in love with it and all their other songs. And Buddy Holly, Elvis Presley, Little Eva, Edith Piaf, Carole King...

Now I had two passions—acting and pop-singing. Pop was banned in our house, my mother loathed it, so the singing stayed secret till I got to Oxford.

Till I got to Oxford. It sounds so easy, doesn't it? How did that happen? Nobody in my family had ever been to university. I don't think I would have tried very hard, or at all, if it hadn't been for my headmistress.

'You?' she said, head flung back, prominent front teeth bared. 'Oxford? Cambridge? The best you'd get is a place at London.'

That did it. I discovered a stubborn streak. And I got lucky again. St Anne's College believed in my potential enough to give me a minor scholarship.

Once there, I acted in everything I could—Chekhov, Shakespeare, Brecht, revue. And I sang. Sang with a student dance band, The Fourbeats, sang anything and everything on the Top 20 and the jukebox—Elvis, Buddy Holly, Piaf, Cilla Black, the Beatles. Acting gave me, to my astonishment, national re-views in all the main papers, while singing was the best fun I'd ever had and paid my way through university. I forged life-long friendships with other grammar-school kids who also couldn't believe their luck.

And when that was over, I went to drama school to learn to be a proper actress. I still loved pop, but it was another world. You couldn't do both, it seemed. Never the twain would meet.

Till one day in 1968, along came a new show into the West End, the American Tribal Love-rock Musical *Hair!* My two pas-sions rolled into one—acting and rock-singing. I got the female lead and my life changed forever. Till *Hair!* I'd been stuck in provincial theatre, which I found dull and uninspiring, not what I'd hoped for when I turned professional. But in 1967, a chum from Oxford, David Wood, asked me to join them in Edinburgh for a new musical he'd written. And at the Festival I saw a New York experimental theatre company, Café La Mama. Their director was Tom O'Horgan and their work was bold and innovative and ground-breaking. It was the kind of theatre I hungered for. I was hooked again.

'I think you're all wonderful,' I said shyly in the bar after the first show. 'I want to do what you're doing.'

'Great!' said one.

'Good!' said another.

'Fancy sleeping with me tonight?' was a third response, which I ignored.

'You better come over and join us,' said Tom.

He meant it, too. Or if he didn't, I never noticed. By the time I'd earned enough for my fare to New York, Tom had left La Mama for Broadway to direct a new show. Three months later, his production of *Hair!* opened. He kindly gave me a ticket.

This time I was more than in love, I was blown away, dazzled, beguiled. It was pure theatre. They broke all the rules, bursting out into the audience wearing nearly nothing, smoking on stage, swearing, burning their draft cards, singing their hearts out. They were having the time of their lives, using microphones like rock stars, for God's sake, never seen before on a Broadway stage. They appeared to be making it up as they went along. And they sang the most amazing, rough, raw, superb rock music, the band on stage with them.

I had to be part of it—I didn't care what part. I'd do box office, wardrobe, usheretting, anything. When I came back to London later that year, they were casting the last few roles for the West End production and I landed one of them. The female lead, Sheila Franklin, a peace protester, with Paul Nicholas and Oliver Tobias to act opposite and twenty-seven of us to be a tribe and sing our hearts out for a cause I could identify with. It went beyond acting for me. It was commitment on a grand scale.

For the first and only time in my life, I wasn't terrified on the first night. I believed in it so totally that I forgot my nerves and was proud to be there. The response was overwhelming. We were swept away on a tide of excitement, goodwill and success. I was acting, dancing and singing in a hit show: my dream come true. Being nominated as Actress of the Year by the *Daily Telegraph* crowned the excitement. Out of the blue, I seemed to have arrived. Life was different all of a sudden. *Hair!* affected everyone, not just me. British reserve, prudishness, safe middle-class musicals like *Salad Days*, all were blown away overnight.

Follow that…

I could have done *Hair!* forever. It was hard to move on. I compromised by going to Paris to do it in French. That got me a great French film, *Le Mur de l'Atlantique*. But once home, things became tricky. Should I go back into straight theatre or should I make an album with a Swedish record company? At that time, you could only do the one or the other.

'Are you an actress or a singer?' they would ask when I went for auditions.

'I'm both!' I should have said, but never dared. I wanted the powers that be to accept me, not just as the hippie from *Hair!* but as a real actress. I thought we'd changed the world, but in fact, the stuffy old British rules still applied. So I said no to the Swedes, joined The Young Vic Company and singing took a back seat.

In 1971, my life changed again. I met a rock composer, moved in with him and started singing again. My acting career continued in the West End and on television. My musical life blossomed at home.

Well, not my home. Don's home. A flat in West Kensington,

off the North End Road. We shared it with two other musician chums of Don's, a flautist and a clarinettist. My new home.

West Kensington Mansions, London W14, April, 1973

I was happy being thirty-one; happy living with Don. Donald Alexander Fraser: crisscrossed with contradictions, beaten up at school for saying he liked classical music more than pop. He didn't even know what they were talking about. If he had, he'd have said it anyway. Told by his headmaster that being a musician was the lowest of the low, of which caste a composer of film music was the lowest. At the Royal College of Music, he won as many prizes as Benjamin Britten a generation earlier. And he ends up doing glam rock with me. I did a drawing of him once, making him a cross between Desperate Dan, with moustache and stubbled chin, and Bugs Bunny with a toothy grin and a gleam in his eye. Stuttered when nervous. He'd get up at six am, stomp off to his music room and compose, arrange, dream and work till midday, or more often right through till six pm. Then he'd emerge, stretching, make a cup of tea, collapse for half an hour in front of *Nationwide* and head for the pub.

Our first night out, he took me down the North End Road to his local Indian restaurant, talked to me about poetry, rock music and Beethoven. He worshipped Beethoven. He had a small version of the famous, frowning Beethoven bust in the music room. He'd copied that brooding look, made it his own. And, unlike me, he had unquenchable self-belief.

After dinner, he sent me home in a taxi without making a pass. That did it. I moved in with him that same week and he proposed a week later. We got to Caxton Hall at four-thirty one afternoon to get a special licence as he couldn't bear to wait. It closed at four. He took me to meet his parents—he was their only son and eldest child—and said, with what I was to learn was his best attempt at diplomacy,

'Er, Mum, meet Annabel. We're getting married.'

His mother, Edith Daisy Maud Fraser, a working-class matron from Dagenham, shrieked, 'Oh no! Oh God, no. No, no, NO!'

It never came up again.

Living with a genius is different. Don was either maniacally genial and could see no problem, or else he was heavily silent—sullen, I thought, until it dawned on me he was living with an eighty-six-piece orchestra playing in his head. Real life can't compete with that. It didn't have much chance in the manic phase, come to that. He would vanish to his music room for hours. It was a small room, the only room in the flat with any furniture to speak of, if you didn't count beds.

Furniture? It contained a grand piano, a set of drums, a Revox tape recorder, microphones, a four-channel sound mixer, innumerable sheets of manuscript paper, tapes, the Beethoven bust and Groves *Dictionary of Music* all jumbled up together gathering dust. And a large heavy glass ashtray, which I remember because he once threw it at me. I'd be left in what was amusingly called the living-room trying to write lyrics, hoping to do well enough to be allowed to collaborate with him. Some hours or, on a good day, minutes later, I'd be summoned to hear the latest creative flourish.

'Listen to this,' he'd say, and play through sometimes several bars of a melody. 'That's a hit, that is. That's thirty thousand quid and a mansion in the country.'

'Great,' I say cautiously, 'How does it go on?'

'Dunno yet. Let's go to the pub. I need a break.'

Quite a few hits were thus lost forever.

His excuse for asking me out that first time was that he wanted to make an album of his songs, with me singing. His songs were terrific, Vanessa Redgrave had recorded one of them, Dusty Springfield had written to him saying she liked them. I felt overawed. He managed to get an album deal for us with an off-shoot of Decca Records and then proceeded to spend so much money on backing tracks they pulled the deal before I began the vocals. I was relieved. I couldn't match up to what he wanted. I'd loved singing with my Oxford dance band and then with twenty-seven other people in *Hair!* It was too scary being a solo singer.

When Julie Covington, a friend of ours, asked him to produce *Day By Day*, her song from *Godspell*, I did backing vocals for them, which I loved. It was a great relief not to be on my own in the recording booth.

Afterwards, I say to Don, 'That was fun. I think I'll ask Julie to form a double act.'

Don: Won't work.
Annie: *(chin out, toast halfway to mouth)* Why not?
Don: Got to be three.
Annie: Why?
Don: For the harmonies.
Annie: Oh.

I could have mentioned The Everly Brothers (all two of them), Simon and Garfunkel (ditto), Nina and Frederick…

Actually, I didn't even think of it. Don was the musician, I deferred to him on anything to do with music. And in this he was clearly right. Girl groups were in a category all their own. Three girls, almost invariably American and black, identical clothes, identical wigs, identical make-up. The Ronettes, the Shirelles, the Crystals. Play around with that at your peril.

But the seed of the idea was planted right there, waiting to be ripened. Three girls singing together. What a great thought.

That was in April. Some seeds ripen fast. This one did. It was fully formed by September.

July, 1973

We walk to the stage door of Her Majesty's Theatre to find the place heaving with bodies. Hundreds of performers line the stairs, up past the stage door, spilling out onto the pavement, a cattle market. Joining the queue behind us, Wayne Sleep, the brilliant, diminutive ballet dancer. We hug.

A shriek from outside makes me jump. 'Oh Christ, Annie!'

My eardrums split. No wonder I'm deaf, it's not just the rock'n'roll.

Gaye Brown is big. Not just tall—*big*. Big mouth, bravura personality, the best one-liners. The confidence of the truly posh. She towers over Wayne, lipstick on her teeth, laughing like an upper-crust hyena.

'Fat chance we've got, darling! Di Langton's already got the lead.'

'Di Langton? Oh my God, we were in *Hair!* together, Don. She played Jeannie, the pregnant one. She's wonderful.'

I introduce Gaye to Don, who's playing for me.

'We'll cheer them up, darling, they're probably bored out of their minds already.'

Gaye, ever generous, is happy just to give them a good laugh. At nearly six foot, she knows she's unlikely to match up to anyone's appearance in the original show. Her philosophy is simple: 'Have fun, make 'em laugh and then go for lunch.'

My turn first. I'm nervous, worse than usual, because I'm singing a song Don and I just wrote—its first public outing. You're never supposed to sing pop for a musical theatre audition. But he wants me to try it out. When I finish there's a silence and then, in the wings behind me, everyone applauds. I'm shocked, this never happens at auditions. I glance over at Don, who grins. They give me a scene to look at and I'm asked to wait. It's hard to prepare with Wayne Sleep auditioning next. In a small, true voice and with irresistible charm, he sings *When I'm Sixty-four* adding a spectacular dance sequence in the middle. Another spontaneous round of applause.

Then it's Gaye. She strides out to the middle of the stage and sings *Won't You Come Home, Bill Bailey* with enormous aplomb, a noduled croak and deafening volume. For someone who never smokes or drinks, she creates an extraordinary impression of a gin-soaked jazz singer in the last stages of terminal nicotine poisoning and too much sex. She too gets a round of applause from the wings. It's turning into a good day. The producer adores her performance and tells her there's nothing in the show for her. They call me back to read my scene. One of them comes up to the edge of the stage, wiping tears from his eyes.

'Thank you so much. That was hilarious. Wonderful reading. The lead's already cast, I'm sorry we haven't anything else for you. Good luck.'

Don and Gaye wait for me.

'Yes?' says GB.

'Course not. You're too tall. I'm too blonde and curly.'

'Shouldn't have had that perm. I suppose they wanted long straight hair?'

'Yup. Just what I had till this week.'

'Serve you right.'

We storm off for lunch, arm in arm. Don, hunched from playing piano, slopes behind us, frowning. I know what he's doing, he's got a sixty-piece orchestra in his head, he's composing. He's always hungry, though, he'll find where we are if he gets too far behind. He'll hear us, that's for sure, even if we're a mile away. Gaye's always loud, I have to match her or give up, so I match her. Same thing on stage. She'll trample all over me once she gets in front of an audience. So I raise my game. It's fun. I'm different with Gaye. For some reason I cannot fathom, I don't feel unconfident with her. She shouts me down, bosses me about, weeps at my jokes and I love her for it. She's my theatrical older sister. Together we're a double act.

In the cafe she tells Don about when she was in the States, do-ing a revue I would have done if I hadn't gone to drama school. Her American accent is New York Jewish, plus a bit black. She'd got to know every stand-up comic there, it appeared. Probably slept with them all, definitely nicked their material. She tries it out on Don, who's stunned but appreciative. It's an education. He's always wanted to go to New York but he's hardly started his career and money is tight. Non-existent, mostly.

'You two girls were great,' he says between mouthfuls of chips. 'I don't know why you waste your time on these idiots. You're far too good for their lousy show.'

'We know that, darling,' says GB, 'but you've got to pay the rent, you know.'

'You're thinking too small,' says Don. 'You got to be inde-pendent of this lot. There's no money in theatre, anyhow.'

Light bulb.

A thousand-watt light bulb.

Time stops still.

I stare at GB, whisper in Don's ear. He comes back into the pre-sent from his internal recording session. I repeat myself. He nods vigorously, spilling his wine.

I turn to GB. 'Don and me—' I announce.

GB splutters. 'Frightful grammar, darling! You're the Oxford graduate, aren't you?'

'All right, Don and I, then—we're forming a band. A three-woman rock group.'

GB blinks. 'What?'

'I'm fed up of going for jobs I'll never get just because I don't look like the girl who played it on Broadway.'

'I'm fed up of being too tall to play anything but dykes, darling.'

The contents of the cafe look round, goggle-eyed. This is 1973, remember, they haven't got used to Julian Clary, or Miriam

Margolyes on *Graham Norton* for that matter. 1973 is still a bit prim.

'Exactly,' I say, cutting in before she carries on at the top of her lungs. 'So I've decided to be independent. Create my own work.'

GB blinks again. 'What sort of work? Building work?'

She hasn't got it. She's not been listening.

'I told you! A rock group. A three-woman rock group. We'll write our own songs. Be in charge of our own careers.'

GB chokes on her wine. 'Like The Supremes? It'll never work. You're not black enough. We're too old, anyway. The time to do that is when you're a teenager, isn't it, Doug?'

'Don, Gaye. He's Don.'

Gaye cackles. 'Oh yes. Doug was your Oxford feller, wasn't he? Sorry, Don. But really, you have to be lookalikes to be a group. Like the Beverly Sisters…'

'No. Not like them. Not like anyone else. We'd be like us. You and me. And someone else.'

She cracks up. 'Girl groups all look alike and sound alike, you nitwit. I'm twice your size, I've got nodules on my vocal chords and my hair's auburn. You're blonde. Anyway, you sing rock. I don't.'

'Of course you do. Can, that is. You will. We can dress the way we want, make not fitting in a positive advantage, be free of typecasting forever. Don'll help you. You've got the biggest voice in the universe. You'll be the only rock singer in the world who doesn't need a microphone.'

A short silence. She stares at us, twirls her glass. Then barks with laughter. The cafe shrinks back against the walls.

'Let's do it. Why not? We're mad enough. You certainly are. We'll be the best bird band ever.'

We drink to that.

'So tell me, who's the other one?'

Don and I look at each other.

'Don't know yet,' I admit. 'I've only just come up with you.'

She purses her lips, frowns. Then chortles again. 'I know exactly who,' she says.

GB's solutions are instant. The quick fix. Terrible or brilliant, there's never anything in between. This one is brilliant, breathtaking, immediate.

'Di Langton, of course. I'll write to her.'

The second it comes out of her mouth, I know she's right. Diane Langton—huge talent, passionate Judy Garland voice, working-class, black curly hair, ex-hoofer, half my size, an elf to Gaye's posh, ex-deb giant. Different in every way from both of us. With me in the middle, middle-class, middle-sized. Almost normal, compared to them. That line-up would break every rule in the book for girl groups. I already adore Di from *Hair!* days, where, night after night, she easily engaged the entire audience with her huge smile and astounding voice.

Perfect.

Poor Di, she had no inkling of what she was in for. Nor did we. None of us had any idea what we were unleashing: the bumpiest ride on the biggest ever rock'n'rollercoaster. Not for the faint-hearted. And not to be missed for any money.

'Right,' says Don, chucking back the last of his wine. 'We better start. Write some songs and that.'

'Can't, love, sorry,' says GB, 'I'm off on holiday for three weeks. But I know where Di is. I'll write to her from Cornwall. I can't write songs, though. I know a great song-writer called Barry Mason. He'll write—'

'Course you can. You'll write with us. Annie couldn't write till last year. She wrote that song you heard this morning.'

Silence.

Finally: 'They'll have to sing the harmonies, then,' mutters GB.

'You'll do harmonies if I say,' says Don.

I wink at Gaye. She looks at us. Don grins back. We all laugh.

Putting Di into the mix is Gaye's genius. It's ridiculous and wrong and yet it feels so right. We're too old, we have totally different shapes, styles, faces, voices. Girl groups just don't do that. All of us actresses, all strong personalities, all lead singers—two of them, anyhow. I'll worry about me later. Upper-class, middle-class, working-class; tall, medium, short; all clowns capable of making you cry as well as laugh. We're on to something, I know we are. How could I be scared with them next to me? Was I excited that day we lunched with Gaye.

A month later we stop laughing. We haven't heard from Di, Gaye's still on holiday. By early September, my hopes are beginning to founder. It doesn't matter quite so much to Don, he has his composing and his personal vision, what he calls his Master Gruppenplan. Rock is only a step on the way. But for me the group is my lifeline, it brings together everything I want—to work as a team, to sing and act, to see something through from start to finish, to bring pop into theatre and theatre into pop. I need it more than I've ever needed anything. I want to fling myself into making it happen. But how can I do that without the other two?

When GB comes back from Cornwall, she has news. Di said she wants to join us, but can't be there yet. In her absence the three of us decide to write a send-up of the worst of the Fifties pop songs, the kind recorded by the endless then-popular girl groups, who all looked alike, sounded alike, if possible claimed to be sisters, and sometimes were. Almost always American. We come up with a ludicrous pastiche of exactly what I sang with The Fourbeats, my dance band when I was at Oxford, songs off the jukebox or Radio Luxembourg. We put in every pop cliché we can think of, banal chord sequences, trite lyrics, overworked phrases. Gaye and I think it screamingly funny.

Di will find it hilarious, too, we're sure, when she shows up—*if* she shows up. I haven't seen her in five years, not since we were in *Hair!* together at the Shaftesbury Theatre in 1968. Gaye and Di had met more recently at the Theatre Royal, Stratford East; Don had never met her or heard of her, except from us.

Getting her there wasn't so easy. I didn't know that was going to be a permanent underscoring to the group. There were always such good reasons: she'd started rehearsing *Pippin* and had a big part; she put paid work first, always had. We couldn't argue with that. None of us had any money. Don and I lived off the North End Road in West Kensington, hardly convenient for a West End girl like Di.

Finally she makes it. Don's eyes bulge when he opens the front door. Five foot nothing, skin-tight white mini-skirt and startling cleavage revealing a scarlet bra under the matching white jacket. Complete Fifties make-up: huge false eyelashes, Kathy Kirby pale-pink glossy lipstick and the brightest, sunniest, ear-to-ear grin anyone's ever seen. And ridiculous, platform, peep-toe ankle-strap heels. She tells us how she'd been called to meet Bob Fosse, the *Pippin* director, then staying at the Savoy Hotel, before she'd been offered the job. To impress him, she'd worn this same tarty little number. Teetering into the old-fashioned foyer of the Savoy, she'd not only caused a sensation, she'd also been refused entry. They couldn't believe she had a bona fide appointment with the famous Bob Fosse and assumed she was a hooker.

After we've wiped away tears of mirth, ''Ere,' she asks, 'What about this song, then? You gonna sing it for me or what?'

We rush to the music room. Gaye and I lean on the piano and give the new song all we've got, sending it way over the top, treating it as a big joke, with Don thumping out the dreadful Fifties chord progressions to make sure Di gets every bit of it. Di stands by the window. I keep a wary eye on her. She's agreed to give the band a try, but if she doesn't like the song, she'll probably back off the whole thing. She stares out at the sky as we sing. I'm not sure she's even listening.

When we finish, there's a long pause while we wait for her

verdict. Finally, she turns back from the window and looks at us.

'Yer doing it all wrong, girls,' she says. 'That's a sad song, that is. It's exactly how I felt when I was fifteen. You gotta sing it for real.'

She opens her throat and starts singing it for real. Don gulps and accompanies her. It becomes a different song, still funny but from the heart, exactly like Di. Gaye and I join in.

Two essential ingredients fuse then and there—passion and piss-take. From this second, I know. We all know. We're a group.

Three voices for the harmonies at last.

Don was right about that.

Gaye was right about Di.

And I had my group.

2

The Master Gruppenplan

We retire to Don's shabby little kitchen to celebrate over a cup of tea. Don makes the tea, we girls swap ideas of how to conquer the world, all shouting at once, too excited to think. You can sing with someone you like and admire, but it may not be exciting. You can sing with a bunch of friends at a party, and it can be tremendous fun, but nobody sane would want to listen. This time, it's a real thrill for all of us. We know we rock, we're high as kites from it. It's a new sensation for us, we're used to doing what we're told, where to stand, what to wear, what to say. For the first time, we see how we can take charge.

'We could do fashion shoots! That'd change the world with our bums.'

'Make a change from all those skinny little models in all them magazines.'

'Yeah. Give other funny-looking people a bit of hope, too. Seeing women up there, not just girls.'

'We could go on the *Russell Harty Show*, twist him into little knots and do the singing spot as well.'

'Take the Theatre Royal, Stratford East, do a whole evening as a fundraiser for them.'

'Whaddya MEAN, Stratford East? We'll take the Theatre Royal, Drury Lane, is what you mean.'

Finally, Don's voice cuts through the babble.

'No, no, girls. You're thinking too small. Now shut up and I'll tell you how it's going to work.'

We shut up. Leaning against the fridge (we only had three chairs), he puts on his Beethoven scowl. 'Now then, this is the Master Gruppenplan.'

'Eh? Master what?'

'G-g-gruppenplan. G-goes like this—'

He stops.

'It goes like this,' he says again. Suddenly there's no hesitancy, no hint of a stammer.

'First we write a few more songs. Then we go into a little studio and demo them up. Larry'll lend me the money. Larry's my music publisher. Then I take the demos round and we get a publishing deal and a recording contract. Then we bring out a single or two, maybe an album. We do radio and TV spots, of course, to help them along, personal appearances, that sort of thing, a few interviews in the papers. Then we do some live shows round the place, a bit of a UK tour. Then we have our own television show, like the Monkees, say, bring out another album on the back of that. Have a few hits, appear on *Top of the Pops*, same time as the series, maybe. Then when we've cracked it over here, we tour the States. Become major stars. Do what we like.'

There's a very long silence.

I'm stunned. He *has* been thinking about it. He's got it all worked out. I had no idea.

'The Monkees weren't a real band,' Gaye objects. 'They were put together for television. They couldn't even sing.'

'Did all right, though, didn't they? You *can* sing and you're a real band, so we'll do even better.'

'Well, I'm not going round the provinces. No way,' says Di with conviction. 'I don't want to do them working men's clubs.'

'Nor me,' I agree. 'I've done my time in rep. I refuse to be sent back to Coventry.'

'We've all done our time, darling.' says Gaye. 'We'll just have to start three-quarters of the way up. Where we belong.'

'Right,' says the genius. 'We'll do all our British concerts in London.'

So we do.

October, 1973

Di's schedule is punishing. We hardly ever see her. Once the initial excitement of forming the group has worn off, she becomes more cautious.

'It's a great idea, this group, but my solo career comes first,' she says too frequently in too plaintive a voice.

If we can get her there, she's with us one hundred percent. More. When she's with you, Di's attention, her sheer presence, is total. She's so generous, so real, so warm, on stage or off, you can't help but love her. When she leaves, she vanishes into another world. Her walkabouts, they're called—she does it in shows as well. She contributes so much when she appears, we forgive her. But it's difficult and unsettling. We manage to rehearse our first song, choose who would sing what, work out harmonies and argue about the feel and the tempo, perhaps once while she's in rehearsal for *Pippin*. It's pretty frustrating.

And then *I* land a job, a wonderful one, the lead in *Verité*, a new play for Thames TV. My agents are delighted. So am I. It's to be recorded in London, too. We'll just have to work round *my* commitments as well.

The night I get the job, Don and I go out to celebrate at our favourite restaurant, The Casserole on the Kings Road. We go there all the time. However broke we are, a meal at The Casserole is just what we need to cheer us up, relax us, commiserate another failure, or, best of all, celebrate.

Tonight is a celebration and a half. Tim Curry, a chum from *Hair!* is to play opposite me in the television play. There are even songs in the show, and although I won't get to sing any of them, music immediately upgrades any play in my eyes. There's a scene where Shirley, my character, tries and fails to tap dance, so I get to do comedy, too. This makes the whole thing irresistible.

Then a magical series of events occurs.

I walk into The Casserole on air and bump straight into Tim Curry. In a shamelessly theatrical fashion—in which we're outdone by all the waiters, especially the Maître d', Ray, a gay Australian, perhaps the most theatrical person I've ever met— we hug and kiss and laugh.

'Tim, darling!'

'Annabel darling!'

'What luck!'

'How fantastic—we're going to work together again!'

'This is great. Must come and see you again in *Rocky Horror*. I haven't seen it for months.'

'How's the group? Got a name yet?'

'Oh, it's great. Really great. On its way. No, no name yet.'

Tim introduces his companion, Howard Schuman. What incredible timing! He's the author of the television play, a charming New Yorker. I take to him on sight. Emboldened by this streak of luck, I ask Howard if he's got music for his songs yet. When he says no, I jump in with both feet.

'Well, the best composer in London is right here. Maybe Don could do the music for you?'

How could he refuse? We all have dinner together. We talk about his play, but not for very long, I'm too obsessed with my group. I'm so proud of it, the first big idea I've ever had myself, I can't help talking about it. They're courteous and indulge me. Not that they have much choice.

Annie: I love your play, Howard, it's the best television script I've
    read in years. You are *brilliant*. I can't believe I'm meeting
    you on the very day I get Shirley. I love her—she's a terrific

character. She's going to be so much fun to do. Especially the tap dancing.

Howard: You like that scene?

Annie: I love it, it's hilarious. I love comedy, it's my favourite. Did I tell you about my three-girl group?

Howard: Your group?

Annie: Yes! Tim knows about it. We haven't got a name yet, but we've formed a rock group. Three of us.

Howard: That's great. Is Don…?

Annie: *(cutting in)* Oh yes. Don's part of it too. He's our piano-player and our composer and our songwriter. He's brilliant, too, like you.

Howard: Well, hey, that's fantastic.

Annie: *(clinking glasses with everyone)* Cheers! Cheers! It's so exciting to bump into you both. It's a magical coincidence, isn't it? What luck. Don, tell them how you worked out how it's going to be.

Howard: Excuse me?

Tim: I think she means her group, Howard.

Howard: Oh. Great. Cheers!

That sort of conversation. Steamroller Annie. They don't seem to mind. Don and I arrange to meet Howard next day to talk about the songs.

A friendship formed over dinner and several glasses of wine can vanish in the cold light of day. Not this time, we get on just as well. We eat and talk and then Don takes Howard to meet his mentor and publisher, Larry Fenton, of Breitkopf and Härtel, who has a piano in the office and lets Don use it.

He comes home well pleased. 'I've worked the basics out. Only took five minutes. Howard liked it. I've got the job.'

Off we go to The Casserole again to celebrate.

Verité goes down well and gets good reviews for me and Howard.

People love Don's music. Over the next few months, a close working relationship develops between Don and Howard, and a close friendship between Howard and me. He becomes a frequent visitor. We play him our songs, I give him half-finished lyrics to read and comment on. He tells me about the plots for the new commissions that start to come in after the success of *Verité*. I like hearing about the scripts, it flatters my ego to hear he wants me to play virtually every heroine. A new writer rarely has any say in casting and I never get interviewed for any of them. I don't mind, the group is well under way and takes precedence for me over anything else. Every little thing we do gets reported to Howard with pride—our new songs, Gaye's eccentric witticisms, her erratic driving, her passion for most things American, Di's ability to walk down the street stopping the traffic with her cleavage, high heels, and plaintive cry, 'Annie, why are they whistlin' at me?'

'Di-Di, ever thought of polo-neck sweaters?'

'Yeah, but I get claustrophobic if me throat's covered.'

Whose throat goes down to their navel...?

Howard keeps using Don to write music for his shows. He's always at the flat, bringing ideas and lyrics. Bless him, he's a great listener and, boy, do I have a lot to tell. The group is growing. Every day, more takes shape. I still have to find a name for us but it's getting clearer where we're going, where we've got to go.

Finding the name is tricky because we can't agree. One afternoon, in Don's music room, we're trying harmonies out, and the argument starts up again. Gaye very much favours 'The Truckers', God knows why, something to do with a current American catchphrase maybe—keep on truckin'.

'Sounds like the heavy leather brigade, GB. And—how shall I put this?—truck-drivers.'

'My dad says how about the Sky Highs?' says Di. 'I told him, that'll give the press just what they need to cut us down to size. We'll be the Sky Lows in no time.'

'I think The Truckers is perfect,' says GB. 'That's my final word.'

I lose it and start yelling. 'No, GB, for the last time, no, no, NO! That is absolutely rock bottom.'

There's a silence while I wait for Gaye to punch me.

Then, as one truck-driver, we all shout, 'ROCK BOTTOM!'

That's it. From now on, we're Rock Bottom.

Our first recording is in the smallest, cheapest kind of studio imaginable. We have our first two songs ready to try out. Don's plan is holding up so far: Larry Fenton, bless him, lends him the money. We borrow a friendly guitarist, Mickey Keane from the *Hair!* band, plus a couple of other musicians who rate Don highly enough to give him an hour or so for free.

So here we are in Central Sound Studios, Denmark Street, off the Charing Cross Road. A tiny, scruffy, stuffy basement, with egg cartons on the walls as soundproofing, no separation between instruments or bodies or sound. Not enough room for four musicians, their instruments and three very over-excited singers.

'Christ, darling, you bring us to the best places,' says Gaye, sniffing at the rich mix of other people's bodies from many earlier sessions.

'Yeah, well, if it was good enough for the Stones, it'll do for us,' Don replies over his shoulder as he sets up the one vocal mike for us. He's in his element: calm, efficient, organised, professional through and through. Just as well, because our expertise lies in working with a script and an audience, not a microphone. The electrical charge attached to being in here to record our own creations sends the adrenalin sky high. Gaye goes highest and loudest, she's most out of her depth. Don handles us with no trouble at all.

'These are only demos, girls,' he tells us over the intercom. We can barely see the control room for the bodies and instruments cluttering up the space between. 'So we'll do a rehearsal of this all together, give it a live feel, get you in the mood, give the boys a flavour. I'll count you in and we'll just give it a go.'

We clear our throats and shuffle our feet and giggle—and give it a go. It's our Fifties piss-take number, our very first song first. The intro has me humming low over a heavy back beat, *mmm, mmm, mmm, mmm*. Di floats an *aah, aah, aah* high above me, Gaye replies with a throaty *oh baby, baby, baby*. Di takes the first verse, while GB and I hum beneath:

> *I've got your number, baby,*
> *The writing's on the wall.*
> *I've got your number baby,*
> *Pride goes before a fall,*

Now we go into harmony under Di's top line for the first bit of the chorus:

> *You told me you loved me true*
> *Now I know our love is through*
> *Cos it's all over, over, oh, oh, oh, oh,*
> *Yes it's all over, over, o-o-o-over now.*

Di is a revelation. We recorded the *Hair!* album together years before, but she didn't have a solo on it so I never saw her in action. It makes no difference where or when she sings—rehearsals, stage, recordings—she flings her head back, closes her eyes, opens her mouth and pure emotion flows out. Whatever images she has in her head translate into a personal, private drama that we all share. I first saw it when she took over as Jeannie in *Hair!* I saw it again in *Pippin* when she sang *Spread A Little Sunshine*. She does just the same here and it's gorgeous.

I'm next—with the middle verse:

> *Thank you for all the good times baby*
> *Thank you for all the good things we've been*
> *   through*
> *Thank you for all the years I thought you'd*
> *   never leave me*
> *I never thought you'd find somebody new*

GB and Di sing the thank-you's, I take the rest of the line. When we get to the chorus, it's all of us again, me now at the top. With them, I can go higher and stronger than I can on my own, it feels great. All at once I get it, right in the middle of the song: this is why I wanted a girl group—those harmonies beneath me give me wings, my voice flies up to where Di's did. Different sound, different feel, but real and complementary. Our voices belong together, I'm surfing on the crest of a sound wave rolling in:

Cos it's all over, over, o-o-o-over now

The heartfelt lyrical *aah, aah, aah,* Di etches over the middle eight breaks my heart.

Then the complete contrast. Gaye comes in low, throaty, broken-hearted for the last verse. At the end I take a phrase very high, echoed by Di, repeated by Gaye. It's bizarre. Each of us hits that top G perfectly, each in a totally individual way. I've never felt anything like it. I've never *heard* anything like it. At this precise moment—as we hold the last chord and the guitar wails the same final phrase—I'm aware this is new and different. I wanted to break new ground? We're breaking it now. In one song we've gone from a sixteen-year-old's lament to a more mature expression of loss to a world-weary woman who's loved and lost and gone through it all and will again. And finally, in the last chorus, we get all three versions of heartbreak blending together. And it's funny, too, with its cowbells, banalities and clichés. It's pure pop. And it's never been done before, I'm sure of it. It's a first.

'Okay. We'll keep that,' says Don.

Mickey nods approval. That means a lot.

'What do you mean? I thought that was just a rehearsal,' says GB.

'I recorded it anyway. It's great. Come and listen.'

We crowd into the little control room behind Don and the sound engineer. We can't believe our ears, start jumping up and down.

'Oh Christ! Listen to that.' 'Oh my Gawd.' 'It's not half bad, is it, girls?'

'Right. Next.' Don's got his eye on the clock. Time is money if he's got to pay Larry back. Things are changing. He's accountable.

He wrote the second song after hearing us sing together in his little music room that very first time. In complete contrast to *It's All Over*, the up-tempo, upbeat, driving optimism of *Boy You're a Big Girl Now* creates a vision of how we could and should and can be, as we take control of our own destiny. My dream of independence fulfilled.

> *Boy, you're a big girl now, yes you are*
> *And everywhere you go you're a bright shining star*
> *People stop and greet you, you're the one they want*
>   *to meet*
> *Girl, you got the world at your feet.*

We have half an hour left to get it down on tape. It's like running a relay race when you haven't practiced, you don't know if your muscles will work and you have no idea how far you have to run. The adrenalin rush from hearing *It's All Over* back, with its combination of soul, lyricism and sheer silliness, its cowbell chimes and sudden ludicrous stops and starts and those dear old well-worn Fifties chord sequences, goes right through us. GB can't keep still, tapping her feet, elbowing us, Di's clutching her parched throat, I'm giggling like a glue-sniffer. We're a bunch of teenage girls escaped from a strict convent, grabbing freedom before they round us up and stick our uniform back on and shove us into detention. We're going to make the most of it.

Don is more than patient, he's a saint. He doesn't seem to mind our screeching, joking and competing. In fact he encourages it.

'Just let's get a guide track down for the boys,' he says, 'and then we'll see.'

That's all we need. Suddenly the pressure's off. If we're only doing it for Mickey and Preston and Rick, we're released from having to impress, we can go for the feel of the song and act it out. After all, the lyrics invite us as much as the beat:

> *So dress to the nines, in your silks and your fines*
> *For the lines of good people who are waiting,*
> *Waiting to rip up their seats! Turn on the heat!*

'How was that? Can we come and listen? Have we done? Where's the whisky?'

'Hold on, girls,' Don snaps. 'I'm going to play it back to you in there. You can just carry on doing what you're doing and we'll record it as background.'

'Ooh, we're fuckin' background now, are we? Cheeky devil. We gave up doing background bloody years ago, didn't we, girls? Who does he think he is?'

Till what we just recorded floods through our head-cans, driving us further.

'Ooh, shit, hark at them!'

'Christ, what's goin' on?'

'Shuddup, you're deafening me!'

Topped by Di shrilling, 'Oh! I only like rock'n'roll!' and we're off. We jabber and chatter and cackle with laughter throughout, the musicians standing by, gazing at us in what seems like horror.

In the final bars, GB is inspired to more foolery. In her best American accent, she starts thanking everyone as if we're at a huge festival. 'I would like to take this opportunity to thank our audience and our producers and the cleaners ... '

She could clearly go on for hours. Di's had enough and cuts her off in mid word, yelling at the top of her lungs, 'Pass me the Southern Comfort!!!' thinking Don's switched us off. He hasn't, he's recorded the lot. Grinning like idiots, we troop back into the control room to hear it back in all its crazy, unmixed lunacy. It's a blast. Singing the actual song, we sound like Rock Bottom on speed. Behind ourselves, we're hysterical, screaming teenyboppers waiting in line to hear Rock Bottom perform, ready to tear the place apart when we do, in true rock'n'roll fashion. Never heard anything like it.

Don looks at the clock and grins.

'A minute to spare,' he announces with some pride. 'Done it!'

From this moment on, I can see where to go with this. If we characterise each song, act it out to the full, we become more than singers, it'll be pop *and* theatre, exactly what I've always longed for. Don gets it too. Exaggerating our differences heightens the effect. Inch by inch, Annabel morphs into Rock'n'roll Annie, Gaye to GB and Di into Di-Di. When we're together we slide almost unconsciously into being Rock Bottom, a heightened version of ourselves. It's an unmistakable shift into a new, collective personality—raunchy, confident, rude, funny. Tim Curry, who spends quite a bit of time with us, wants me sitting on a barstool reading Proust, while the others just behave badly around me.

Either way, we can't lose. It's original, I know it. Off the wall, outrageous, bold—it's never been done before. We're on the road.

The tapes are completed in late November. When we play them to record producers and A&R men, they're truly amazed. In fact, they're amazed by the whole enterprise. We take our little demo forty-fives round, dressed up to the nines, each of us at Don's insistence keeping our own individual style and the way we project our personalities, heightening the contrasts. He stands back to let us take over the entire office, performing nonstop for anyone who cares to stay. They know it's new and striking, they don't want to lose us in case we're on to something. And they remain flabbergasted. Jaws drop quite often from now on round Soho. They take us out to dinner and offer us ludicrous contracts, which we refuse to sign. They come to admire Di in *Pippin*, where she's giving a gloriously vulgar, vulnerable performance, with a voice that boomerangs from the stage to the back wall of the auditorium and back and a delicious sense of comedy. They ask for more tapes, which we haven't got. We even get on radio, without a recording contract and without a proper record. Word's got about. LBC, only a month old, invite us onto Tony Palmer's rock chat programme, and we proudly play our scratched, faulty, unfinished demo.

We stun them by all talking at once, telling them some of the master plan, certainly about the as yet un-booked concerts in London (no dates, no venues, no ideas) as if they are already fact. We also talk knowledgeably about doing our own television show. For some reason Tony and his producer, Jason Pollock, seem to find our exuberance refreshing. It's excitement rather than arrogance, but how are they to know? It's our first public performance and we're well pleased. Another dinner at The Casserole, then.

Something else wonderful—we're invited onto Capital Radio, also just starting out, a month behind LBC, still with only our scratchy acetate demo. Eleven pm, the *Sarah Ward Show*. Who cares how late it is? It's the trendiest of the trendiest. In the hospitality room, we're waiting to go on air when the legendary Gene Pitney walks in. We gasp. It's ten years since his hit *24 Hours from Tulsa*. We could all sing it to him right away but we chat him up instead. He's taken aback but gallant, wishes us luck when we go into the studio first. The usual mayhem live on air, as we giggle and fool around and talk over each other. Our song bounces off the walls. We burst back into the hospitality room, and listen to Gene on air just after us. When he comes back in we say, 'You were great! Come and have a drink with us! Let's go out on the town. How long since you've been here? We should celebrate!'

Gene grins and shrugs. 'I really, really wish I could. I have to go on to yet another show right away, I'm afraid.'

Quick as a flash, Gaye snaps, wicked as ever, 'It's tough at the top, love.'

Gene, deadly serious, nods. 'It really, really is.'

Outside the building, we fall about. We'll tell it all round London.

'We mustn't ever take ourselves that seriously.'

'Huh. Chance'd be a fine thing.'

'You never know.'

'Well, we'd never *not* take the piss, would we?'

'With GB around? Course not.'

By Christmas nothing definite—or paid—has shown up. Rock Bottom's been going for three months and we need a result. Don's tireless, he must have seen half the music business in the time, crashing every office party, playing the tapes to every single person who might have ears and/or influence. We want the rest of the world to catch up. We need them to, we're skint. At one of the office parties, I bump into Tony Edwards of Purple Records, a chum who'd briefly managed my singing career. I drag him out of the party and back to his office to play him our tapes. I never go anywhere without them, just in case. He's intrigued. I take Don with me for another meeting to discuss the group's future. More pieces of the Master Gruppenplan are aired. Tony mentions a television producer at the BBC he's working with, Brian Degas, who might be interested when the idea has developed a little further. He can tell we're going to be visually exciting, as well as being a recording act.

Most people see that if they meet us, but the oddball nature of the line-up also confuses them. Finding a recording deal is taking longer than the two or three days we'd assumed. Never mind, it's Christmas.

1973, after a rocky start, has proved a winner. Rock Bottom is alive and well.

3

Television Dreaming

West Kensington Mansions, W14, a night in January, 1974

'Don?'

'Mmm?'

'I've had an idea.'

'Yeah?'

'Yeah. About the television series. A brainwave, actually. I know exactly who we have to talk to.'

'Mmm?' Don sighs and turns over. We're in his bed from when he was a kid. Small even for a kid, about two foot six wide. When one turns, we both turn, there's no choice. 'Brainwave?'

'Yes. A genius one. Jack!'

'Who?'

'Jack. Maureen's husband. Jack Rosenthal. He's a television producer, isn't he? He's a brilliant comedy writer, the best TV writer in England.'

'Already spoken to him.' He sits up and clasps his hands behind his head.

'What? When?'

'Er, sometime before Christmas. I was in Hampstead and dropped in. He's thinking about it.'

'Oh, my God. This is brilliant. You idiot, why didn't you tell me?'

'Forgot, I suppose. Meant to. Why did you mention Jack now?'

'I was just thinking we owe them dinner and I was wondering what I'd cook.'

'Mmm.' He settles back down, puts an arm round me, nuzzles. 'Can we have spaghetti?'

Polydor Records come through with a deal for two singles. They heard us on Capital Radio. Just six weeks after finishing the demos, it seems a long time to us. Handling the contract will be a new challenge, none of us has a clue how to go about it. This is where you need a manager. Of course you have to sign a contract with him, too. It's a kind of Catch 22: first find your manager. A boyfriend of Gaye's, Troy Dante (once of The Infernos) proposes himself. We don't feel like handing over control to an unknown quantity. We'll have to deal with Polydor ourselves without help. The minute their offer comes through, Gaye and I go to Stratford East where Di's rehearsing her next show and entice her into a meal at the local Chinese restaurant. We giggle and gossip and eat like pigs and finally tell her it's make-your-mind-up time.

'It's a record deal, Di. Can't mess around with a record deal. You in or out, doll?'

Di wriggles and squirms and talks about her solo career and her need to be free and her fear of being tied down.

Finally I say, 'Di, darling, we know all this. Nobody's forcing you. It's your decision. But you need to make it now. We're about to sign a recording deal. This is your chance to come with us— or quit.'

There's a long pause. Then her face brightens. 'Sorry, girls, I gotta go to the toilet.'

Flashing a brilliant smile, she walks off.

GB and I look at each other.

'Is there another exit she could take?'

Gaye snorts. 'She'll be back. Don't worry.'

We wait.

And wait.

And there she is, in the doorway, radiant.

'Course I'm in, you nitwits. How couldn't I be?'

We rough out an agreement on the back of a paper napkin. I'll get Sandra, Don's sister, to type it up for us and make it look professional. It all helps.

'I need biographies, girls, for Polydor and the press,' Gaye announces at the end of the meal.

I groan. 'I hate writing about myself, I'm useless at it.'

'Me, too,' says Di. 'Can't our agents do it?'

'Of course not, darling. They'll just hand out a list of credits. That won't do.'

'No, I suppose not,' I admit. 'Even so, I loathe the thought. Honestly, I could write either of yours better than mine. I know them just as well.'

'Can't be helped.' GB is brisk. 'It's just a paragraph to hand to the press. To give a flavour.'

I groan again. Then a light-bulb moment: 'Wait a minute! Why don't we write each other's? See what we come up with?'

Di beams. 'I could do yours, Annie.'

'And I'll do Gaye's.'

'Huh. That leaves me with Di-Di's, then,' sniffs GB. 'Paper, Annie! Napkins at least! Quick, before the mood passes. Let's do it. Pens!'

'Wine!' shouts Di-Di.

'Ready? Steady? Go!'

Twenty minutes of swapping details, drinking and scribbling, we read them out, giggling at our own creations. Simple, funny—and different.

GB is satisfied. 'Brilliant, Annie. That'll show the bastards.'

When I get home, I type them out:

GAYE BROWN—by Annabel Leventon

Northumberland-born Gaye Brown was a film star from

the age of six in "The Happiest Days Of Your Life", "The Blue Lamp" and various other Ealing comedies. SUCCESS. From here she could only go down—to a convent school in Devon at eleven years old. Despite this expensive education, a posh background (Gaye was a deb, her grandmother a Gaiety Girl) and drama school (Guildhall), she has no qualifications and always plays tarts. Her first part, hot from the Guildhall, was starring in the West End as Chief Weasel in "Toad of Toad Hall", followed by a revue at the Savile Theatre "The Lord Chamberlain Regrets". SUCCESS. Then two years' total unemployment, when she learned to hustle, run Circlarama, P.R. for others, and grew tall. Joan Littlewood rediscovered her, put her into the best Stratford East shows—"Oh What a Lovely War", "Marie Lloyd," etc. Since then she's had hundreds of film, T.V. and theatre jobs, touring the U.S.A. in the revue Annabel did in Edinburgh, played Chicago's Second City—SUCCESS. Currently to be seen as the opera singer in "A Clockwork Orange" and in "A Touch of Class"—playing... a tart. She claims she never works.

DIANE LANGTON—by Gaye (Silver) Brown

Diane was born in Fulham some time in 1950!—small, vivacious and a born star! Danced and sang her way up and down North End Road and finally into the Palladium as a chorus girl—various summer seasons—Bruce Forsyth show in Bournemouth was a favourite!—various gigs in dodgy pubs for 30/- a night and then into the West End! In "Hair" with Annabel—then she did the Rock Musical Circuit—Jesus Christ Superstar—Two Gentlemen of Verrona—then discovered under the auspices of Victor Spinetti by Ron Hill of Stratford E.15 to star in "Is Your Doctor Really Necessary"—success—a starring role in "Pippin"—success—back to E.15 for the new show opening on January 29th—joined Rock Bottom at the birth and who knows...

ANNABEL LEVENTON—by Diane Langton

She was born in Blackheath—a star by the age of three
as the Queen—admittedly in the "King's Breakfast" by
A.A. Milne! But a start! She was then educated—and
made it to Oxford—singing her way through the years and
finally gaining a degree in 1964—and took Greek Street
by storm later that year at the Establishment Club—in
revue! (Where she did not meet Gaye Brown, who was at
the time about to take her place to go to Chicago, U.S.A!)
More studying—Drama School—kicked all the awards—
graduated into rep—closely followed by New York and
then—Eureka—back to England to star in "Hair"—
total success—on to Paris—other West End successes—
created her own clever chat show "Cover To Cover" for
London Weekend Television—has made numerous records
quietly—joined Rock Bottom and writes a lot of the songs.

West Kensington Mansions, W14, late January, 1974

Howard's eyebrows arch up in comic surprise, his jaw open.

'You have Jack Rosenthal coming for dinner? *The* Jack
Rosenthal?'

'Yup.'

'Oh, my God, he's my hero! I worship Jack Rosenthal. He's the
greatest television writer on the entire planet.'

'I know.' What a gratifying response. I didn't realise Howard
felt this way. The kitchen walls expand a little as I pass him his tea.

'How come?' he asks.

I rattle the biscuit tin to bring Don in before the tea gets
too cold.

'We're friends.'

'How come?' he says again.

'Mo, that's Maureen Lipman, and I were at drama school
together. We've been close friends ever since. She just married
him. First Jewish wedding I've ever been to. Laurence Olivier

was there. Not that I got to speak to him. But we were in the same room. At the same time.'

Howard sips his tea. 'Oh, my God. Jack Rosenthal.'

Laurence Olivier clearly doesn't mean half as much.

I rattle the tin again and open it. Not a great assortment: one crumbling digestive and half a dozen broken Rich Tea. 'We thought he'd be the perfect person to write the television series for us. And now we've got a record deal going, it seems it might happen sooner than we'd thought.'

'I can see that. Of course. You're right. He produces as well, doesn't he?'

'Yes. Don mentioned the idea to him before Christmas. This is the first time we could get together to discuss it. Find out what he thinks. And spend some time with both of them, of course.'

Don puts his head round the doorjamb. There is no kitchen door. Well, it's a sort of door, a sliding one that doesn't slide, it stays open. The whole kitchen is a bit of an afterthought, design-wise.

'Any tea left?'

'Get a mug, darling, will you? I was just telling Howard about Jack and—'

'Tell you what,' cries Howard. 'Not only is that a great idea, but do you think you could introduce me? I'd kill to meet him.'

'Course. Come over Friday,' says Don, grabbing the last two biscuits.

'Only it's not just dinner,' I say. 'It's a business meeting for Rock Bottom. We're going to discuss the series idea properly, in detail. So maybe just come for a drink and vanish before I serve up. Would that be okay?'

Howard beams. 'More than okay!'

He's as good as his word. He shows up on Friday, has a drink, chats for half an hour and goes.

'Nice feller,' says Maureen.

'Good writer, too,' I say, as we sit down to eat. 'You saw *Verité*, didn't you?'

'Good piece of writing,' Jack agrees. 'He's got talent.'

We tuck in. It takes a while to get to the heart of the conversation. Not just because of the spaghetti bolognese, there's always so much catching up to do. What we're up to, what our friends are doing, Philip Sayer, Lesley Joseph, Ruby Wax.

We're on to pudding before Don says, rather abruptly, 'Er, so what about the idea, then? The TV series for Rock Bottom? What do you think?'

Jack pauses, wipes his mouth, then his glasses, puts his spoon and fork together.

'The thing is,' he begins.

Oh dear. That doesn't sound so good.

'Don't get me wrong. It's a brilliant idea. Original, bold, everything you could want for television.'

'Great!'

'The thing is: I don't think it's for me.'

My heart plummets.

'But you're so right for it. You'd make it so funny, you know us all, you—'

'It's not that, love,' says Jack, with his usual kindness. 'I know nothing about the music business, you see. I'd be writing from ignorance. That wouldn't do at all. It's not my world, pop. Or rock. Or the music business in general.'

'But—'

'And I want to get away from writing series. I did *The Lovers* for too long. I've got several plays I want to write while they still *do* single plays. Sorry. I've thought long and hard.'

Mo comes to the rescue. 'We truly think it's a great idea, don't we, Jack? It'll make great television. You three lunatics together. The very thought of it makes me laugh.'

I cheer up. 'Wait till you see us on stage!'

'*What?* On stage? When?'

'Straker's asked us to do a concert with him this summer. We'll share the bill with him. He invited us to do backing vocals,'

I say. 'Cheeky bugger. We said only if we have our own solo spot, so we're doing it. You'll come, won't you?'

Jack beams. 'Wouldn't miss that for the world. We'll be there. If we can get tickets. You really are going for it, aren't you? And I'm so sorry to turn you down over the television idea. I know you understand.'

Mo and I clear the plates while Don takes Jack to the living-room to play him our demo—again. *Boy You're A Big Girl Now* blasts through the walls.

'He's heard it already!' I yell over the noise.

'Who cares?' Don shouts back. 'It's great!'

It *is* great. Mo and I dance as we wash up.

As they leave, Mo suddenly turns to us. 'It's a real shame. I did my best to persuade him, you know. Maybe you should consider Howard as the writer?'

'I've thought about it,' I say. 'He's not got much track record.'

'Or clout,' observes Maureen, ever practical.

'Exactly. And his style is just a bit…'

'Surreal?' she asks.

'Yeah. Rock Bum is so earthy and real. It might be a bit weird. But who knows?'

We kiss and hug and they go out into the January chill.

'Do you think I should, Don?' I ask when we're in bed.

'Mmm?'

'Talk to Howard?'

'Why not? Can't do any harm. Shame about Jack.'

'Mmm.'

'Nice dinner, though.'

I meet Howard for lunch. It takes a while to find the right moment. There's so much else to talk about and I feel cautious. I don't know whether Howard'll be interested. And I don't want to promise anything, not yet. Unwittingly, Howard leads me in.

'It was so great to meet Jack. Maureen, too, of course. I can quite see why you're friends. Jack is my hero, as I've undoubtedly told you too many times.'

'It was fun, wasn't it?'

'It really was. That guy has inspired me, you know.'

'I'm not surprised, he's the best. His writing is so truthful. And funny. Down-to-earth, human kind of funny. So real.'

'Exactly.'

I'm getting towards it now. 'That's why we thought he'd be perfect for Rock Bottom.'

'What did he say?'

'They both loved the idea. But he said no, he knows nothing about the music world. And he wants to be writing single plays now.'

'That's such a shame. Never mind. Did I tell you Thames have commissioned another one of mine?'

That's that till pudding.

'By the way,' I say through a mouthful of tiramisu, 'Maureen wondered—and I wondered—if you'd be interested in maybe coming on board as the writer at some point—if we ever get the series off the ground?'

Howard sits back in his chair. 'God! That was good. Nice place, this.'

'It is.'

'I suppose there would be things for and against, Annie. I want to get into writing series, you know that. The reverse of Jack's position, really. I'd gladly swap—he does the one-off plays, I grab the series slot. Wouldn't that be great?'

'It would,' I agree. 'Coffee?'

'Mmm, why not? Of course, it'd be interesting as I know you and Don so well, and the girls a bit, mainly through you.'

'That's what I thought.'

Howard hesitates. 'Two things. One, I have no track record except at Thames. Even then it's only with the drama depart-ment. My name means zilch anywhere else, unlike Jack. His name'd open doors everywhere for you. I wouldn't be much use. And second, I have so many projects of my own to develop, like *Loony Tunes*, for instance. Let's wait and see, shall we?'

'And obviously,' I add, 'I couldn't guarantee anything at this stage as we don't know who might pick it up. They might have ideas about what writers they'd want to use.'

'Obviously. As I said, let's wait and see, okay?'

I ask for the bill. 'Oh, did I tell you the best, best news?'

'What's that?'

'Peter Straker's doing a concert in July. He's asked us to do it with him.'

Howard's face lights up. He leans forward and pats my hand. 'That's a truly great next step. I'll be there. That's so exciting for you, Annie.'

'I know. I can't get over it. I'm really nervous, too.'

'Nonsense. It'll be fine. I'll bring people.'

'Bring the world, please!'

'Maybe Andrew Brown.'

'Andrew Brown? Oh, the guy who produced *Verité*?'

'Yeah. He might talk about it in the right places. I could ask someone from the drama department at Thames, too.'

'Bring anyone you can think of, Howard. This could be our real break. Though I can't see how a drama department would be interested in a pop group, can you?'

Howard shrugs. 'It's more light entertainment, really. But they're the only television people I know, so I'll give it a shot.'

'You're an angel.'

'I have a great part lined up for you, by the way, if I can get this next idea off the ground. Did I tell you yet?'

And we go on to the next-project-that-might-one-day-see-the-light-of-day.

Peter Straker never, ever admits his age. Caramel skin, chronically myopic, exquisite BBC English with the faintest hint of

West Indian, mainly when he's had a drink. Black afro halo during *Hair!* morphing by degrees into a severe, slicked-back plait down his back over the intervening years. Owns nothing but some solid silver rings and a spectacular, soaring voice, which cracks now and again as he will *not* take care of it. And, of course, his records. He and I used to hang out together during *Hair!* Absurdly generous, not to say grand, his wages trickled through his fingers like water, mainly on running up restaurant bills treating his friends: La Popote in Walton Street, then The Last Resort in the Fulham Road, frequently The Casserole.

His private life is very private. He wears beautiful silk suits to do cabaret, outclassing the paying customers. It takes him years, literally, to learn a song. Once he's got it, like *Carousel* by Jacques Brel, he goes on refining it and deepening it forever. He'll never own a flat or be able to pay his bills, but he can rustle up a record deal from the wreckage of the one before as if they're ten a penny.

He and Don took to each other like long-lost friends. Now Don produces his records, some of them our songs. For one of them, *Piano Player*, Don rushes me into the studio to do a guide track, so Peter can hear it in his headphones and follow me. He's had the piano track for three weeks and when he gets into the studio he still has no idea how it goes. I don't have time to get nervous, it's not me on show, and since I've co-written it, I know it backwards. I come in straight off the bus, stand in front of the microphone and do it in one take.

Afterwards, Don takes me aside. 'That was beautiful. Best you've ever done it, I'm going to keep it.'

It's not even in my key. I leave feeling very good about myself.

Later, when he gets home, Don looks shamefaced.

'I don't know how it happened. I'm so sorry.'

'What?'

'The sound engineer wiped your vocal. It was perfect. Better than Peter's.'

'Never mind,' I say. 'After all, Straker's got the recording deal.'

It's a shame. Who knows what might have become of it? But praise from Don means just as much.

At the end of January, Gaye, Di and I sign our very first Rock Bottom agreement in Breitkopf and Härtel's, in front of Larry Fenton and Sandra, his secretary, who also happens to be Don's sister. She files it away for us. Whether it keeps Di with us we have no real idea, we're just doing the best we can to keep her on board. She's proved elusive since she joined us. Not just the rehearsals for *Pippin* or the show at Stratford East, she's more wayward than that. She gets a bad throat, or she doesn't notice the time, or she's been up all night. Or she panics. We can't have a go at her or she might deliver the ultimate threat: she'll leave the group.

'But, Di, you agreed it last week. The musicians are booked and everything. And the studio.'

'Yeah, but I can't just drop everything, you know. I got to earn a living.'

'We all do. Rock Bottom is supposed to help us.'

'It's all right for you. I got my solo career to think about.'

'You're coming this morning, aren't you?'

'When did you say?'

'This morning, Di! Now! Please!'

Alarm bells rang so loudly after one of these frequent conversations, we actually talked about replacing her, recasting before it's too late.

'Elaine Paige?'

'She's great.'

'Julie Covington?'

'She's great, too.'

It was no good, we couldn't do it. The minute Gaye first mentioned Di's name, we felt it. The second she came in to hear that first song and agreed to join us, the group became tangible and concrete, a living thing instead of just an idea in my head. We belonged together, we knew it. There was a chemistry between us that money can't buy and words can't explain.

It was simply unthinkable to regroup. We gave up trying.

Don's sister Sandra does her best to organise things for us, whatever there is. Nothing much, we don't write anything down, we're much too busy.

This is our first attempt at a proper agreement, drafted on napkins in the Chinese restaurant in Stratford East:

We the below named:

GAYE BROWN
DIANE LANGTON
ANNABEL LEVENTON

agree collectively to work together as singers or however else required, and to be known as

ROCK BOTTOM.

To do everything possible, in whatever way, to promote the group.

Any member leaving the group will relinquish and forego the use of the name ROCK BOTTOM and may not use the name in any way whatsoever. Any member leaving the group will give such notice as may appear reasonable, but in any case not less than two months. No member may leave ROCK BOTTOM until six months have expired from the date of signing this agreement.

GAYE BROWN
DIANE LANGTON
ANNABEL LEVENTON

29th JANUARY, 1973.

None of us notice the date's wrong: 29th January, 1973. It should, of course, be 1974. But that's what happens in January. And of course it completely invalidates the six months' notice to leave we agreed on. But it's a step forward in our commitment to the group.

February, 1974

While the Polydor deal progresses, two things emerge from it. First we get a publishing deal with Ronnie Beck at Feldman's. Then we sign another piece of paper formally booking Don as our producer, giving him an equal share of anything Rock Bottom earns. All our publicity is geared to us being three independent broads striking up on our own. But there's never, *ever*, any question of us girls being separate from Don. He's an essential part of the team.

We have to start planning the Peter Straker concert. We're all working in different places. Through most of February I have television work, Di's at Stratford East and Gaye's doing the *Barry McKenzie* film. There are songs to write, Straker's repertoire to learn, costumes to plan, make-up, staging—the concert's potentially a bigger break than the Polydor deal, it could be the great launch pad. On stage we'll all be on home ground, it's where we belong. I have to focus on my *Second City First* play for the BBC, to be filmed in Birmingham, before I get to grips with all that. Then I've a *Dixon of Dock Green* for the BBC. And a *Crown Court* for Granada.

Meantime, I've been auditioning over and over again for a new musical. New songs, dance auditions, no script. Very odd. All I know is Michael Crawford's playing the lead and I'd be playing opposite him. It's called *Billy* and it's a version of *Billy Liar*, the Keith Waterhouse film, which starred Albert Finney and Julie Christie. Another lookalike job: my brother Patrick thought she *was* me when he saw the film. My agents keep telling me what a great part it'll be. The only problem is they need a Fred Astaire/Ginger Rogers dance sequence. Neither Michael nor I are trained dancers and the choreographer is justifiably worried, she wants a dancer in there. The rest of the team want me, my agents say. There's a simple little song to learn, then a dance session with Michael, who couldn't be nicer. We have fun treading on each other's toes. Easier for him, he's got the job. Then total silence for weeks. I get on with planning the concert.

It sounds so straightforward, planning a concert. Nothing much to it, you'd think: choose a few songs, get some musicians, do the show. With less than five months to go, reality starts to bite. Little teeth nibble at me in the middle of the night, wake me up with another thought—backing vocals for Straker, rehearsals for maybe twenty songs, as he hasn't made up his mind which ones he'll do. That's just his set. Ours—a fifteen-minute slot, perhaps? That's four songs. Five, maybe. We've still only got two, *It's All Over* and *Boy You're A Big Girl Now*. Christ! Only two? Turn over, try to get back to sleep. I've got lines to learn for tomorrow.

Don and I grab what time we have. 'Got to start routing Straker's songs.'

'We have to write some more for us, Don.'

'How many have we got?'

'Two, Don. Just two! That's all.'

'All right, keep your hair on. We got anything?'

'What about *We Were*?'

'Straker's singing that.'

'*Ragtime Piano Joe*?'

'Straker.'

'Why don't we do one of them?'

Don's adamant. 'Straker's doing them.'

'Don, those are our best songs.'

'Yeah, but he's going to record them.'

'What're we going to do, then?'

'Better write some more, hadn't we?'

It's amazing what fear can do. While Don's in the music room doing band parts or something equally mysterious and time-consuming, I sit in the living-room, stare out at the grey February sky for inspiration and adopt Don's Beethoven scowl, in case that helps. It does. In less than a minute, I come up with an idea. The first of only two prizes I ever won at school was for playing the triangle when I was six. The prize was a book about a fox, with a dark green cover and a very red fox standing on its hind legs. For no good reason, I remember it vividly. Triangle? Nothing much rhymes with triangle. Not the most romantic image, either, except maybe a warning triangle. That won't do. I go back to my younger self:

> *When she was a young girl back in school*
> *They wouldn't ever let her sing—*

Quick—a rhyme for school—fool, tool (no!), mule. Ah!

> *Weren't they cruel?*
> *The teacher was so mean*
> *Made her play the—*

Triangle? No way. What, then? Recorder? Piccolo?

> *Made her play the tambourine*
> *That's why she is a tambourine queen.*

'Got it! Don, I've got it.' I rush into the music room. 'Listen. I can't give you the exact melody but something like this—and this sort of rhythm.'

I hum a bit and sing a bit and tap out the rhythm. Don thinks for a minute, starts finding chords. The whole thing is roughed out in less than twenty minutes. The chorus writes itself:

> *Hey baby you're a tambourine queen*
> *Ribbons and bows you know what I mean*
> *Hey baby you're a tambourina queen*
> *A tambour, tambourina, tambour,*
> *   tambourina queen.*

It looks stupid on paper, I can see that, but it's fun to sing. Harmonies appear as if by magic and Don makes it thunder along.

'We're going to have to use tambourines, aren't we?'

'Any of you know how?'

'I doubt it.'

'Not as easy as you think,' says Don. 'I'll get Gary in.'

He means Gary Kettel, his whizz-kid percussionist friend from Royal College of Music days. 'He'll teach you. Maybe get him to do the concert while he's at it.'

'I can't play the fucking tambourine and do harmonies at the same time,' GB objects when I tell her.

'Let's just give it a go, all right? We'll worry about real tambourines later.'

No lead vocal on this one, we all decide. Harmonies all the way through, except for the bridge to the last chorus:

> *Her school days are over*
> *Now she's a star*
> *One girl and her tambourine*
> *Have gone so very far!*

It's really high. Don gets us to sing it in turn. I'm too sweet up there, Di too soulful, GB hits it full on, a buzzsaw with an edge of satire, half talking it. Genius.

Another one done. Two, maybe three more to go.

March, 1974

My television shows start being screened and I get publicity in the *Radio Times*, the *Daily Express*, the *Sunday Times*. I'm so excited about Rock Bottom, I can't stop talking about it and they love it. When we get a provisional release date from Polydor for the single, the same thing: loads of publicity comes our way without us trying, from local papers to the music press to *Titbits*, with accompanying photo shoots. We're starting to feature our differences of style and photographers, though bemused, all go along with it.

When an offer for the Julie Christie part in *Billy* comes through, I have twenty-four hours to answer, still without being given a script to read. It means a commitment of over a year, with the first eight weeks performing in Manchester, just when our single will be coming out.

I turn it down. My agents fire me.

Am I the only one apart from Don who sees Rock Bottom's potential? After the trouble Don and I went to, bringing them on board, playing them our songs? I write an angry song about them, *Go Away Daddy*, which Howard loves. I get a new agent, much nicer, much more supportive. I tell her all about Rock Bottom right away. She thinks it's great. Meanwhile, she sets about finding me 'real' work, as she puts it.

April, 1974

When the Polydor deal falls apart, we're on such a wave of confidence we tell each other recording deals are like buses, there'll be another one along in a minute—and focus on the concert.

'When is it again?' asks Di in a plaintive voice. 'I hope it's gonna fit in with the Royal Court.'

'Bound to, darling,' says GB. 'It's on a Sunday, isn't it? *Tooth of Crime*'ll be open by then so you can rehearse with us.'

'Yeah, but when is it?'

'July 14th, Di-Di. Put it in your diary,' I say.

'I ain't got no diary.'

GB snaps, 'Bastille Day, darling. That's easy to remember.'

'What's that when it's at home?'

'Oh for goodness sake! French Revolution, of course.'

Di nods, humbled by Gaye's superior general knowledge. 'Oh.'

We fling ourselves into preparation. This is a way forward over which we have at least some control. We need to write, we need to rehearse, we need costumes, we need theatrical ideas, we need lists of important people to invite. If things go well in July, we might be able to jump several stages of Don's Master Gruppenplan, get another record deal for sure, even get a television company interested in making the series with us. It's a wild hope, but by now we're all equally infected with belief in the group. We could go anywhere, anything's possible.

What we most need is a director, someone to stage the numbers, create the look of the whole show, someone strong enough to keep us in check without stifling us. We all have opinions and such different views it's hard agreeing things. We need an outside eye, we're all used to theatre where you have someone in command.

It takes about a second to work out whose arm to twist— David Toguri's.

David, a superb dancer, was assistant director on *Hair!* so Di, Straker and I all know and love him. We also know he's tireless, endlessly encouraging to actors with two left feet and, last but not least, we trade on the knowledge that, generous to a fault, he's unable to turn down work however busy he is, even when it's a lot of work for no money, like this one. He agrees at once, bless him.

GB keeps coming up with solutions to other problems. She knows someone for everything.

I get as far as, 'How about my designer friend Harry Waistnage for costume? He adores us.'

'Willie Burt, darling, we'll have Willie Burt, he's brilliant. You'll love him. He'll do it.'

'For nothing?'

'Oh, yes!'

I give in. A small, pale, unassuming Scot, Willie has an eye for detail and colour and line. We want two sets of costumes— one for backing singing and one for us as front-liners. Quick changes might be tricky if we're nervous. If? That's hilarious, we already are, with over three months to go.

'Maybe we should open the second half, then stay in whatever we're wearing through to the end?'

'How are we to look really striking, really different and still go well together, Willie?'

Willie pulls some material out of his magic bag. It's very, very, very bright silver. Searing stuff. 'How about this?'

We crowd round. It's certainly showy.

'Might it be a bit stiff? We got to be able to move.'

'I could cut you straight skirts with panels.'

'Panels?'

'Aye, like Roman soldiers—slits all round, up to your hips.'

'If we're all in the same colour and same material, how will we look different?'

Willie raises his eyebrows. 'You'll not have a problem with that, dears. What I propose is that each dress is a different design.'

'How d'you mean?'

'Well,' picking up the silver material, 'We'll accentuate your strong points, highlight them. Look.'

He drapes the fabric round Di. 'High neck, cutaway sleeves for you, Di. Gaye, wide square neck to show off your great shoulders. And you, Annie ...'

He puts his head on one side and studies me.

'Off the shoulder, dear, for you. One shoulder completely bare, both arms bare, draped fabric softly over the bust, leave it simple. All of you with a straight skirt, short, just above the knee, quite demure, backing singers mustn't grab too much attention. But the minute you move, the panels will swing and reveal glimpses of thigh, all the way up. How does that sound?'

It sounds great. And that's just for us as backing singers. He promises to make the main outfits really rude.

GB scores another bullseye when her hairdresser, Douglas Trout, offers to do our hair on the day and volunteers his wife Petra, a model, to do our make-up. This is a real bonus, it's a new kind of show for us, so different from what we do solo, we need serious help presenting ourselves. We can't pay anyone, we're dependent on kindness and generosity. I'd better go and meet Douglas, check he really means it. Gaye is hard to refuse, she comes on so strong, but people don't always want to commit themselves. We need commitment.

Stephen Way's in Bond Street is chic, shiny, expensive. Oh dear. Douglas is a strange mixture—small and neat, very quiet, with a penchant for extremely tight trousers, fetching little blouson jackets and Cuban heels. He won't be rushed. He goes at his own pace, even if fifteen clients with wet hair are dancing with frustration.

I wait till he has a moment.

'Been messing around with your hair, haven't you?' he observes. 'Used to be long, didn't it?'

'Long and straight, yes. I had it cut last year. Big mistake.'

'Yes. Permed, too, judging by the state it's in.'

'Even bigger mistake.'

'Don't think you want to wear a wig, do you?'

I'm shocked. 'It's not that bad, is it, Douglas?'

He shakes his head. 'You want to look glamorous, we're going to have to come up with something. Can you get the other two to come in with you? I better see you all together.'

He has no idea how difficult that might be.

'I'll do my best,' I promise, without much conviction.

A group called Abba have just won the Eurovision Song Contest with a song called *Waterloo*. The girls are pretty and feminine. Nice. Very different from us. The blonde one wears high silver platform boots, which I rather like. I might look around for something like that once the concert's over. Maybe for the next one.

Next one?

Of course there'll be a next one. If we don't blow this one.

May, 1974

The list of people whose arms we're twisting is getting longer. Straker, more used to this than me, knows all the right people. He takes me to see Michael White to persuade him to give us a theatre for a Sunday night, preferably free. Michael's an impresario, the coolest, *The Rocky Horror Show* is his. It started at the Royal Court Upstairs and is now playing in a converted cinema on the Kings Road. I like Michael, he's young and gorgeous and one of us. He twinkles at our boldness, hears my impassioned views on Rock Bottom's potential and my desire to bring theatre and pop together to create something truly theatrical and gives us the Kings Road Theatre free—almost. We'll have to pay the staff.

'One condition,' he says, 'White Light supply sound and light for us. You'll have to use whatever lighting is already rigged and negotiate their fee with them.'

His generosity silences me. I nod and try to stop a grin of relief spreading right across his office.

'Who are White Light? Do you know them?' I ask Straker as we zip out before Michael can change his mind.

'Of course I know them,' Straker replies. 'So do you. They're fantastic. You've seen the show.'

'Loads of times, it's always immaculately lit. And the sound's terrific.'

'Nobody better. They know about rock. We'll go and talk to them next.'

In the end, Straker goes by himself while I grapple with the rest of the huge list of people and things to get on board and be decided: make-up style, rehearsal space, rehearsal schedule, songs, posters. No need to worry about publicity with GB around, I can leave all that to her. My ideas are about concept and structure: running orders, how to stage a number, putting comedy and drama in. That's what I love. I want to put *It's All Over* into a Forties office, with old-fashioned phones and us three as typists filing our nails, each one mourning a man who got away. Not that we can afford to do anything like that yet, but one day…

In the middle of all this, Gaye, who talks about Rock Bottom just as much as I do, it appears, strikes gold.

'Guess what, Annie? I bumped into Brian Degas at the Beeb today. He wants us all to go to meet him and talk about the Rock Bottom series. He heard about it already, from a mate of yours, accordingly. Tony Someone from Purple Records? Anyway, he loves the idea.'

GB always uses 'accordingly' for 'apparently' so I know just what she means.

'Tony Edwards? Of course, he mentioned Brian Degas months ago. That's why he sounds familiar.'

'Darling, he should do, he's the producer of *Colditz*. He wrote *Barbarella*, for goodness' sake. He's top of the range, Brian is. King of the Beeb.'

'Oh my God, *Colditz*? It's brilliant.'

'He devised it, wrote some of it, produced it.'

'And you say he likes the idea of Rock Bottom as television?'

'Annie, I'm telling you he loves it. He'd be perfect for us. So would the Beeb. We're to go in ASAP, all of us. I'm calling Di now. One afternoon next week.'

A BBC producer with his track record? Oh my God, indeed. This is happening so fast, maybe Jack Rosenthal turning it down won't matter too much. Brian will write it. Or think of someone terrific. If he likes us, that is.

We breeze in to Lime Grove, heels a-clatter, hair bouncing, dressed up to the nines. In Di's case, tens. Decibels are off the register. We all talk at once, picking bits of fluff off each other's shoulders, checking for smudged lipstick, high as the proverbial corn in July. Well over the top, there's no other way to describe us. Brian wants to know how the show might be? We're here to show him.

Seeing is believing. So is hearing. He must be able to hear us in reception from his office, four floors up. By the time we tumble through his door, we are in such an advanced state of performance you couldn't switch us off. Brian Degas is a tougher nut to crack than he looks. He sits back in his chair, hands behind his head, throwing in the odd question to which he gets fifteen answers. It's total chaos. He doesn't seem to mind. After forty minutes of cabaret, he gets to his feet, laughing, hands over ears.

'Ladies! Ladies! Enough, have mercy on me. I beg a moment's silence, then we'll repair to the bar. I need a very large drink.'

'Yeah! Great.' 'Me too.' 'Not me, I got a show to do.' 'Di, you're being ridiculous. When did that ever stop you?' 'Shuddup, Gaye, that's not—'

'Please, girls. I beg you. Let me speak. I'll tell you how I see it.' Unwilling, we tone it down, just a bit. Not for long.

He doesn't need long. 'I buy this, I buy it totally. It's genius. You're all brilliant. It'll make brilliant television.'

'We haven't got a writer yet. Gaye knows someone—'

'And Annie knows—'

'Hold it! Hold it. You don't need writers, my dears. You've just given me enough material for three series yourselves in this very room. It's hilarious. You girls are something else. This is what we'll do. We shut the three of you up in a room with a stenographer each—'

'What's that when it's at home?'

'Stenographer? She writes down everything you say.'

'How could anyone get it all, the way we talk?'

'I know. You all talk at once. What I'm trying to say is we put you in a room with a stenographer *each*. We pick a few themes— from what I caught, could be anything—marriage, show-biz, bodies, songs, fellas, break-ups, clothes, children, musicals, friends, politics. My goodness, you covered the lot. Anything you say—'

'May be taken down and used in evidence against us.'

'Anything you say, they'll write down. You get a stenographer each, we'll pick a theme at each session, you go for it, they catch it and put it down. And one good editor can clean it up, shape it and make thirteen half-hour comedy episodes.'

'No writers?'

'No writers. Your material is enough. More than enough. Too much, even.'

'Lovely, darling. That's fine by me. How about that drink now?' GB starts for the door.

Brian turns to Di. 'Di?'

'Yeah, sounds okay. If you think we can really—'

'Annie? What about you? What do you think?'

No writer? We do it ourselves?

Once again, I can't trust myself to speak. I nod so hard I think my head's going to fall off.

4

Making It Real

June, 1974

Don asks Howard to collaborate with him on a new song. It's called *Memory Lane* and it's a tribute to the Beatles, using only their lyrics. It's brilliant. And far too difficult to do on stage. But now Howard has a brainwave; he introduces us to a friend of his, Judy Raines, a lyricist. Small, dark, American, she brings Don the lyrics for a couple of songs. One of them is so perfect for us, Don sets it to music right away. She loves it, we love it, it's a piece of pure theatre called *Dirty Rat*. The style—rude, breathy and sexy—falls into place on the first rehearsal. Toguri knows just how to stage it. We'll come down the catwalk which runs through the middle of the stalls and seduce the audience with it, in their faces. We have another number.

By some miracle we all crowd in to Stephen Way's together to see Douglas, mercifully before the salon is too full of normal clients. It's such a buzz to be together, we're as boisterous as if we're on stage already. Stephen doesn't seem to mind. He smiles gently, waves us towards Douglas and stands back in a bit of a daze while we make the salon very much smaller.

Douglas is unfazed. And laconic. He leaves a haircut halfway done, looks at each of us, turns us round, runs fingers through our hair, moves us together till our shoulders touch.

'Right. Thanks.' Turns back to his client.

'That it, Douglas?' says Di. 'I got up early and come in just for that?'

'Yup,' he says. 'I said thanks.'

'Ideas are brewing, though, aren't they?' I ask.

'Yup.' He snips away at the head in front of him. She keeps her eyes closed, either to protect herself from falling hair, or because she can't bear to look at us. 'Gaye, you better come in for colour.'

GB bristles. 'What's wrong with my colour?'

'That auburn. Doesn't suit you anyway. Scarlet. Or orange.'

Gaye blinks. 'Scarlet, darling? Are you sure?'

'Yeah. Scarlet. Bright pink round your face if you like, instead of orange.'

Di and I watch Gaye's mouth opening and closing and start to giggle. She's met her match.

'That's you sorted, GB,' I say.

Di hesitates. 'What you gonna do to me, then? I'm in a play, you know. I can't just do anything you fancy.'

He doesn't even glance at her. 'You're perfect, now you've got your own colour back. Annie's the only real blonde. You suit dark hair. We'll make yours very curly, put it on top of your head, add a green streak and a bit of glitter if you like.'

Di beams. 'Suits me.'

She and Gaye turn to me. 'What about Annie?'

'I got to think about that. Not sure.'

Since the horrible perm, my hair isn't blonde enough, long enough or shiny enough. I'm just relieved he agrees. He'll come up with something. Gaye's right, he's brilliant.

We wave and shriek, run down the stairs and out into the sunshine.

'Scarlet, Miss O'Hara? Ooh hoo.'

'Black, glittery and green? Sounds like Hallowe'en.'

'That rhymed. Might be a song there.'

'Do you mind? He got me right away. Mitzi Gaynor in *The I Don't Care Girl*!'

'You nana. She didn't have black hair. It was a black head-dress with ostrich feathers. And feathers coming out of her arse as well.'

'I don't care, girls. I'll be Mitzi Gaynor. Willie Burt will do me arse-feathers, too, so there.'

'And Doris Day for Annie, I think. *Annie Get Your Gun.*'

We whip-crack-away down posh Bond Street, Di wiggling imaginary feathers behind her. The traffic stops.

Don and I go to see Di in *Tooth of Crime* at the Royal Court. Di has a spectacular monologue which she does superbly, where she's fighting a man off while he's undressing her, her hands being his. The punchline is a desperate 'I might get pregnant!' once he's ripped her bra off. It's touching and hilarious.

Afterwards, when we go backstage to congratulate her, she's furious. Apparently her bra broke in the middle of the scene and ruined things for her. Not us. Her greeting to me:

'Oh no, Annie. Why'd you come tonight? The greatest actress in the western world sitting there watchin' it all go wrong.'

And in the same breath, she exclaims, 'Blimey, Annie, 'aven't your tits dropped!'

I am lost for words. It remains a running joke for me and Gaye ever after.

All I've had for income is from the *Second City First* television play last February, a radio play and an episode of *Dixon of Dock Green* in March, all for the BBC. The dear old Beeb pays me a pathetic salary because, they say, I got a job as an extra in one of their costume dramas as a student and that fixed my pay level at lowest of the low forever. Money is stretched thin. Don's music room is all very well for singing rehearsals, but we need space and proper flooring for the staging. Carpet won't do. We have to have rehearsal space and we have to pay for it.

With David Toguri on board as director, things gather momentum. By the middle of May, we're rehearsing regularly. Well, fairly regularly, not as often as I would like, but the best we can do. I'm the organiser, my job is getting us together for dancing, singing, costume, shopping expeditions for shoes, tambourines, glitter, booking rehearsal studios, typing out lyrics, distributing them, guest lists, artistic coherence. Not that there's much of that, it's something to dream of.

Di emerges as dance captain, pouring oil on the edginess that develops between me and Gaye over which foot where and how to remember what David's asking us to do. I have the least confidence when it comes to dancing. Gaye, though confident, never remembers anything from one rehearsal to the next. Di knows exactly what the moves should be and more important, just how to manage us.

With Di's show up and running we can only work Sundays and some afternoons. She must be exhausted, but she doesn't complain. I find dance studios in Fulham on the North End Road, then get another *Crown Court* to do, recording in Birmingham, but rehearsals for it, thank goodness, in London. This involves running backwards and forwards from rehearsing in Soho for the Beeb to dance rehearsals for us in Fulham, with costume fittings for both shows in between. No time to eat. I grab an apple and jump on the Tube, adrenalin flowing nonstop. The upside is I'm losing a gratifying amount of flab. In fact by June I'm leaner and fitter than at any time since I was fourteen, and that includes my time in *Hair!*

'Good grief, Annabel!' observes an Oxford chum, Peter Sibley, at a party one evening. 'You're wasting away.'

'It's excitement. It's the group.'

'Watch it!' he says. 'It's becoming Magnificent Obsession.'

He's right. Magnificent Obsession it is. I feel as if I've been waiting all my life for this.

I've never undertaken a project of this magnitude before. And I love it. Directorial ideas bubble up all the time, I can't wait to try them out. Most importantly, I'm not trying to do it alone, it's all shared out. GB comes into her own. She's terrific on publicity, having run big fundraisers at Stratford East. Her ability is astounding. Not only is she full of ideas, she also knows everyone in the business. I know how hard it is to say no to her, she simply won't have it. A large steamroller bears down on you and you say yes and run for cover. Don takes care of all the music, the band, the band arrangements, Straker's needs. It's a team effort. I feel I can achieve anything with all of us in it together. It's how theatre ought to be. And I'm right in the middle of it.

Between us all, we know quite a few journalists. Each of us is well enough known in our own right to generate publicity. Together, we're a journalist's dream come true. The response is overwhelming. They vie for our attention, from David Wigg in *The Daily Express*, to *The Evening News*, *The Sun* and the music press. Crowned by the wonderful Molly Parkin, who takes us out to lunch and promises us a full-page spread in *The Evening Standard*. With a photo. Taken outside the Royal Court stage door so Di is close to work, we look outrageous and camp, grouped round someone's motorbike (not ours). Lunch is very noisy indeed. Our usual cabaret act is in full swing. And Molly loves it. Loves us, loves the idea of the group. Promises fame and fortune. Promises to come to the show.

Meanwhile, David Toguri doesn't let us down. He gives Sundays and evenings, whenever we're free, pushing and exhorting us and treating it like a properly paid West End show. The tambourines show up. I spray them silver and add ribbons and bows. They're a pain to use, Don was right. For our main set, Willie Burt has come up with Hollywood-style costumes of marked vulgarity and over-the-top glamour. It's scarily great looking in the mirror, even with pins sticking in us all round.

Molly Parkin's as good as her word. Two weeks before the concert, her article comes out in *The Evening Standard*. *Molly Parkin's People*, it says, with a cartoon of Molly at the top and a huge photo of us looking as outrageous as she makes us sound.

Three Courses of Rock and Raunch, says the headline. We gasp as we read. She compares us to the Marx Brothers and proceeds to nail us as bossy, rude, sexy and the most exciting thing to happen to rock'n'roll ever. It catches the spirit of the venture beyond our wildest dreams.

'She'll be our script editor when we do the TV show for Brian Degas,' Gaye declares.

A genius idea. GB scores again.

Two days later, the show has sold out. We decide to make the afternoon dress rehearsal a public show, too. Might as well get 'em all in.

July, 1974

The posters arrive. A big close-up of Straker looking soulful, wistful and wise. 'Nothing like he really is,' snorts GB. Hmm. We didn't take quite enough care of the poster, perhaps, it's *all* him. Underneath, it says: '*with Rock Bottom*'. Not big letters, no photo, but we exist in print, it makes it real. The fervour with which we gather friends to do a little illegal fly-posting up and down the Kings Road at midnight testifies to our belief in the concert as The Big Launch. We know we risk arrest—or knee-capping if the uncrowned king of flyposting catches us. It only adds to the fun.

GB and I spend an afternoon taking posters to the stage door of every theatre in the West End.

'They all know us, they'd better come in support,' she says.

'And what else will they have to do on their night off? Might as well come and have a wonderful time.'

I'm beginning to believe it might be just that—wonderful.

Straker is a bundle of nerves and needs nursing. I sit him down to devise the running order, while he puts an ice pack to his head and moans. Someone's got to get this together, might as well be me.

'You're a few numbers short, Strakes,' I say, looking at the list.

'I know, Belle. Oh God.'

'What else is in your vast repertoire?'

'That's it, darling. That's it.'

I have loads of sheet music collected over the years. I riffle through a few hundred.

'*Pennies From Heaven*? *Ain't Misbehavin*? *Girl From Ipanema*—that'd be good for you. *Summertime*?'

Groan.

'*Laziest Girl in Town*? It's easy-peasy to learn.'

'Is it?'

'Yes. Listen, it goes like this:

> *It's not cos I wouldn't, not cos I shouldn't*
> *And you know it's not cos I couldn't.*
> *It's simply because I'm the laziest girl in town…*

Marlene Dietrich sang it. Should be good enough for you.'

The melody is a simple little phrase repeated over and over. A doddle to learn. And it would be funny having Straker sing it. His songs are mostly quite serious.

He perks up enough to say, 'Put it to one side. I'll go through it with Don,' and lies back down again.

'Come on, Straker. It's going to be fine. You've got *Ragtime Piano Joe* to learn and *We Were* and this and it's done. I'll help you.'

He moans again. 'It's not just learning them, Belle. It's routining them with Don. The band, the arrangements. We've hardly begun. There's no time.'

I nag and cajole till we have a solid set for him and a great running order. I never knew I liked planning. Straker seems relieved to have me shoulder the burden. He just wants to sing, while I want to be part of every last scrap of it.

I have an unworkable idea for *Ragtime Piano Joe*, which Straker is singing. It's about a silent movie pianist who dies of a broken heart when the talkies come in. We've put it in as one of the last numbers in the show. We'll be on stage too, as it's almost the finale and we're backing him on it, but I think it needs something extra. There's a section where you hear the ghost of Ragtime Joe playing softly in the empty movie house. I know it backwards because I helped write it.

'Wouldn't it be great,' I say to Toguri, 'if all these dream figures from the silent movie era came out on stage like ghosts, really, while we hear Joe's ghost playing the piano? You know? The bit where it says,

> *If late at night into the movie-house you go,*
> *Sit at the back, stay out of sight,*
> *You can still hear Ragtime Joe.*
> *When the crowds have gone, the old-time songs,*
> *The ones we used to know,*
> *Can still be heard, but very faint,*
> *It's the ghost of Ragtime Joe*

and out they all come for the instrumental to do a little dance. I know we can't afford it. Not this time. One day ...'

David thinks for a moment.

'Leave it with me,' he says. 'I'll work something out.'

I imagine he's thinking of some back lighting so we have shadows on stage behind the band. At the next rehearsal he comes up to me.

'I've got it,' he says. 'They can come off stage down on to the catwalk. I'll get twenty dancers, they'll have to supply their own Hollywood-style costumes, and I'll rehearse them somewhere in the theatre on the day, I don't know when or how yet. They can do a slow motion tap sequence during the instrumental. Would that work?'

'Would it work? It'd be brilliant!' I throw my arms round him. 'Genius, David. But how will you get twenty dancers? You know we've got no money.'

'Oh,' says Toguri, 'They might do it for love. Like me. We'll see.'

It would be a tour de force. I know it's impossible. I keep my fingers crossed.

In the last week before the concert, Straker drops a bombshell down the phone.

'White Light are being very difficult.'

'What do you mean, difficult?'

'They want all their money up front, before the concert.'

'How much?'

'Three hundred pounds.'

I whistle. 'Oh Christ, Straker. Is that what you agreed?'

Straker pauses. 'I can't remember. I assumed I'd pay them out of the proceeds.'

'Oh dear. What are you going to do?'

'I don't know. I haven't any money.' He sounds affronted, like Mme Arkadina in *The Seagull*—I'm an actress, not a banker.

'What if they don't get it?'

'If they don't get it by Friday, they'll pull the plug on it. We'll have to cancel.'

'Jesus.'

Three hundred pounds is a huge amount. Straker never told me.

Over supper, Don and I talk. 'What do we do?'

Don munches away. Nothing puts him off his food. 'Dunno. Nothing I can do. Haven't got any.'

As if I didn't know that. 'Could you ask Larry?'

He shakes his head, pours himself another glass of wine. 'He's already put in so much, I can't ask him for any more.'

'We can't cancel either. I'd die if we did.'

I lie awake all night. In the morning, I call Straker.

'Can you borrow anything from your bank?'

'You must be joking, Belle. I'm hopelessly overdrawn already, you know that. Always am. You got anything stashed away?'

'Long gone, I'm afraid. There's nothing in my account. Nothing.'

'You're not overdrawn, though, are you?'

'No. And I never want to be. I'd be terrified.'

Straker laughs. 'Dear girl, you need to join the rest of the human race. It's a way of life!'

'Not for me.'

I'm stubborn on this one. My parents were penniless when I was a child, I've always been anxious about money. It's bad enough having nothing, borrowing would only make it worse. I can't go down that route.

'Tell you what,' he says. 'If I come with you to meet your bank manager, I can say I'll pay it all back after the concert's over. I'll write him a letter of promise. Do you think he would lend you then?'

I think of Mr Skillern. Solemn, strait-laced, proper. It sounds very unlikely.

'We can try,' I say doubtfully.

Mr Skillern comes up trumps. £300 is made available for a week, on Straker's letter of promise. On Friday, July 12th, I pay White Light their money, with a heart beating far too fast, just in time for Sunday.

We're still on the road. Just.

5

The Smell of Success

Boy you're a big girl now yes you are
And everywhere you go you're a bright shining star (Fraser)

The Kings Road Theatre, Sunday July 14, 1974

Backstage, there's only one dressing-room for all of us—Straker and his extensive entourage, plus hair, make-up, costume, musicians and us. Willie hangs up our costumes while we grab a little space each. I unpack our new, glittering platform shoes. Nowhere to put them where they won't get trampled on. I put them on the dressing table till I work it out. We paint our nails, compare earrings, look through the running order. Straker lies back to have a head massage, apparently exhausted already. It's eleven am. Douglas and Petra have taken the far end for make-up and hair. Combs, hairpieces, pins, electric rollers, towels, hair spray, hair dryers, hair nets, eyelashes, make-up sticks, hand mirrors, all laid out in perfect order. Petra files her nails and waits her turn.

Toguri runs in, ignoring the chaos our end. 'Girls! I need you down on stage in five minutes. I need to do the opening of the show. You, too, Straker.'

'Ok, darling. On our way.'

He's just running out again when he screams, 'No, no, no!'

We all look up like startled rabbits, except for Straker.

'New shoes on the dressing-table? Never! Terrible bad luck!'

I grab the shoes and put them on the floor. 'Sorry, David. Sorry, darling.'

He runs off.

'That's one I didn't know,' remarks Gaye, 'but I like it. I think I'll adopt that.'

She tries it out at full blast in a Canadian/Japanese accent: 'New shoes on the table? Never! Frightful luck!'

'I bloody hope it isn't,' I say, 'I put them there.'

'You broke a few mirrors this year, didn't you?' scoffs GB, 'and you're here to tell the tale, aren't you?'

'Got to respect other people's superstitions. Like not mentioning You-Know-What in a dressing-room. Just in case.'

'What's that?' asks Di.

'And what about whistling backstage?'

'Yeah, I know that one. What about the other one?'

'The Scottish play,' we chorus.

'What play's that?'

'Can't say, darling. We're in a dressing-room. Just don't mention it or quote from it, okay?'

'Spoilsports.'

'Come on, girls. Shoes on. Toguri's waiting.'

'Can we forget the fucking tambourines, please!'

'No, GB,' says Di. 'Toguri'd kill us.'

'The routine may kill us first,' says GB. 'I hate the sight of the damn things.'

'They look gorgeous,' I protest, having decorated them myself. 'Just this once, GB. If it doesn't work, we'll drop them for the next show.'

'What next show?' she shouts to my disappearing back.

What next show indeed? Getting through today will be quite enough.

Toguri has about two hours to do everything, instead of a normal show when he'd have days or even weeks. We can't manage doing the tambourines and the choreography at the same time, the ribbons keep flying into our mouths and driving us mad. But he wants his choreography and he's going to get it. GB keeps tapping her foot on stand of the microphone we're sharing. It bashes her teeth with a noisy clatter and the clunk of her foot reverberates round the theatre and drives me barmy. She covers her nervousness by joking with the band and delivering wisecracks, which also drive me barmy. I'm as tense as a brick. We all are.

Backwards and forwards from the dressing-room to the stage for lighting, sound, backing singing for Straker and running through our own set. Douglas grabs us as we fly past, as does Petra, so we find ourselves being photographed by Straker's brother Paul in whatever state we're in—big electric rollers in our hair, eyebrows half done, dressing-gowns over undies. We insist on wearing the shoes for all rehearsals, whatever else we're missing. We haven't worn them before. They're enormous—*enormous*—platform, open-toe, ankle-strap sandals with a big bow right on the instep, all painted silver and then sprayed with silver and gold glitter dust. I'm proud of my handiwork, they look terrific. Gaye now stands at well over six foot and even Di looks average height instead of her usual diminutive self. I feel a million dollars in mine, as long as I don't move too far or too fast: I'm afraid I'll fall off.

Still no idea what Douglas will do with my hair. Too late to worry about that now. I put my faith in the people around me. After all, they're putting their faith in us. And their time, expertise, creativity and generosity. Anyone who says theatre people are shallow, jealous, or backbiting ought to be here today. Their support, loyalty and kindness are overwhelming. I'm humbled. More so when towards the end of rehearsal I see a bunch of people in the dark at the back of the stalls, quietly practising dance moves. They must be the tap dancers. Where did they come from? David's worked some kind of magic.

All I can do is try to work some of mine and not panic. Terror must not be allowed to rule. This has GOT to work, there are too many people to let down.

Their belief sustains me. God knows I need it, my mother's coming. She hates pop, hates amplified sound, hates me singing like this. She'll hate *me*. I curse my sister for bringing her. And try to blot that out. We can't, mustn't, think about the audience. Though of course I do, all the time. Half the cast of *Hair!*, half my year from drama school, half the cast of *Rocky Horror Show*, Straker's recording company RCA, our music publisher Ronnie Beck, even Michael White says he'll try to look in. Jack Rosenthal and Maureen. Tim Curry. Of course Howard Schuman, maybe with someone from Thames, if he's lucky. All on our side, really. Except for my mother. I decide to think of Philip Sayer, my chum from LAMDA, the best support in the world, and how he'll snort with laughter and applaud and cheer if anything goes right (or wrong, come to that) and get everyone else round him reacting, too. He's brilliant at that. I know he'll love it. I focus on him and try to stop shaking.

Don spends his time trying out the piano, rehearsing the music, checking the sound, handing out half-finished arrangements, keeping the musicians happy, keeping us focussed, following Straker's erratic path through songs he still doesn't really know, busking while we try our quick changes. Authoritative, calm, funny, he's in his element. White Light seem to know exactly what they're doing. David and Don consult here and there about the odd lighting or sound effect. I can no longer take any part in that. *Think about the performance.*

Our silver backing-singer dresses feel great, look great. Gaye's hair is a miracle of hot red and dayglo pink, Di well pleased with her black curls, green flash and little silver stars. And my hair is a tour de force. Douglas has sprayed it silver, added an extra piece at the back and turned me into a version of Rita Hayworth.

'Oh, Annie!' says Di in wonderment. 'You look like a goddess. A Hollywood goddess. You really do.'

Here we go. Public Dress Rehearsal. Straker does the first half, we can ease ourselves into the feel of it all while Straker warms them up. Dressed in our silver, we're Straker's backing singers. The Silvertones? The Hi-Ho Silvers? The Strakettes, we decide. We get through the first half, our costumes don't fall off, I don't fall off my shoes, Straker remembers his words, the audience is at fever pitch.

Interval.

Frantic costume change in the crowded dressing-room, touching up hair and make-up, re-glueing eyelashes, getting lipstick off Gaye's teeth and reapplying onto lips, jewellery, tambourines. Becoming not just backing singers, but Rock Bottom.

'It's like the Folies Bergère in here,' someone says.

'It's too darn hot,' Di moans. 'I'm melting.'

GB bursts into song at the top of her voice, 'Too darn hot, too darn hot.'

My ear drums burst.

When Willie's finished dressing us, we crowd in front of the mirror. It's the first time we've seen each other's costumes, first time we've looked at ourselves dressed as Rock Bottom. Willie's been as good as his word. We look glamorous and raunchy at the same time, Di in lime-green stretch glitter fitted top and matching pedal pushers which reveal every tiny everything. She looks as if she's naked and spray-painted. I'm in gold hot-pants edged in black, with a lot of cleavage and not much else.

'Best legs in the business, dear,' Willie says in my ear.

GB's in a dayglo-orange satin halter-neck with skin-tight skirt slit up to her hip bone, with the scarlet and pink hair clashing wonderfully. All of us in sheer black stockings.

We're awesome. Spectacular.

'Wow. Double wow, Willie,' I say.

'Triple wow, darling! Can't you count?' GB counters. 'Whatever happened to your education?'

'Beginners, please,' someone shouts.

We stagger down the stairs in our impossible shoes.

In the wings, shaking like leaves and clutching each other for support, except Di who's clutching her parched throat, muttering 'Port and lemon, gimme port and lemon', we listen to the audience on the other side of the flimsy curtain baying for blood.

'Jesus, it's like throwing Christians to the lions,' I mutter to GB.

'Rubbish,' she says, 'It's just a rock audience, darling.' Her teeth chatter.

Di murmurs, 'Think green and blue. Green and blue. Sea and sky. Keep us calm.'

We have a group hug, so tight we can't breathe. We can't breathe anyway.

What I need is a hug from Don. I haven't spoken to him all day, I can't go on without that. But Don's already onstage, sitting at the piano, smiling at the musicians, waiting to give them the down beat.

What can I do? Next to me is John Simpson, from White Light, with his walkie-talkie and nice suit and good looks. I lean towards him.

'John,' I whisper in his ear. 'John, please will you ... ?'

He can't hear a word, the noise from the audience is deafening. 'What?' he shouts.

I give up all pretence at discretion. 'WILL YOU MARRY ME?' I scream.

'YES,' he yells back and pushes us on.

With the intro to *It's All Over* chiming out, we bump into each other in the dark, trying to fumble to our places. GB's facing the wrong way.

'Upstage! Face upstage!' I snarl. 'Arse to audience!'

'Keep your fucking Hollywood hair on!' she hisses back. This makes me laugh so much I nearly wet myself.

The audience are screaming like banshees. When three spotlights focus on our behinds, they roar. We hold position and hum the opening bars. When we look over our shoulders and start to sing, they yell approval. By the time we get to the chorus, they're on their feet. Even with the microphones, it's hard to hear each other or the band. We're off. We're launched. They love whatever we do, we're giants bestriding our world. We finish the show in triumph. And this is just the public dress rehearsal.

Tonight it's standing room only. We have thirty minutes to change, catch our breath, eat half a banana and panic some more.

Di's almost in tears. 'I gotta have a port and lemon *now*!'

I try to comfort her. 'Di-Di, darling, the pubs are still shut, it's Sunday. If you can get through these two without a drink, you'll never need one before a show again, will you?'

She touches her throat, looking agonised. 'Can't Straker's guys find an off-licence somewhere?'

Straker's guys are busy keeping people from bursting the dressing room walls asunder. They're squeezing through the doorway, waving and cheering. The heavies politely keep them out. No time for compliments, we've only got half an hour. Mistakes have to be put right, David wants to give us notes, tears me apart for not dancing more vigorously, ('Marking it!' he says savagely), Don wants to gives us notes, Douglas wants to fiddle with our hair, Willie to adjust costumes. My tummy's rumbling, but I can't eat, there's no time. Get out of costume, pee, have a slug of water and get back into the silver again.

The second show takes us further and higher. This time I'm freer, I manage to move a bit, breathe a bit, drink in the atmosphere. We're welded together, Gaye and Di and me, charged with electricity. A flow of dynamic energy connects us and leaps across to the audience, connecting them to us and completing the circle. The current lets me fly like I've never done before. Together we are something else. Bizarre, joyous, unstoppable.

When we get to our set, *Tambourine Queen*'s a spectacular mess, tambourines everywhere, in each other's faces. The audience don't care, we can do anything we like. In the instrumental section, we dance off the stage and down the catwalk, the audience roaring, mouths wide open, eyes shining, reaching out to touch us as we sashay past, shaking the tambourines in their faces. We're close enough to see people we know. There's Philip Sayer, doubled up with laughter, Tim Curry grinning at us, Dougie Fisher (my boyfriend from Oxford days) looking amazed, darling Molly Parkin in a hat with a veil and just as much make-up as we're wearing. We wave and yell and grin at everyone.

With *Dirty Rat*, we do it again, inching down the catwalk as far as the mike cables will allow, hissing, making faces, shrugging shoulders at the bastards who've let us down. They go mad.

After our set, while we take a tiny breather to leap into the silver dresses, Straker gives us a little time by going on solo to do *Laziest Girl in Town*.

'*It's not 'cos I wouldn't, Not 'cos I—*' he starts and forgets his lyrics immediately, has to say *hmm, hmm* instead of *shouldn't* and *couldn't*, covers it by retreating behind the curtain and waving a leg demurely at them. They think it's planned and find it hilarious.

We're on the home stretch, we can let go and enjoy ourselves. Sing out, in fact. It's impossible to drown Straker, his voice can top anything, but we give him a run for his money, all restraint abandoned. We're no longer just his backing singers, we're Rock Bottom, matching him decibel for decibel, proud to be out there, full of ourselves.

Proud Mary takes the theatre roof off. We do three verses and three choruses, then we take the chorus alone while Straker nips off to do a quick change, which, being Straker, he hasn't rehearsed. It should take two choruses, he thinks. We sing two choruses. In the wings we can hear cursing and see black tabs flapping. No Straker, though. We sing it again:

> *Big wheel keeps on turning*
> *Proud Mary keeps on rolling*
> *Rolling, rolling, rolling down a river*
> *Rolling, rolling, rolling on a river*

Still no Straker.

Seventeen choruses later, we're exhausted. Round and round we go, adding movements and gestures and whoops, our throats getting hoarse and our legs giving way. When Straker finally gets back on, with tight trousers and shiny new boots, Di shouts at the very top of her considerable lungs, 'Straker! WHERE THE *FUCK* HAVE YOU BEEN?'

It brings the house down.

When we get to the last number, *Ragtime Piano Joe*, we're so spent I've forgotten the treat in store. We get to the last verse and the instrumental:

> *If late at night, into the movie house you go*
> *Sit at the back, stay out of sight,*
> *You can still hear Ragtime Joe.*
> *When the crowds have gone, the old time songs*
> *The ones we used to know*
> *Can still be heard, but very faint*
> *It's the ghost of Ragtime Joe.*

The band goes very quiet, just tinkling piano and Gary's soft cymbals. It sounds really eerie, sends the shivers up my neck. This time I'm relaxed enough to take it in. Just.

And then I notice a group of people creeping silently along the catwalk from the back of the auditorium towards us, bowler hats, Twenties head-bands, pretty little floaty or beaded frocks, wide-legged trousers. Twenty of them, they spread out from the back of the stalls to the edge of the stage, illuminated by a ghostly green light while they do a mournful, lyrical tap dance. Toguri has surpassed himself. It's utter magic. My dream of fusing pop and theatre is happening right in front of my eyes—and it works. The audience is as spellbound as I am, the applause never-ending. It's a triumph.

We're a triumph.

Afterwards, it's mayhem backstage. People surge into the communal dressing-room as we arrive, struggling to get past the hordes in the corridor outside. Howard manages to squeeze his way in, beaming. 'You were great, girls! Andrew Brown was here, really, really likes it.'

It's too hot in here, too full. There's nowhere to be quiet with the girls for a minute, nowhere to take my costume off. 'Tony!' I call, 'Help!' and burst into tears. The friendly RCA strong-arm takes one look at me and empties the room as if by magic. So that's why stars have bodyguards. I get it now. And am I grateful. I change and pack up, making no effort to lose the silver Rita Hayworth hair or the huge amounts of make-up. The Casserole, across the road, will have to take me as I am tonight.

Don and I float down the stairs in a cloud of glory, bumping straight into Andrew Brown in the foyer. He bounds up to us like a Walt Disney cartoon dog—Pluto? Howard was right, he *is* ecstatic. I daren't stop moving in case I fall over. I leave Don chatting to him on the pavement while I drift across the road to the restaurant. Ray flings his arms round me. 'I hear you're a triumph, darling!' and escorts me to our usual table. The place is heaving. It's all audience, applauding and shaking my hand and kissing me. Doug Fisher and his girlfriend greet me.

'I screwed up the movement, David's furious,' I tell them.

Doug shakes his head. 'Bella, looking like that, all you have to do is stand there. Let the others go overboard. That's what works.'

I don't get compliments from Dougie very often. I glow.

When Don catches me up he relays, in his best New Zealand accent, what Andrew said. '*Mar*vellous group. *Mar*vellous idea. It'll make *mar*vellous television. How would you feel if I talk to one or two people on your behalf?'

'What did you say?'

'Told him fine, of course.'

We sit down, hold hands and look at each other.

'Blimey.'

'Blimey.'

'The Master Gruppenplan's working, Don.'

'Yeah. Seems to be.'

'Shame Brian Degas couldn't be there. He'd have loved it.'

'He'll hear about it, though, won't he, when he gets back.'

'With Gaye around, how could he avoid it?'

We both sigh out a long breath, still holding hands, shaking our heads, stunned into total silence.

'Love the *riah*, dear,' says Ray, waving the menu, smiling down at us. 'Very Rita Hayworth.'

> *So dress to the nines in your silks and your fines*
> *For the lines of good people who are waiting.*
> *Waiting to take up their seats.*
> *Turn on the heat!*

6

Cloud Nine

Next morning, I'm still on a cloud. I lie in bed for an extra half hour, my hands behind my head, listening to the traffic below counterpointing the faint piano chords coming from the music room. Don's already at work. Outside, the sky is bright blue, clean. Morning has broken. Shame that's already been used, I'd have it. The way forward is clear for the first time in years. I'm Moses on the mountain looking at the land of milk and honey. Everything is different because of last night.

Through the week, the phone never stops ringing. Congratulations, compliments, crowing, approval. We're no longer the only ones who believe, Rock Bottom has a life out there. RCA, Straker's record company, want to sign us up, Michael White, London's most celebrated rock musical producer, loved us, Brian Degas wants to do a series with us, Andrew Brown thinks the idea *mar*vellous. After ten months of bluffing our way through meetings and conversations and interviews, ten months of shooting our mouths off to record companies, publishers, press and radio, till Di's boyfriend Derek observed after the Capital Radio show, 'You girls have got some front. You'd better be able to deliver the goods', it seems we've now delivered the goods for the coolest, hippest audience in London. Praise and encouragement from all sides. (Leave my mother out of it— it was an endurance test for her. 'Very loud.' was all she said.) I can even pay back the bank loan.

And encouragement from Howard at last. Howard, who's heard all my hopes and dreams about Rock Bottom since the day we met and showed only polite interest till now, Howard is a convert. Whether it was our brilliance on stage, or the crowd's response or Andrew thinking it'd be *mar*vellous television, I have no idea.

I bask in all of it for a few days, till it's time to start writing some more songs to record for RCA. Larry Fenton can lean back and keep his hands in his pockets finally, his faith in Don more than justified. From now on, record companies will pay, first for Straker's singles, then for ours. Don will get paid as his producer and arranger, we'll get paid as session singers. Life is suddenly very, very good.

It gets even better the following week. Straker's brother Paul brings over the concert photos. I gasp when I see them. We look magnificent—strong, sexy, alive. I order lots of them and tell the girls they'd better see them, too.

I also call Howard.

'You've got to come over and see our photos,' I tell him. 'We *rock*, Howard.'

He's very short with me. 'Have to call you back, Annie. Excuse me.'

I tell Don.

'Did we do something wrong, d'you think?'

'Dunno. He was over the moon yesterday. Prob'ly nothing to do with us. Come on, let's get started on those lyrics of yours, what's-it, the new one.'

'*Stars*,' I say. 'Provisional title only. The last line of the chorus is 'a star in a newspaper sky'. I quite like it, actually.'

'Show me.'

We go to the music room. This time, I have the format, the lyrics, the rhythm and quite a bit of the melody ready for him. He sits at the piano, adopting his Beethoven scowl, while I sing it through. Once again, he gets the feel so fast we're halfway through the whole thing before the phone rings again.

'Damn. Might be Howard. Shall I?'

'Yeah, go on. I've got a chord sequence to work out.'

I run down the passageway to the living-room.

'Hallo? Hallo?'

A strangled cry at the other end.

'Howard? Is that you?'

'Of course it's me.'

'You all right? You sound a bit stressed.'

His voice spirals to a top C. 'Stressed? Yes, I'm stressed! I'm way more than stressed. This is a total disaster.' He's almost in tears by the sound of it.

'Howard, darling, what's wrong? What's happened? Can I help?'

'I doubt it. I doubt if anyone can help. That asshole Andrew ...'

'Andrew? You mean Andrew Brown? What about him?'

'I'll kill him. He's ruined everything.'

My heart sinks into my boots. Christ, what's happened?

'I'm so mad with him I don't know what to do.'

I try to stay calm. This is horrible. 'What's he done, Howard? Put me out of my misery!'

'He's only gone and talked about the Rock Bottom series to two companies at the same time. That's what he's done!'

I'm confused. What's the problem with that? And why hasn't he told *us*? 'Which companies?'

'Thames *and* Stella Richman.'

'Stella Richman. Isn't she London Weekend Television?'

'That's hardly the point, Annie!'

'I would've thought it's rather clever of him. London Weekend are much more likely to be interested in comedy rock than Thames Drama. You always said—'

Howard hits the roof. 'Don't you get it? Don't you see?? They both want it. They're fighting over it!'

'But that's great.'

'No, it is not. It is NOT great. It is, as I have said, a total disaster.'

'Why?'

'It'll slow everything down, that's why. It might kill the whole thing.'

I make soothing noises down the phone, calm him down as best I can and go back to the music room.

'Took a while, didn't you? I've finished this.'

'It's very odd. I don't get it.'

I report what Howard said. 'Why would Andrew tell him and not us? I know they're friends but Andrew was going to them about us, on our behalf, wasn't he?'

''S'what he said.' Don gets up, stretches his fingers and looks out of the window. Below is the pub. 'Might be time for a beer. What d'you think?'

It's certainly time for food. In the pub we mull over the strangeness of the whole thing.

'What I don't get is why Howard is so upset.'

'Doesn't make any sense.' Don swallows a mouthful of beer and stuffs some crisps down for good measure.

'Unless,' he says, frowning, 'Unless he's worried about London Weekend. They don't know him. He keeps saying Thames are the only company who use him. Maybe London Weekend'd want their own writers. Or do the same as Brian Degas and get you girls to write it yourselves. That'd cut Howard out, wouldn't it.'

'Yes,' I say, slowly, turning my glass round and round, 'I suppose it would.'

Then I cheer up. 'The good thing is Howard must really want to be involved now.'

'Jump on the bandwagon, now it's rolling, you mean.'

'Darling, that's a bit cynical! If he needed assurance it's a potential blockbuster of an idea, he's got it now.'

'They're all getting it now.'

'Just as long as they keep getting it.'

We drain our glasses and go back to finish my song.

The girls come round to see the photos.

'We look bloody marvellous!' says Di. 'I love my hair like that. And yours, Annie.'

'Ta very much, darling,' from GB.

'You always look marvellous, silly.'

Don puts his head round the door, bleating, '*Mar*vellous! *Mar*vellous!'

'What's he on?' asks GB. 'That supposed to be Kiwi? Useless. Sounds more like South African.'

She does her version of Andrew Brown. It's much better. We all have a go.

'Come on, you got to bound as well!'

A line of four idiots bounds along the corridor chanting '*Mar*vellous! *Mar*vellous!' Poor Andrew. It's going to be a catchphrase.

'That's enough!' says GB, panting. 'Tea, Annie, tea! Heard anything from him yet?'

'Pass me the Southern Comfort!' I shout from the kitchen.

'I never said that, did I?' Di sits and rubs her ankles, going through the contact sheets again.

'You lost your copy of the demo?'

'Never had one, did I?'

'Course you did.'

'Oh, Annie! Look at this. I got to have a copy of this one. We look as if God's sent a shaft of light down on us.'

'Maybe He has,' I reply. 'And no, we've heard nothing from him yet, not directly. Andrew, that is, not God.'

We tell them about Howard's weird phone call and his weirder state. Then we plan the next few weeks, discuss the new recording contract, run the backing vocals for *Ragtime Piano Joe* and *We Were* for Straker's recording session next week and go back to gloating over the photos, still glorying in our recent triumph, secure in the knowledge the group has the beginnings of a real future out in the real world.

'Oh, I just remembered. Want to hear my new song?'

Into the music room we go.

'It's lovely, Annie,' says Di. 'Don, we got to record it. Pisces, Aries, Gemini, what's that?'

'It's us. Our star signs, GB, you and me. *Pisces, Aries, Gemini will combine today.'*

'*Hey, hey, hey,*' they take over. 'What's it called, then?'

'*Stars*—I think.'

'Hasn't Janis Ian just done one called *Stars*?'

'Then maybe I'll call it—'

'Horoscope?' says Don.

Horoscope it becomes. They insist on me singing the lead.

'It's so you, Annie,' says GB. 'Anyway you've only written two verses. Don't want a fight, do we?'

August, 1974

When Howard rings again, he sounds triumphant. And seriously excited.

'Annie, it's happened!'

'What?'

'It was a long shot, but it paid off. Thames Television's Drama Department. They're interested. Verity Lambert likes the idea!'

'Extraordinary. We never thought a drama department would—who's Verity Lambert?'

'Oh really, Annie. Verity Lambert? She only did *Doctor Who* and *Shoulder to Shoulder*. She's taken over as Head of Drama at Thames. I'm telling you, she's interested in the series.'

'Well, that's great news. What about London Weekend?'

Howard ignores that. 'I really want to present the Rock Bottom idea on your behalf. Andrew's set it all up. I think it should be me to take it to the next level. I know you all now, I know what they're looking for, she needs someone who talks her language.'

'Oh. Well, I suppose you're more used to pitching ideas than we are.'

'It's not just that, I know how they work over there, I tell you. I think you should leave it all to me.'

'Let me talk to Don. Maybe we should meet and discuss this.'

'I think I better get everyone's say-so on this, don't you?'

'Maybe we should all go to jolly things along. They might need to see us in action.'

Howard laughs. 'I don't think so, honey. No-one would get a word in. No, no, better leave it to me. After three shows in the can with them, I know how to handle them. I'll be best on my own.'

'Then you *will* need everyone to agree to that. I'll roll it past them.'

'Actually, sweetie, I thought I could take you all out to lunch and explain things. My treat.'

'Wow. Double wow, Howard. That's so generous. But we'll pay our way. We're all in this together.'

'Oh, it's the least I can do,' he says carelessly. 'I want this series to go as much as you do. You'll have to get the girls there, though.'

'I know,' I groan. 'I'll find a way.'

Recording Studios, Soho, mid-August, 1974

A basement room. They almost always are. Better for sound-proofing, perhaps. A small, square brown box with stained brown carpet on the floor, three walls also carpeted and hung with woofers, cardboard egg boxes, cables, hooks. The floor is littered with music stands, drum-kit, chairs, mike stands, head-cans. Cables everywhere. The musos have been and gone, we're here to do the backing vocals for Straker's single. Don decides we should share a microphone. We put head-cans on, large ones, black furry earmuffs. Flats are wheeled round us, separating our sound from the rest of the room.

The fourth wall is glass. Triple-glazed, with the control room the other side. A huge twenty-four-track mixer desk takes up most of the space, the rest of it by the sound engineer, pushing knobs up and down, nodding to Don on the big black swivel chair. The glass wall is triple-glazed to separate us from them. The sound is entirely one way: we can't hear a word they're saying, they can hear every little mouse-squeak from us. No wonder Don's frowning.

Don: Okay girls. We're going for a take. Gaye, step back an inch. Annie, step forward an inch. Di-Di, perfect.
GB: It's like a steam bath in here, darling. We're dripping.
Don: Let's get on with it then.
Di-Di: *(whispering)* I'm sweating like a pig.
Annie: Do pigs sweat? Ouch. Stop it, Gaye!
Gaye: It wasn't me, honest, guv'nor.
Annie: Huh. Gottcha.
Gaye: Ow.
Don: Shut up, all of you. Stand by.

Annie winks at Howard, cross-legged on the studio floor.

'Wass he doin' in here?' Di had hissed. 'There's no room. He oughta be in the control room.'

'Darling, it's fine,' said GB. 'He buys us lunch, he can sit where he flipping well likes. He wants to sit at our feet, good luck to him.'

'I wouldn't want to,' muttered Annie, 'Not your feet anyway.'

Di-Di giggled. 'Gaye's feet are lovely. I think it's mine. Wass 'is name again?'

Gaye: Join us by all means, Howard, darling. Sing along if you want.
Don (from the control room): No way.

All laughed. Howard had squeezed himself in and now sits amongst the cables, back against the control room wall, grinning up at us.

I know how he feels. There's something about being in a

recording session, creating something new. I like having him in here. He's been party to so many stories and jokes and hopes and fears, one stage removed, all via me and Don. Now he can see what we're like with his own eyes, up close, from the inside. One of us, almost.

Don: Stand by. Tape running. Take one.

After the recording, Don stays behind, with mixing still to do. He'll follow us. We go off, relieved and full of ourselves, with Howard.

'Where we goin', Howard?'

'Just up the road. La Tavernetta, on Dean Street. Don knows. He'll catch us up.'

'This is fun, goin' out to lunch.'

'Darling, you're always out to lunch.'

'Hey, the recording was fun, too. I really got into it. You girls are amazing, you sound fantastic. Those top notes, Gaye!'

'All part of the job, darling. Glad you enjoyed it. I'm starving!'

'Me, too.'

'Me too, beyond starving.'

'Nearly there.'

La Tavernetta is small and cosy and family-run. They don't seem to mind the shrieks and horseplay. Gaye flicks her napkin at me, Di tucks hers into her front. All of us chatter at once, flirting with Howard, the waiters, anyone. Being together is a triple shot of adrenalin.

'No need to ask if you girls will drink something? Not that you need to, obviously.'

Why not? It's not a business meeting, we're being treated to lunch. It's rare. It's lovely.

'Well, champagne'd be good. But it might be a bit previous, mightn't it?'

'Let's save it till we've got a ruddy great contract in our hands, signed.'

'And the money in the bank.'

'Why're you buyin' us lunch, Howard?' says Di in a friendly tone. 'I mean, you got no reason really. Don't think we don't appreciate it. We do, don't we? Just we don't know why.'

'Didn't Annie tell you?'

'No. Just you'd be turnin' up and wanted to talk to us.'

'I thought you'd like to tell them yourself, Howard. After all, it's your news, really.'

While Howard tells us, the white wine arrives, then the food.

'Bloody hell. The drama department? We thought only light entertainment would ever be interested. We're rock, not drama.'

'Why not drama queens as well?'

Howard is apologetic. 'They're the only people I know in TV. That's why I brought Andrew Brown to your concert.'

'Who's he?'

'He's *mar*vellous, *mar*vellous, darling,' says GB.

I chime in over her. 'He's the producer who did *Verité*, the play wot Howard wrote, the one Tim Curry and I—'

'A toast! A toast to Thames TV, God bless 'em. It can be the sports department if they want, as long as they like the idea.'

'Well. We thought we'd get there, but not this soon, honestly. Did we?'

Howard says, 'It's great. I want to write the series for you, you see. And I want your permission to go to Verity Lambert and pitch the idea. She's Head of Drama. If she buys it, it'll be plain sailing. We could be in production by September.'

Di gasps, chokes on her wine. 'September? No way! That's a bit soon, innit? I don't know if I'll be free then.'

We girls pat her on the back, refill her glass. Howard looks puzzled. Then laughs.

'No, no, Di. Not *this* September. *Next* September!'

'Oh! Thank God for that!'

'Me, too. What a terrible thought! Even next September will mean a whole lot of pressure on me. If they go ahead, that is.

There'll be so little time to write it. I want to do six one-hour episodes, you see.'

'What?' I'm choking on *my* wine now. He never told me that.

'Yes,' he says, 'I think it's the kind of story that needs to be developed properly. In depth. Half-hour slots would be too short for what I have in mind.'

We digest this over the first course.

'Well, but what if—'

'The thing is,' says Howard, 'you have to like the idea of me going to talk to them on your behalf. I honestly think I'm the best person, but you have to be comfortable with that. I'm a writer, I'm used to pitching ideas.'

'Great. Why not?' says Gaye, her mouth full.

Howard pauses dramatically, looking solemn.

'Well,' he says, twirling his glass round, looking at the reflections dancing on the white tablecloth. 'There's just one thing. There's a one percent chance that they'll go with the series and not with you girls.'

'How d'you mean?' asks Gaye, still chewing.

'I mean,' he says with precision, 'there is a risk. There's a one percent chance that Thames will decide to go ahead without using you girls in the parts.'

We laugh. 'That's ridiculous. You're writing it about us, aren't you?'

Howard nods, 'Yes, I certainly am.'

'And you're writing it *for* us, too, then, aren't you?'

Howard nods again. 'I am. Of course I am. But I think it's only fair to warn you that if they give me the go-ahead, if they decide to do the series, then it is just possible—'

We're up in arms. 'Darling, if you're writing it for us and about us, how could they not use us? It doesn't make sense. What on earth are you worrying about?'

'Then you give me permission on that basis?'

We look at each other. This is crazy.

'Of course we do. We'll cross that bridge if we ever come to it. But it couldn't. It's not something to worry about, is it girls?'

'No way. It's us. It's our story, they have to use us. Don't even think about it. It's impossible. Ludicrous. Ridiculous.'

When Don walks in, we're onto dessert, talking and laughing and competing for Howard's attention.

'Everything all right, then?' Don enquires, sitting down and grabbing my wine glass.

'Fine. All fine. We've told Howard he can go and talk to Thames on our behalf.'

'Right, then. Any food left?'

It's only when we've all watched Don eat and we've ordered another bottle so he shouldn't feel too left behind, and Howard has to go rather suddenly, that we realise he's left us the bill.

'He must have forgotten.'

'Rubbish, darling. He invited us. How tawdry. How tacky. I'll have another glass if we're paying,' says Gaye. 'I thought it was too good to be true. Short arms, long pockets. Bastard!'

September, 1974

While Howard talks to Thames, we have plenty to do: publishing deals and recording deals and plans to discuss. Brian Degas is due back from the States soon. Maybe that'll bear fruit. White Light want to manage us. They've never done management before. We think it might be the blind leading the blind and say no, with some regret as they're all so nice. Especially John Simpson. I don't mention the proposal I made on the night of the concert, nor does he. It was the heat of the moment, I tell myself. RCA, now officially our record company, ask us, with Straker, to do the after-dinner show for their annual sales conference at the beginning of September, at Selsdon Park in Croydon. So we have our next show—unpaid, but an important one. If the salesmen like us, they'll be better at selling our records.

Selsdon Park, Croydon, September, 1974

Gaye is all energy, all gaiety. She shrieks hello to the doorman, shrieks when she sees where we were supposed to get ready, a bare, almost unlit back room like a sort of school detention room, with windows so high you can't see out to dream of freedom. She joshes Douglas about his heeled boots, strokes his silk blouson jacket, teases his wife who's busy laying out make-up brushes on a wobbly plastic table; 'Only the best for us, Petra darling. We bring you to the best establishments.' A bumptious one-woman whirlwind. It drives us mad.

Don frowns and tries the piano. In tune at least. The stage is truly tiny. How will we ever get the Goldring twins with their guitars, plus Preston and his drum kit and the Count and his electric guitar and three microphone stands and us three behind Straker for the backing vocals without someone being injured by an elbow in the eye or one of us falling off our platform shoes trying to avoid the others and breaking an ankle?

It doesn't bother Gaye. 'Think of the money, darlings!'

She's a big three-year-old with the prospect of an audience this evening, it's all she needs to be over the moon, over the top, high. Di and I wink at each other and find places to put our day clothes while Gaye flirts with the musos, towering over the twins and their guitars. She knows there's no money in this gig, it's an audience of three hundred salesmen. They go out to all the record shops and persuade them to stock new records. If they like us tonight, they could help make us a hit. Gaye knows they're going to love us. How could they not? They're all men, we're all women, done deal.

God, she's impossible, today more than ever, the bit gripped between her teeth. I'm always nervous before a show, Di's always desperate for a drink and Gaye can't wait to get out there. The success of the first two triumphant Rock Bottom concerts has gone to her head. She's forgotten Di and I exist, forgotten we're

a trio. She's back to being a one-man band. Don has forty minutes to do the sound check and rehearse us with the band after
a two-month gap. While he's trying to establish the tempi, the
hooks, the breaks, the sound balance, she cracks jokes, gets her
harmonies wrong, thumps her foot loudly on the mike stand so
we're all deafened.

Suddenly, Don hits down on the keyboard very hard with
both fists, glares at her and shouts at the top of his voice:
'SHUDDUP, GAYE!'

Di and I freeze and wait for the storm. The Count smirks
and retunes his Gibson, the Goldrings jiggle from one foot to
the other without looking at anyone. Don sits back down on his
piano stool. Gaye, big, bold, bumptious GB, draws in a breath,
swallows and bursts into tears. Apart from the gusting sobs, and
the blowing of her nose, perfect peace descends. Not another
squeak out of her. Don can now rehearse.

And once Douglas has made our hair into tributes to
Hollywood stars (today I've asked to be a Walt Disney fairy-
tale princess with soft blonde waves flowing down to my waist,
Di is Mitzi Gaynor, Gaye is—well, who knows? David Bowie
maybe) and Petra has given us make-up to match—huge eyelashes, exaggerated eyebrows, scarlet outsize lips, glitter on our
cheekbones—and we're about to squeeze into our slashed silver
backing-singer dresses for Straker's set, I know what women
we'll be. Superwomen, irresistible, all-conquering.

'Where's Willie?' asks Di.

GB throws her head up and looks round the room.

'Willie?' she repeats, eyebrows shooting up through pink hair.

'Yeah. He should be here by now.'

'Willie! Oh God. I'll just run and make a phone call.'

'Why?' I ask.

'Back in a minute!' she yells over her shoulder and zips
through the door.

Di and I exchange another glance. Willie, our designer, is

Gaye's contact, not ours. We don't even know his phone number or where he lives. Quiet, methodical, precise, he cocks his head on one side, surveys our best points and highlights them. We trust Willie. I love my silver off-the-shoulder dress with wide strips of fabric falling from the waist like a Roman soldier's skirt, flipping as I move, exposing glimpses of black fish-netted thigh. He dresses us on the night, packs our outfits away, mends them, adjusts them, cleans them, keeps them safe. And he should be here. There's less than an hour till we start.

GB poses in the doorway, head high, a picture of non-chalance. 'Slight problem, Bird's Egg.'

'Where is he then? Didn't get lost, did he? You did tell him where to come?'

'It's not that.' She won't meet our eyes.

'What the hell is it then? Something awful?'

'Umm, we had a bit of a barney yesterday. He got the wrong end of the stick.'

'And?'

'All stupid nonsense. I thought everything was all right. Anyway, when I rang just now, he was at home. Hadn't left.'

'What? Why not?'

'Apparently he thinks I told him he'd get paid before the gig.'

I gape at her. 'Paid? No-one gets paid. He knew that, didn't he? Didn't he?'

GB inspects her fingernails. 'I may have promised something.'

'Fuckin' Ada—he's expecting money now?'

Gaye shrugs. 'It's all ridiculous.'

I swallow. 'Have you got the costumes then?'

'No.'

'Well, is he bringing them?'

'Not till he gets paid, he said.'

'Jesus, GB. What did you promise?'

She shrugs again. 'Can't remember.'

A pause. Douglas puts his curling tongs down and stares

at us. Petra stares at us. Even Straker opens his eyes and turns to look.

At this moment, Don puts his head round the door.

'All right girls? Bit quiet in here, innit? All meditating, are you? Hope you're ready. They're gonna start letting them in in five minutes, okay?'

I run to him. 'Don, Don, we've got no costumes. Not for backing singing or our set or anything.'

Don blinks. 'Christ. Well, music's ready. You better come up with something,' and vanishes.

So here we are in this school-room, huge Petra-painted eyes, exquisite hair, fishnet tights, silver platform ankle straps shoes, undies—and no costumes.

No costumes.

In the silence, Douglas clears his throat. 'Could lend someone my blouson jacket. Gaye? You keep stroking it. Perhaps you could get into it.'

It fits. What's more, it looks sexy on her.

'What about yer arse, Gaye?' says Di. 'That only just comes down to yer waist.'

Douglas dives into a black plastic bag. 'Feather boa, anyone?'

GB grabs it, wraps it round her hips. 'That's it. Sorted. Thanks, Douglas.'

Di and I look at each other, dumbstruck. Then I wake from my dream. 'I brought something. Must've been psychic,' I say as I pull out the gold lamé Marilyn Monroe dress a fan gave me last week. It's skin-tight on me, tighter than tight. No idea why I brought it along today, I can't breathe in it, let alone move. As I pull it out of its carrier bag and shake it out, Straker says, 'One of you could wear my jumpsuit with the cock feathers. I'd rather wear my dinner suit anyway with this crowd.'

This is absurdly generous. It's very beautiful, a shimmering, blue-black, slender one-piece with flared trousers, slashed to the navel and below, edged with shiny blue-green cock feathers.

Long, lean, Seventies male glamour. Straker's legs are very, very long. Put Di in there, her head'll just about get up to the waist.

She shakes her head. 'Thanks, Strakes, don't think that'll work. I'm too short.'

GB says, 'I'm too wide and my boobs are too big or I'd swap with you, Di.'

There's no help for it.

'Di,' I say, keeping disappointment out of my voice as well as I can, 'Di, you'd better try my gold dress. I'll try the jumpsuit.'

Thank God for Petra. Between them, she and Douglas provide instant solutions. An outsize safety pin concealed under a huge brooch holds the jumpsuit together near my navel—just. No underwear, it'd show. The legs are so long my platforms are completely hidden. It'll be a miracle if I don't trip up and kill myself just getting on stage. But I'm in it. And it's dead sexy.

Di wriggles and struggles and tugs and curses her way into my new dress. She may be short but she's far from thin. The Monroe confection creaks and protests.

'Don't breathe, kiddo!'

'I can't, Annie. I'll never survive this.'

The dress won't survive, more like. But once she's in, she looks terrific. Damn, I'll never get it back.

GB and I look rude, even for us. It's disgraceful. Nobody ever goes out on stage, even strippers, looking like this, GB all fishnet legs and a feather boa, not hiding much—or anything, me in a man's jumpsuit slashed so low I can't wear bra or knickers. So much for my fairy-tale princess look, she's gone right out of the window, except for my hair. Douglas has added a fall, it now flows all the way down my back, totally romantic, and totally at odds with the jumpsuit. I love it. Di, boobs and hips straining every stitch and seam of the clinging stretch gold lamé, with a little gold net frou-frou at her shoulders and knees, looks positively demure compared with us.

Then a miracle. On stage, Gaye behaves. We get the right

harmonies, no foot-tapping on the mike stand, she remembers all her lyrics, every single move. A submissive angel. It's heaven. We have the RCA salesmen's entire attention throughout. At one moment I'm singing the solo and I see all eyes fixed on a single point. And it's not me. Di-Di would never pull focus on stage, she's generous to a fault. So why—? The more we do, the more they gawp at Di. I know I look great with my tumbling hair and cock feathers and endless cleavage. What's going on?

We come off stage, hot and sweaty and triumphant. And I look at Di. The Monroe dress has split right up the front, from knee to crutch. No wonder all eyes were on her.

Di is horrified. 'Annie, love, I'm *so* sorry. I didn't know. I didn't mean—'

The dress is ruined. We laugh till we cry.

Don bursts in. 'They love you, girls. They'll die for you. Especially Di.'

We curl up with mirth and relief. Willie Burt's let-down has become our triumph. From now on, I decide to please myself how I look.

Afterwards I have this little nagging doubt. Did Gaye know about Willie? Did she know yesterday he wouldn't show up? Is that why she was so over the top earlier? And why butter wouldn't melt in her mouth for the show? I'll never ask and she'll never tell.

'Anything from Thames yet?' GB asks, a week or so later.

'Nothing. Nothing from Howard either.'

'It's been weeks. All mouth and no trousers, that one,' she observes.

'He didn't have much chance of success over there, did he?'

'He's a bit of a creep, Annie, if you don't mind my saying so. I know he's your friend but really, all that talk and then nothing.'

'I know. I'll jog his memory.'

Don and I have a drink with Ronnie Beck, our music publisher, to clinch our new deal. We bring Howard with us, as he might like them to publish him on *Memory Lane*. Ronnie loved the concert, loves our songs, loves Rock Bottom. The sun shines on Soho. Till Don happens to mention to Ronnie that Brian Degas is back and planning a visit to Thames, either to Verity Lambert, or maybe Philip Jones, Head of Light Entertainment.

'What?' says Howard, putting his glass down rather hard, and standing up suddenly. 'Who did you say, Don?'

'Verity Lam—'

Howard's face pinches, his mouth tightens. He walks out.

'Excuse me, Ronnie, I'll be back in a minute,' I say and follow Howard outside.

'This is a disaster! It's a disaster.'

It's becoming a bit of a catchphrase. His voice is strained and shrill. He paces up and down, rubbing his forehead. 'This could really, *really* screw things up.'

'How?'

'Don't you see? Anything could blow this deal. It's not a sure-fire thing, nothing's signed, nothing's...'

I try to explain our position.

'Howard, excuse me, but we've heard absolutely nothing from Thames, ever. Or you. You went off to see them over six weeks ago, nothing's been mentioned since, so we presume they're not interested. You always said it was a long shot and I agree. We can't wait around. If Brian Degas comes through first, that's what we'll do. This is our future, we have to explore all the possibilities.'

I can't pretend I'm being diplomatic, I don't like him being upset, but it's better to be truthful. We part awkwardly. I report back to Don.

'Tough,' says Don, draining his glass. 'We didn't promise him anything. If he can get us a deal, fine. If Brian Degas comes through with one first, we'll go with that.'

At the end of the month, the RCA contract comes through. We're going to make proper versions of four songs to be released as singles, *Tambourine Queen*, *It's All Over*, *Memory Lane* and *Horoscope*. I'm thrilled, I've co-written three of them.

We book the girls for the recording dates and are about to start rehearsing when Howard calls in a cheerful mood, all gripes forgotten.

'Annie! It's happened! Verity's come through. She likes the idea. They're interested in making the series. She wants to meet you all.'

He's a different person.

'Well, this is great news. I'm delighted. They haven't contacted us, you know.'

'Never mind, never mind, it's all going ahead, I tell you.'

'Wow. I'll get Don. He'll want to hear it from you. Well done, Howard. Whatever you said must have worked. This is brilliant. Brilliant!'

7

Thames Television

Thames Television Drama Department, Teddington Lock, October 4th, 1974

Here we go, another group audition. Verity doesn't know our music, hasn't seen us perform, probably knows our names as individual actresses, but may not have seen any of our work. This is a big pitch. *The* big pitch. Harder than with Brian Degas. At least Gaye already knew him, so the door was halfway open. And he's a man, which made it easier. This is a woman, known to be heavy duty, just made Head of Drama. How do we convince her we'd make wonderful television? Has she a sense of humour? Will she buy our brand of comedy? Should we play her a demo of one of the songs? What has Howard told her already? It's scary. And exciting. This will be our most important performance yet. In an office, not on a stage. The stakes are high.

We prepare to do battle, nervous, keyed up to fever pitch. Don's working, we'll have to start the meeting without him. I want him there, he'll steady us, make us look more… more… businesslike? Substantial? Trustworthy? I don't know. I just want us all together. There's four of us in this group. He's now our unofficial manager as well as our composer and Master Gruppenplanner, she ought to know all of that. And meet him, too. All for one and one for all.

So dress to the nines, in your silks and your fines… In Di's case, as usual, the tens. By the time Gaye's car shudders to a halt at Teddington, adrenalin is flowing pretty freely. Our walks get more exaggerated as we strut down endless corridors behind the casting lady, Liz Sadler, the jokes wilder, the decibels higher. The receptionist probably thinks they're being invaded by lunatics.

We barge through her door. I'm too high to take much in, no idea what the office looks like, what Liz Sadler looks like. Verity makes an instant impression. Dark and friendly and smiling, shaking hands, telling us (when she can get a word in) that she loves the idea of the Rock Bottom series and what wonderful television it will make. Are we happy to have Howard write a pilot? You bet we are. We'll go along with anything, just as long as she'll do it.

This isn't quite the audition we'd expected. Whatever Howard said to her has already done the trick, she doesn't need this cabaret act, she's made up her mind, she wants to go ahead with it. Too late. We're so strung up, we can't stop. In this state of keyed-up performance mode, all about giving out, not taking in, it's very hard to grasp what she's saying. She wants to stop us talking about the idea while they develop it? That means they *want* to develop it? Yes, apparently that's what she means. She's got it all planned out. Not thirteen half-hour comedy slots, but six hour-long drama episodes, just what Howard had said to us two months ago. It all depends on him, she says, it's now the first week in October, he hopes to have a draft of the first episode by the beginning of December, they'll give it to us before Christmas for approval. If they like it and we like it, we could have everything decided by January.

We try to get our brains in gear. This is so totally unexpected. Gaye manages to sober up enough to say, 'Quite tricky to decide the whole thing on one script, isn't it?'

'That's true. We're in the same position,' agrees Verity. 'I can't make promises, obviously, but if Howard finds the right approach, I'm hoping to go ahead. Meanwhile, I want to put the idea under wraps. That means none of you talks about it to anyone else while we're developing it.'

None of us *talks* about it?

'But, excuse me, Verity,' I say, 'We've got concerts booked through to Christmas. We've got our first single coming out soon. Our recording company are talking about us going on *Nationwide* to promote it. And we're expecting more television and radio bookings once it comes out. We can't *not* talk about it.'

Verity laughs. 'Oh, don't get me wrong. I don't want to limit what you do as a group. Far from it. The more you do, the better for everyone. One-off appearances are all to the good. I just want to stop you appearing in anything which could conflict with us. This is a big commitment for Thames. And we're taking a big risk. A drama department doesn't normally go into this sort of territory, a show about the pop world. With music, of course. We don't want to waste our time and money having you go to the opposition.'

'Like us talking to Brian Degas at the BBC, you mean?' says GB.

'Exactly,' says Verity. 'Not while we're laying out a huge amount of money developing it ourselves. I don't want anyone else to get there first.'

Wow. That means it's a very good idea indeed.

'Excuse me,' Di says in her poshest voice, 'Excuse me, but may I ask if this contract you're talking about will stop us working as individuals?'

Verity laughs even louder, throwing her head back, showing her beautiful teeth. Of course she doesn't mean anything like that. We can do theatre, television, film, anything as solo actresses, separately or together.

'I simply want to stop you as a group doing anything that could steal Thames's thunder, in other words, anything that could compete with what we're planning.'

'Oh. That's all right, then,' says Di, brightening up, but still very posh. 'Because I've got a *Carry On* film to do soon.'

The posh accent laid onto the *Carry On* makes everybody laugh.

Three months' option to keep our mouths closed, all decide together, Thames and us, on the basis of Howard's first episode, go in September next year if we all like it. If in the meantime, Verity adds, we become the female Rolling Stones and really, really famous, too big to want to do a little drama series—screams of laughter from us—we won't stop Thames going ahead without us, will we? As if! The female Rolling Stones in four months? We're going fast, but nobody could manage that. Another absurd bridge to cross later. Then she offers us money to keep quiet. Eyes light up. Anything! Anything! We're performing seals, oink! oink! clap! clap!, agreeing with everything, happy she likes us.

By the time Don comes in, we're old friends and everything's been agreed, except for him doing the music, which she'll sort out later, she says. And the actual amount of money. He just has to vanish with Liz Sadler to agree the sums. Verity promises to come to a concert and Liz says she'll send us a letter confirming what we've agreed.

And then they'll send us the money.

Exhilaration and relief hit us like a blast of oxygen as we leave the room. We peel the offer like an orange, savour its contents, hug each other, dance through the swing doors, divide the meeting into morsels of triumph.

'They liked us, Annie! They loved us!'

'They bought all of it!'

'Fancy her saying we might turn into the female Rolling Stones.'

'And in the next five months!'

Don turns round. 'She said that?'

'She said, what if we become the female Rolling Stones before they do the series? Would we accept our normal fees as actresses—they couldn't pay more.'

'Blimey,' says Don. 'O'Reilly.'

'Yeah.'

'Girls, we are definitely, *definitely* going places.'

'As long as it's funny as well as drama, that's all.'

'You said Howard's writing's funny, dincher?'

'In more ways than one, darlings,' says GB. 'We have to keep him off the surreal, you said.'

'Listen, he's got his work cut out just trying to get us down on paper. He won't have time to spiral off anywhere stupid. We're funny enough and real enough not to need any of that rubbish.'

'I'm so relieved she said that about our solo careers.'

'Well done for asking, Di. That was brave.'

'I had to know, Annie. I thought she was saying we couldn't work at all while Howard's doing his pilot. I can't afford not to work.'

'She had a good laugh about that, didn't she? We're only not to talk about us as a TV series or do anything like it with anyone else, till they decide if they want to go ahead. That's what she said.'

'*We*. If *we* want to go ahead. It's us, too, remember?' says Don. He looks as pleased as we do.

'I felt really daft.'

'The last thing you are is daft, Di.'

'Anything else, do what we like, that's what she said, innit?'

'The more the merrier, darling,' says GB. 'And I quote.'

'Christ, I need a drink!'

'Cuppa's your only chance round here. It's four o'clock. Even that's unlikely—look around. We're in the middle of nowhere.'

'River's lovely though, innit.'

'Drink that, if you're thirsty.'

'Oh, shuddup, clever.'

Teddington Lock is indeed dry, apart from the Thames.

The pubs are closed, there aren't any restaurants but they'd be closed, too, if there were any. It's a bit out of the way. For TV studios, that's useful. Plenty of parking space—just as well, as there's no public transport. One station a mile away in one direction, more than that in the other. Thank goodness for GB's car. We'd never get anywhere without her. We certainly couldn't have walked far in our heels and Di would have been arrested in that outfit. It's Indian summer still and we rock, dancing through the carpark, spinning on the lamp posts. Our dream is coming true. And fast.

'Are they really going to pay us just to do nothing? Did she really say five hundred quid? Is that each?'

'Er, no. Five hundred quid between all of us. Lotta money, just the same.'

'You bet.'

'Was it hard getting it out of them, Don?'

'No, as it happens. Howard told me what to ask for. He told me what their budget is for development.'

'How much, then?'

'A thousand pounds, he said. Andrew Brown told him and he told me. We each asked for five hundred, see?'

'Do you think Jean should take a look when they've written out the agreement, before we sign it?'

Don is firm. 'No need. It's not for agents, this. It's for the group.'

So it is. This'll be the first bit of money we've ever earned as Rock Bottom. Serious celebration is in order.

When the letter of agreement comes, several weeks later, we try to take it in. It's okay. Not exactly what I understood at the meeting, but not way off. We don't show it to our agents. Or a lawyer. We need the money too much—and the series. It slips past me with only a second's unease. It'll do. They want us.

After the cheque is paid in, and before the money has cleared, we celebrate again. 'I'll get the champagne.'

'I already got it. Bubbly, anyway.'

'A party. A party for everyone we know.'

'A day trip to Brighton. Hire a minibus.'

'Steak. The very best.'

'Half a minute, cheque's not cleared yet.'

'Have to be The Casserole, then.'

Five hundred pounds would keep us all for several months in beer, chips and hope. Or could have done, if we hadn't spent it many times over. But those first few days of elation and the hope of more to come, buoyed us up and kept us going. And even when the money ran out, its memory sustained us till the real thing came along.

Into the studio to record the tracks for RCA. Don's always at his happiest in the studio, totally in command. We can relax and sing. We don't have to worry about the bills, they're taken care of. Recording bills, that is. Other bills still give me sleepless nights. But the music gets recorded. The tracks aren't one hundred percent perfect. The two that are the most complicated technically, *Tambourine Queen* and *Memory Lane*, sound phenomenal, Don gets them absolutely right. *It's All Over*'s a bit slow for the comedy to be inescapable, secretly I would have liked it to be a bit more vulgar and off the wall, like the demo of *Boy You're a Big Girl Now* a year ago. I want more raw energy pulsing through, more of a live feel, the way it felt in performance. But it's our first go, Don's first go at recording us properly, it'll take time to get it right.

Howard sits in on the recording of *Memory Lane*, which he co-wrote, and takes Don and me to meet his agent, Jenne Casarotto. She's very friendly, and seems to love the music and the whole idea, and says that although she's only a literary agent, she'd like to help in any way she can. She enquires about management. Suggests Robert Stigwood.

'Already tried him, Di has. Not interested,' says Don.

'I could put in a word,' she says.

So kind and helpful. She wants to know every detail of the

Master Gruppenplan, what, when, how, who. We're not sure exactly why, but it's good to have positive feedback.

We've got plenty to do this autumn. RCA need us to choose a logo, approve car stickers (!), do a photo shoot in a studio with a professional photographer, John Haynes. We have three more concerts before Christmas and a date for the release of the first single, *Tambourine Queen*, with *Horoscope* as the B side. Things keep leaping forward, though not in the way my agents would like. They aren't pleased when I turn down six months' lucrative television drama, because it'll clash with the single release. I have to be available for that, the TV series will be filmed in Leeds, I'd never get home. We take our tapes round there as well, hoping they'll understand when they hear the music. They don't.

Chancery Lane, WC2, October, 1974

A strange place for a photographic studio, right in the middle of wall-to-wall lawyers. We have new black costumes from Willie Burt, all disagreement resolved, as well as the lime-green, orange satin and gold ones from the concert. We get the full treatment. Douglas and Petra devote a whole day to getting us ready, holding our hands, helping us change, pointing a toe, rearranging hair, lending jewellery, rushing in between shots with make-up brushes and suggestions, laughing at our jokes, as excited as we are. It's a cold day and the studio's unheated. We freeze and our nipples stick out to prove it. More jokes. John Haynes isn't used to doing studio pictures, we know him from theatre: action shots, movement, drama, so we're all making it up. By the time he's finished, we're blue under the Max Factor and late for our meeting at RCA.

No time to take the glitter or the eyelashes off, or their offices will close. Lugging carrier bags full of shoes, electric rollers, make-up boxes and props, we run out onto Fleet Street in the middle of the rush hour to hail a taxi. We split up to give us more chance.

GB has the loudest voice, I have most leg showing but Di wins, stops the traffic instantly, fluttering her eyelashes at an elderly taxi-driver. He brakes, pulls over and frowns when she gets near. When two more harpies bundle in as well, he's not pleased.

'Curzon Street, please, driver,' says Di.

At that he brakes again.

'Out you get,' he says grimly.

'What?'

'Out of my cab, you lot. You goin' to Shepherd's Market, eh? Not havin' the likes of you in here.'

In vain we tell him RCA lives there, it's our record company, they're waiting for us. He's not going to take prostitutes. No argument. Out we get again.

We arrive at RCA late, breathless and apologetic. They love it, it's another good piece of copy and they need every bit they can get. They go on a bit about this: we're not the norm, we'll be hard to sell at our ages, looking as we do, it's a hard world out there, we'll need to reach a broader audience than the cool London folk we're building up, people who won't have seen us live, won't have heard of any of us. We're competing with The Eagles, Slade, Charles Aznavour, Mud and The Wombles.

Yeah, well.

As for girls, only Suzi Quatro, a new Swedish group called Abba and The Three Degrees.

Ah, yes. The Three Degrees, a black American three-girl group with a hit single *When Will I See You Again*, in London to promote it, the first girl group to get to Number One over here since The Supremes ten years earlier, which gives us a bit of hope—and a brush with the big time, as our next outing is supporting Straker, who's supporting them. Not a jolly little affair in a small theatre on a Sunday night this time, it's the Apollo Victoria, a huge barn of a place. We're only doing backing singing, without a single song of our own, but we tell each other it's all experience. Not uplifting, perhaps, but experience. We arrive to do our two hours on stage for the sound check and rehearsal. Nothing. None of the sound equipment has been set up. We hang around all morning, twiddling our thumbs, hoping for a glimpse of the main attraction. Not that they'd be here yet. They'll make an entrance when everything's all ready for them and they've had a nice lie-in.

By the time we get on stage, it's mid-afternoon. Roadies stroll across with cables, shouting to each other, walking into us if we stand in their path. They have A Job to Do. Before Don has done more than line up the band, and Peter's trying out a few explora-tory bars, they cut the sound off.

'Get off,' we're told, 'Your time's up.'

Don protests, Peter protests. Before we can open our mouths, the heavies manhandle us offstage. In the evening, with bruised arms and egos, we go out in front of a vast crowd of people who've come to see the Three Degrees and have no intention of listening to the warm-up act. Straker is ignored, we're stuck behind huge speakers. Not only can we not hear ourselves, or probably be heard, we're not even visible.

Afterwards we hear this is the classic rock circuit treatment. And I thought theatre was hierarchical. We decide never to be a support band again and wonder how much we should attach ourselves to Straker from now on. Perhaps it's time to go it alone. RCA, bless them, give us a chance. We have two pre-Christmas shows booked with Straker at the King's Road Theatre, but once Alan Sizer, our A&R man, realises we're not so happy being 'with Rock Bottom' at the bottom of the bill, he offers us an-other concert. We can share the bill equally with another band, a rock'n'roll revival band called Fumble.

'You have the first half all to yourselves,' he suggests, 'they do the second half and you can have a jam session at the end. How would that do?'

That would do very, very well, thank you. More songs, new costumes, a longer set. Loads to do. Our first single's due out in November. RCA get us the promised TV appearance on *Nationwide*, various radio shows are sent the single. One of them makes it their 'Pick of the Week'. RCA are well pleased. They drive us all up to Birmingham one Sunday morning to go on the show. Except Di, who's doing her *Carry On* movie. We do our best, but it's not the same without her.

And that's all we can do to promote our very first single, because GB and I are in the middle of a lovely job. Michael White, producing a film version of *The Rocky Horror Show*, asked us all to be in it.

Di's still Carrying On, so it's Gaye and me only.

Two out of three. It's becoming a common theme.

Bray Studios, October, 1974

Fake rain, a cobweb machine, motorbikes. Our first scene is as Transylvanians roaring up on real motorbikes in real dark and hosepiped rain to Frank N. Furter's fake-cobweb-strewn mansion, for the party to celebrate Rocky's birth. It's like being a teenager again, clutching the driver's waist, zooming round corners, shrieking with excitement. The make-up and costume's a bit different, though, we weren't Goths when I was sixteen.

Or Trannies. This is *The Rocky Horror Picture Show*.

Transylvanians in order of height—from the shortest: Sadie Corre, four feet eight in her high heels (main job playing the cat in Dick Whittington pantos), pretty little Kimi Wong, not much taller than Sadie, Henry Woolf just about making five feet—all the way through Imogen, Tony, Tony 2, Perry, Ishaq, Anthony, me (in the middle—ha ha) past Lindsay—going up—Chris Biggins, Gaye and tallest of all, Stephen at six foot seven. Not forgetting Peggy, eighty-three and game for anything, and Fran Fullenwider—as her name suggests. When she shimmies, she's going one way and her hips are still going in the other, trying and failing to catch her up.

It's the *Hair!/Jesus Christ Superstar/Rocky Horror Show* crowd together again—Tim Curry, as brilliant as he was on stage, Richard O'Brien, ditto, David Toguri choreographing, we're amongst friends. Rock'n'roll in the ballroom with cobwebs, food in the studio canteen with plastic cutlery. On the second morning, GB brings her own stainless steel knife, fork and spoon wrapped in a linen napkin.

'They may be paying us shit, but I refuse to eat with their filthy plastic!'

Eight weeks of singing, dancing and fooling around. As Trannies, we're trapped a lot of the time on and off the set. Gaye and Biggins are a lethal combination. We are hysterical from five in the morning till seven in the evening. Biggins has a car, so Sadie, Kimi, Perry and I endure the agony of his jokes before we've had breakfast and are sick with laughter before we ever get to Bray. Once we're there, Gaye joins in and if we had time, we'd feel sorry for Tim and Meatloaf and Susan Sarandon and Richie, because they're working too hard to join our party.

At the cast and crew screening in Leicester Square, we carry on behaving badly. Worse, if anything. The minute we get together, it's mayhem. Amazingly, they give all of us a credit at the end.

'Oh, Annie, how hilarious,' says GB. 'Did you see? They've spelt your name wrong. Nice big letters, too. Can't miss it!'

Hilarious. Ha, ha. Both names. I'm immortalised as Annabelle Levington, in the longest-lasting, highest-profile film I'll probably ever be in. I don't care, we're on a permanent high, we've got someone writing a television series for us and about us.

The single doesn't get anywhere, but RCA, that is Alan Sizer, pleased with the 'Pick of the Week', tells us it's a normal debut. Don and I are more disappointed than he is. This time last year our demo got more plays than the real thing. But if we're only available as a group for the occasional Sunday, what can they do?

'We'll need more time from you guys if we're to get you off the ground. This isn't plain sailing, you know,' Alan warns.

'You're not your average stereotypical teeny-bopper group the media can soak up. We need your help.'

We promise to give them more time.

December, 1974

We're so busy with the three Kings Road concerts, it's a while till I realise the pilot script should have been delivered. Howard's locked away trying to finish it, he says, and can't talk. He'll let us know when he's sent it in and then they'll send it to us. I can't let myself think about it, it's too exciting. I spend a happy evening with my new neon-yellow satin halter-neck cowgirl top with the short, tight, button-through skirt, adding shiny buttons, decorating the lapels with bits of costume jewellery, sequins and bits and pieces of sparkle. Custom-made.

I spend another evening transforming my new cheapo, North End Road tan platform boots to match the new costume. First I spray them gold all over and before they dry, chuck gold and silver glitter over the toecaps. Then I cover the tops and all down the outside seam from knee to ankle with whatever spare buttons, glass beads and sequins I can glue on. When I've finished, I ignore Toguri's superstition and put them up on the kitchen table for Don and me to admire. Nobody has ever had a pair of boots like this. They'll catch the light on stage, they'll sparkle when I move, just like my costume. I am pleased with my work, it felt just as creative as writing a song lyric or dreaming up the ghost dancers for *Ragtime Piano Joe*. Next thing you know, I'll be designing my own costumes.

Three more concerts and it'll be Christmas. This Christmas will be different from any other. Don and I have a future. Also, for the very first time, we have the entire flat to ourselves. The clarinettist moved out to live with his girlfriend, the flautist and *his* girlfriend are on holiday. We'll be alone together for the very first time. Time to enjoy a bit of peace and quiet. It's been a tumultuous year, a year of spectacular achievement, a year of hope. Christmas will be an oasis, a honeymoon.

The RCA-funded concert with Fumble, back at the Kings Road Theatre, is an even bigger success than the one with Straker last July. New songs, new outfits, freedom to try out anything we like. Our costumes are more in character, more vulgar, sexy and jokey. We decide we can rely on wit as well as music. We start the way we mean to go on with a new introduction.

Di steps forward: 'Hi. I'm Di-Di.'

Cheers.

I step forward. 'I'm Annie.'

Roars.

Gaye jumps in, grinning, lipstick on her teeth, her hair searing scarlet, and in her most piercing voice tops both us and the audience: 'And I'm gay and we don't give a damn!'

They go berserk. It takes minutes to control them enough to announce the next song.

We go down a storm. Fumble are all delightful, if a little stunned by us. Des Henly, the lead guitarist, tells me afterwards they stood at the back of the auditorium after their set watching us, unable to believe their eyes as we stretched the boundaries of rock. The new material includes a ten-minute solo spot for Gaye to do her stand-up comedy routine and insult the audience, rather than having her swamp the rest of our act with one-liners and improvisation. We need the show to be tight as well as funny.

'Let her do that, and rein her in for the rest of it,' we agree.

It works a treat. GB with the bit between her teeth is a fearsome sight. She has them screaming in seconds. She's perfectly happy, more than happy, to seize centre stage, drive them into a frenzy and bring them back, too, when it's time. The jam session with Fumble at the end is such fun we decide to keep it in from now on.

Verity Lambert came. We didn't see her, but Howard says she was there. Her boyfriend didn't like us.

'Not rock'n'roll,' he was heard to say.

Howard reports this in a state of high anxiety. 'God, I hope it doesn't blow the whole thing,' he keeps saying.

We know how the audience reacted. Verity saw it. Does she care about her boyfriend's views? We have no time to wonder, we're on to the next.

'Good thing she didn't come to the Three Degrees concert,' I say to GB. 'She'd have dropped the whole idea if she'd seen that.'

'Who knows, Bird's Egg? Might make a wonderful episode.'

Of course, she's right. Everything's useful for a show based on our lives. Verity can't lose. Nor can we.

'Why "Bird's Egg"?' I ask.

She's gone.

Four days later, on December 21st and 22nd, we have the last two concerts with Straker. We hurl ourselves into them, adding carols, jokes and general mayhem. The first one goes like a sky rocket. Afterwards, we're happy but exhausted, the pace beginning to tell on us. The autumn was non-stop, not just with Rock Bottom and *The Rocky Horror Picture Show* but other acting work. I did another *Crown Court*, and the running around has allowed me to lose a few more pounds, though I'm not trying, I just don't have time to eat. Di's still filming her *Carry On*, with a young child at home and an hour's drive back to Hampshire before she can fall into bed. As we change into our clothes to go home, knowing we're doing it all again next day and Christmas is next, eyelids start to droop, hanging clothes up gets slower, and we run out of juice. Di looks at my new trim self.

'It's not fair, Annie. You look spectacular. I've got a right paunch on me. Trouble is, I'm too tired to diet.'

'And you're too tired to drive home, darling,' says GB in a brisk tone. 'Better come and stay at my house tonight. Save you that journey.'

Di and I look at each other. We both know what staying at

Gaye's entails. Ever generous, Gaye doesn't always realise that guests need sleep. We'd both been woken at six in the morning by Gaye hoovering round the bed, flinging the curtains open and chatting at the top of her voice.

'Thanks, Gaye, but I want to be home,' she says.

Don and I are deep asleep when the phone rings. It's GB.

'Mmm? What is it?' I murmur.

'Di's had an accident.'

'What?' I'm fully awake in an instant.

'Fell asleep at the wheel, only five hundred yards from home, accordingly,' says Gaye. She often says accordingly for apparently, I'm used to that.

'Is she all right? Is she hurt?'

'She's fine. Bruised her knee, that's all. Wrote the car off, though. They found her in the gutter, crawling around after her hairpiece moaning 'Mum, Mum'. It was up a tree. That's the only casualty. Nothing wrong with her, if you don't count that.'

'This is terrible. Poor Di. Is she in hospital?'

'No, but the doctor says she's got to stay in bed for a couple of days.' GB barks a laugh. 'So it's you and me tonight, babes.'

Oh, my God, the show! We've rehearsed without her, we've done radio shows without her, meetings, even a recording session, but a performance? How can we do that? Everything's geared to three, not just the harmonies but the line-up, the contrasts, the look, every reference, musical and visual, is based on three: small, medium, large; dark, blonde, redhead; upper-crust, middle-crust, working-crust. And jokes go in threes—a Scotsman, an Englishman and an Irishman, Ready, Steady, Go. 'I'm Annie and I'm gay' won't be quite the same. Tonight's going to be interesting. Gaye's ability to busk, and mine, will be stretched to the limit.

Amazingly, it works. I never want to go through it again, but it works.

'How did it go, Annie?' asks Di, sounding weak and faint.

'I'm ever so sorry to let you down. I just couldn't.'

'I know, Di, it's all right, don't worry. You missed quite an evening.'

'Go on, tell us how it went.'

'Well, we added a couple of numbers. GB sang the *Marrow Song*, you know, *I've never seen one as big as that before*, that one, I did a solo number, we told a few jokes. And GB did her stand-up routine and I left her to it.'

'What d'you mean?'

'She was getting on so well with them, I just walked off down the catwalk to the back of the auditorium and got myself a glass of champagne.'

'Annie, you didn't. You don't even drink.' Di giggles.

'And I stood around like Lady Muck watching her gee them up and drive them hysterical. I'd nothing left to do really except a few backing vocals and a verse of *Away in a Manger*. We'd talked about you and they were all so—*with* us, so warm, Di-Di, we were really swept along on this big tide of affection for all of us. It was lovely. I should have gone to change really, I was wearing the yellow satin halter-neck with the little button-through skirt, you know, and I looked really rude, even ruder than the night before. My stocking tops and suspenders were showing and quite a bit of thigh.'

'Takin' over from me, then,' Di observes.

'Something like that,' I admit. 'And I knew we were going to do some jiving in the jam session so I needed to get out of my platform shoes and into sneakers. But there wasn't time. I was just sipping my champagne, minding my own business, when GB suddenly shrieked, with no warning, honestly, Di, 'ANNIE! WHERE ARE YOU? Ladies and gentlemen, if I can call you that! I give you my friend Annie!' So I went back, right up the catwalk, pretending I do this sort of thing all the time, bowing and waving and spilling champagne all over people, I expect. And they loved it!'

'Oh damn. I missed all the fun.'

'Most of the fun was because you were missing, silly. We can write it all in from now on. Not you being off, or having an accident but all the other stuff. I tell you, Di, we can do as we like. We really can. They love us.'

The next day, just in time for Christmas, our advance from RCA comes through. £1,200. Twelve hundred pounds! A fortune, even divided between four of us. It'll get us sailing through to the New Year. Possibly not GB, though. She's invited the world and his wife for Christmas, just as she did on October 10th for election night, 'the night we lost' as she put it, the night Labour got in. It's one of her eccentric talents to gather everyone of every political persuasion to come to a party to support the Tories and we all show up—Tim Curry, Howard, now one of the inner circle, Sean Curry, who will never recover from the sight of Di twirling about in her Roman outfit with no knickers as far as he could tell, and every leftie in town. Never mind the red final demands piling up for electricity, phone and Harrods, GB demands and provides the best: the best soap, the best olive oil *at all times* and at Christmas, the best champagne.

This time, Don and I have other plans. With the flat to ourselves, we want to be at home this year, snuggle up, gloat over our wonderful year, have a bit of peace, quiet and self-congratulation. We're going to have a second honeymoon. For perhaps a couple of weeks. Not that we'd ever had the first.

A couple of weeks? It turns out to be rather less than a couple of days, more a couple of hours. My mother comes down from Scotland to stay. Don's mother won't have her installed unless she's there, too, so the Fraser family decide to move in, all three of them—with the dog. On Christmas Eve my brother Hugh calls from Heathrow, saying he's back from Australia with a girlfriend and can they stay too? So on Christmas night, we give Don's parents our bedroom, my mother has the little box-room vacated by the clarinettist and Don and I enjoy the peace and quiet of our little honeymoon on a mattress on the floor of the only other room, surrounded by his sister Sandra, my brother Hugh and his girlfriend Geraldine, also on mattresses. And the dog.

Still, Don and I are happy. So happy. Everything's going our way. As we snuggle up together on a lumpy old mattress on the floor, a song Don wrote for me long before Rock Bottom keeps running through my head:

> *And now that this long day's work is done,*
> *I think a little peace has been well and truly won.*
> *It's been a little hard and sad and a struggle*
> *   getting through*
> *But you know I'm glad, there's been a lot of help*
> *   from you*
> *Oh the feeling's good when we're together*
> *Yes, together's fine.*

8

Extended Honeymoon

The honeymoon mood, despite the multiple family invasion, survives all the way through to January, when my mother goes back to Scotland and Don's family go back to Dagenham. Hugh and Geraldine sign on for the Harrods sale, so want to stay on with us as it's only a few stops on the Tube. They're out all day and the flat becomes relatively peaceful. Till Don reports that Liz Sadler rang to extend the option and offer us £250 for one more month, just till the end of January. Is that good or bad?

'I thought we were all supposed to decide by the end of December?'

'Howard can't have finished the script yet, can he?' he replies, not bothered too much.

I'm bothered. The money's all very well, but Howard was supposed to submit the script before Christmas and we should have got a copy of it by now.

I call him up.

'I haven't finished it,' he says, sounding harassed.

'Any idea when you think you might?' I ask.

'Believe you me, the minute I can. I don't want this hanging over my head.'

'You having trouble doing it? Can I help?'

'Oh, no, Annie! Of course not. This is *my* part of the job. I'll get there.'

I leave it at that.

Don comes home one day towards the end of the month, looking pleased.

'I bumped into Howard in Habitat,' he says.

'How was he?'

'All smiles,' says Don. 'He's finished the script. It's gone off to Thames.'

'Oh, great. Wonderful! Did he say how he'd felt doing it?'

'Oh, he was very chipper. He told me all about how your characters are all coming along. And mine, thank you very much. He's calling me Henry Huggins, Henry Hyper Huggins, in fact. And you're Anna. He loves your character best, he says. She's middle-class and an Oxford graduate, surprise, surprise.'

'Why Anna instead of Annie, I wonder? Hardly worth changing if it's going to be that close. Though I don't see why he's changing our names at all, do you? And Hyper's a bit unkind.'

'GB's called Q now, he said. Still an ex-deb, though. And Di is Dee.'

'And I suppose she's working-class. It sounds bizarre. I hope he's not going to be too boring and factual.'

'Howard? Shouldn't think so. He doesn't do factual, does he? You'll soon be roaring round on broomsticks or stripping or something.'

Why didn't Howard tell me all this himself? Especially about getting the script in. There's a strange air hanging over our friendship that I can't quite grasp.

February, 1975

No script. No word from Howard.

'What's the problem?' Gaye says. 'Thames have got it. Just call them up, ask them for it. You know I'm off to Birmingham shortly, I can't do anything.'

I call Howard again.

'We haven't got a copy of the script yet.'

'I gave it to them,' he replies, very terse.

'When?'

'Oh, I don't know. January some time. They have it for sure.'

'Well, they've not given it to us. And it's part of the agreement that—'

Howard's voice goes up a notch. 'So you keep saying. I gave it to them, I'm telling you. It's their job to give it to you.'

I have a version of this every day for a week before I lose patience.

'They're out of contract now,' I say. 'As are we. We're free to go elsewhere.'

At this, Howard's voice spirals into the stratosphere. 'You say that? I've spent months on this. Go elsewhere? Without me, I suppose.'

I look at white tendons stretched over my knuckles, squeeze and release tense fingers.

He says, 'This is intolerable. How can I go on writing—?'

He stops.

'What? What do you mean, *go on* writing? I thought you'd finished it and handed it in.'

'The others, how can I continue with—'

He stops again.

'With what?'

He doesn't answer.

'You're not writing the next episode, are you, Howard? Not before we've all agreed to go ahead with it? That's the deal. You know that. All of us, all of them. We decide to go ahead on the basis of the first script. Surely you can't—'

At the other end of the line, Howard clears his throat. 'Annie, they've given me the go-ahead.'

'Oh.' I'm stunned. 'Oh. Are you sure?'

'Yes, of course I am. Isn't it great?'

'That's so weird. They haven't spoken to us at all, except to extend the contract till the end of January. What's going on?'

Howard says, 'You have to ask *them*, not me. I'm under such pressure. I have to focus.'

'Dear Howard, I don't mean to pester you, you know that. You're the one I *can* talk to. We can't keep calling them. We get nowhere.'

'It's your agent's job, not yours. Tell him to do it.'

'Her.'

'What?'

'Her. It's a her. She's not involved in this. Don's arranged everything. She doesn't represent Rock Bottom.'

'Then he should go through the proper channels. Do his job. This is a disaster, it's doing my head in. You guys have to fix it. It ain't my problem.'

'Rubbish,' says Gaye, when I report this. 'Absolute rubbish, darling. I thought he was your friend. It's fine, Annie, don't panic. It's great news they want to go ahead. They've just forgotten to send it to us, that's all.'

Forgotten? Forgotten? A whole television series held up because they've forgotten to send a script on which the whole thing rests?

'They've forgotten they need our approval, more like. He carries on writing and we never even get to see the bloody thing.'

'It'll be fine. Calm down. I'll call them when I get to Birmingham. If I have time.'

Oh Christ, yes. She's on her way to Birmingham for six weeks' filming. Just when our second single is coming out. Great. *Great.* Di about to start rehearsing for *A Little Night Music*, Gaye away. I'm not Rock Bottom, it has to be all of us together, it's not a performance I can do on my own.

It doesn't matter. No-one asks me. *It's All Over* is met with a profound silence, a great big nothing. The launch is such a non-event I begin to doubt my own judgement. I can't find it on any radio station. Has anyone even bought one? I doubt that, too.

Just as I'm spiralling down, I get a call from Rae Coates, David Toguri's right-hand man, our dance captain from the first concert, the one in charge of the tap dancers in *Ragtime Piano Joe*. 'You know our club, dear?'

'What club?'

'Smacked wrist for you, naughty girl. By the Troubadour. You've been there. In disguise, probably. What did she come as, Chris?'

I laugh.

'Sorry, Rae, I go to so many gay clubs, I wasn't quite sure for a moment.'

Rae is offended. 'I didn't say gay clubs, dearest. I said *our* club. You young things need your ears washing out.'

He's years younger than me.

'Sorry, darling, my mistake. *Your* club. Of course I know it.'

He's talking about The Catacombs. Right round the corner from the Coleherne pub in Earls Court, infamous as a hangout for mustachio'd, muscled gay men. The more adventurous ones go on to The Catacombs.

'Well, dear, we'd like to invite Rock Bottom to make a personal appearance there on Sunday week. Can you gather your little flock and get your arses down here by eight pm, please?'

I promise to do my best. And I don't even have to try. Two phone calls and it's done. Gaye's back for the weekend, Di's willing, we're in business.

The Catacombs is heaving with happy, sweaty gays dancing, drinking, screaming over the music, or just screaming. Our crowd, in fact. We'll have to come up with something good or they'll obliterate us. No sign of Rae or Chris, but we're greeted by someone who leads us to the front, claps his hands and calls for shush. Nobody takes any notice. He grabs a microphone and roars, 'Ladies and gentlemen, shuddup and please welcome to our little club the famous rock group—ROCK BOTTOM!'

We clamber onto the tiny stage in our platform shoes,

towering over the massed bodies and grin round at everyone. Some of them are looking, some are even listening. A Chinese boy is talking loudly right in front of us, his arm round his blond friend.

GB grabs the mike. 'You see what I'm seeing?' pointing to him. 'They come over here, take our men!'

That does it. The place erupts.

'And now ladies and gentlemen, boys and boys,' continues the master/mistress of ceremonies, 'you are now in for a Catacombs special! Rock Bottom are going to perform their new single *It's All Over!*'

What?? We look at each other. Didn't know about this.

'Clear the stage, if you please, dearies. And you girls. Off you go. Once again, for the very first time in the Catacombs, I give you ... ROCK BOTTOM!'

He shoves us back onto the dance floor and removes the mike. The opening chord's so loud we block our ears. Onto the stage come three drag queens in full slap—a short dark one, a tall red-head and a blonde in the middle. They proceed to take the piss unmercifully as they mime a shameful parody of us singing *It's All Over.*

The GB impersonator, very tall, very thin, with a blond moustache and a scarlet wig is instantly recognisable as Rae's friend Stephen. Chris as Di is tattooed and hairy with pumped-up muscles from (presumably) hours in the gym. He looks like he's been rejected by the Merchant Navy, every one of 'em. He clutches his throat when it's his verse, looking agonised, muttering 'my throat, my throat' and we cry with laughter, Di more than anyone. I glance round. The crowd clearly know us, they must have been to our concerts, they're completely with it. I can't work out who's playing me. He's bigger and squarer but the likeness is uncanny. He moves just like me. It's like watching a twin brother in drag. When he starts singing the second verse, I get it.

'Oh, Jesus!' I yell in Di's ear, 'Look! It's Rae.'

Tears are rolling down our cheeks. He's caught me exactly. We are helpless. It's the most fun we've had together since the first concert.

The three of them bring the house down. If this is fame, I love it.

Afterwards, Stephen hands us each an A4 envelope, the cardboard-backed kind you put photos in. Inside we each have a drawing of ourselves in Rock Bottom. He's caught our costumes, our shoes, our hair, our personalities and made wicked cartoons of each of us. The gays have done us proud. Now we have to make the rest of the world catch up.

West Kensington Mansions, March 3rd, 1975

I love having Howard over. It's only eighteen months since we all met and did *Verité* together. The three of us have shared so much since then. The ideas we've discussed, Howard and I, the laughs, the songs he and Don have developed in the music room down the corridor, to which I've hummed along while laying the table and scrubbing potatoes in Don's funny little kitchen in his West Kensington flat. I love living here, W14's a lot more interesting than Paddington, especially if you're in love with the person who lives here. We don't call it W14, it's *Wuh Quatorze* to us, our private joke. I don't miss my flat in Westbourne Terrace, with its huge kitchen and freezing cold living-room and big double bed. I belong here now. Loads of sky on the fifth floor, just sky and roofs. All the stairs keep me fit, the North End Road market is my local store. Best of all, the people who pour in here. It's a hive of activity—music and theatre talk all day long. I'm at the centre of my world.

Tonight I'm doing spag bol. Money's a bit low this week, mince is cheap, onions and tomatoes are cheap, spaghetti's cheap. Salad I couldn't do without, money or no money. Howard's a good guest, he'll bring a bottle of red. Always does. Sometimes flowers, too.

The kitchen is an odd shape, a sort of long triangle with the window at the narrow end, looking out over trees, past the housing estate just going up, not quite hiding the landmark tall green building on the Old Brompton Road. Something to do with the Admiralty. Must ask Gaye, she'll know. I slice onions, chop tomatoes, spin the Webbs Wonderful, put oil in the frying pan. I'll get a new one sometime, when all this is sorted, we can't afford it yet, don't count chickens till they've crossed the road. Nearly there. We're so nearly there, Thames have given Howard the go-ahead.

What a year! It's only just March.

I'm all ready, table laid and absurdly happy by the time he arrives.

'*Loony Tunes*. That's my absolute favourite, Howard. Dr Paul Whiteman and the Whitecoats. What's happened to that?'

Howard laughs and opens the bottle. 'Dear girl, as if there's time. One day. One day. We're on a roll with this one first. Great you haven't forgotten, though.'

'Forgotten? A musical set in a loony bin with Rock Bum as nurses? Come on!'

I pass him three glasses. The table looks nice. I wanted to make an effort this evening, even though it's just us. Family, really.

He smiles. 'Plenty of time. Let's get this little number on its feet first. I need all the help I can get, you know.'

'So do we, Howard. Don! You coming? Grub's up.'

I serve the avocado and French toast.

'No, Annie, darling, you don't understand. The pressure's really on for me to get these scripts in. It's impossible, really—they're talking about a September start date. You have no idea how impossible that would be for me.'

'What's impossible?' says Don, sitting down.

'Hi, Don. Thames. A September start date for the series. Can't be done. And what about the music? How'll we get that in?'

'*We* don't have a start date,' observes Don. 'Well, Annie's agent had a possible one. I've had another. Nothing definite.'

I cut in. 'The main thing, darling, is that they haven't even sent us a copy of your first draft. They aren't supposed to go ahead till we've okay'd it. Nor are you, I suppose.'

'That's what I keep telling you, Annie. How can I go on writing unless I know you like it? Think what pressure I'm under. You haven't seen it. They keep bringing the studio dates forward. I'm squeezed every which way. And as for the songs, Don—'

'No need to worry about them,' says Don, helping himself to the last scrape of butter. 'I can do them at the last minute.'

'*You* can, maybe. I certainly can't.'

Howard's brow is more creased by the minute. What are those dogs with lots of folds in their skin? Shar peis?

'You have to push them for the script. You have to.'

'Thing is, it's up to them. Not much more I can do. I've asked and asked.'

'Yes,' says Howard, leaning forward earnestly. 'But what I don't get is why you wouldn't let Jenne give it you. It'd speed things up.'

'Not right,' says Don, briefly. 'She's your agent. The agreement is Thames give it to us. That's the deal. Has to be done professionally, see? Properly.'

'Properly? Properly? I have to do the scripts "properly"! I have no time. This is too much pressure. Really.'

'Why do you think,' I ask, to stop an argument growing. Howard, always excitable, is in a right state this evening. 'Why do you think they won't hand it over? Are they just inefficient? Or have they forgotten they need our say-so? It seems bizarre to me. Unless they think we wouldn't like it. Might they?'

Howard plays with his fork. 'Annie, I have no idea. I'm not a mind reader. All I know is, I have to know I'm writing it for you. I have to know you're on board, that you buy it. How can I write unless you are?'

'I don't see how you can, really,' I agree. 'It's impossible.'

'Yeah. That's what I just said. Impossible. Someone needs to do something. Don, it's up to you. Can't you put some pressure on?'

'Me?' says Don, mouth full. 'I got no say over there. They don't answer my calls half the time. Something's going on, I reckon. Dunno what.'

'Howard, would you get the salad? The dressing's over there. I'm going to serve up the next course, Don, do you mind?'

'Be ready in a sec.'

Howard puts the salad on the table.

I pass him two dessert spoons as servers. 'Best we've got, sorry.'

Howard says, 'You should write to them and insist on them sending it.'

Don wipes a finger over the last bit of avocado and sucks it. 'I suppose I could. I need to know myself. Been offered another job, see. If they go ahead in September, I'll be a bit pushed as well. Probably be in Edinburgh then. At the Festival. If it comes off.'

Howard leaps up, spilling his wine over the white sheet, my version of a tablecloth. 'That's my whole point, Don. That's exactly it. Sorry, Annie, I'll clean it up. It could be a disaster going ahead so soon. I need your help on this. We'll never make it.'

'Up to them, isn't it?' repeats Don. He can be stubborn sometimes. 'Unless you call them, put some pressure on as well.'

'I'm writing, Don. All the hours God gave. I can't write and I can't afford to stop writing. Spaghetti's delicious, by the way.'

'Thanks. There's no pudding, guys, so eat it all up.'

'No pudding?' says Don, clearly surprised.

'Sorry. Forgot. Could do custard if you're still hungry.'

I didn't have enough money for pudding.

'Pudding shmudding, darling,' says Howard. 'This is great. There's another thing on my mind, by the way. Di and *A Little Night Music*. She's doing it, isn't she? For Hal Prince?'

'What about it?' asks Don.

'Isn't she about to start rehearsals? Won't there be availability issues?'

'Not our problem. If it goes ahead now, they'll have to work round her schedule. Can't ask her to turn it down for something that isn't written, has no date and might not go ahead anyway. Thames couldn't schedule it for before September, could they? Her show might've closed by then. Any more spaghetti?'

'Yeah, but what if it runs and runs?'

'Oh,' says Don, 'then we'll have to come up with something, won't we? Get her out of matinee days, say, or Thames record on a Sunday. Main thing is, we can't deal with any of that till we approve the script. Till we've read the bloody thing and we know we're going ahead, can we?'

Howard is shrill. 'My point exactly! Please, please, insist on the script. Insist, Don, I beg you.'

No good begging Don to do anything. 'I'll have another go,' is the best he'll offer. 'Worst come to the worst, she can pretend to be pregnant, can't she? Get out of the show that way.'

Not the funniest joke in the world. I laugh anyway. I've had enough of this circular conversation.

March, 1975

Don tries again. He gets Sandra to write formally asking for the script. He speaks to Liz Sadler and reports, a bit shaken, that she's furious about Di being in *A Little Night Music* and told him he'll have to repay all the option money.

'What?' I can't believe it.

'The whole flipping lot, she said. Breach of contract, she said, Di doing a show. And I have to pay back what they paid Howard as well. The deal's off.'

He looks very pale.

'Don, that's ridiculous. Did you tell her we haven't seen a script yet? That's part of their contract, too.'

'It's no good talking to her. I need to speak to Verity. Jesus.'

April, 1975

Don finally manages to get through: 'Verity, we can't do anything about anything, d-dates, planning the music, Di's availability, till we've seen a script. It's our right.'

I heard him, he was very firm, apart from that one little stutter. Perfectly clear.

Verity says she'll send the script. She sounds surprised we haven't got it, Don says. Maybe it was just a mistake. An oversight.

It's April. They've had it for two months. Anyway, we all get a copy. Everything's all right with the world after a nasty few weeks. Don's Master Gruppenplan is still unfolding as he predicted, Thames want to do our series, the script's arrived. I sit in my wicker chair in the living room to devour it.

My part is Anna Wynd. Is that a joke? Not too funny if it is. Not to me, anyway. Thanks, Howard. I read the first half without cracking a smile. Any more than my character does. She's tense, humourless, insecure, permanently on Valium, propped up by the other two. Hmm. As a character she's well defined, but it's hardly me. Unless that's how Howard sees me.

The biographical details are almost too correct: straight actress, known for leading roles in Shakespeare, yearns to do musicals to have more fun (sounds like a Lonely Hearts ad); wears contact lenses, blonde hair, not much of a dancer, widowed mother. Yes, yes, yes. As for my persona in Rock Bottom— Annie, as distinct from Annabel—there's no sign. Where's the sense of fun and mischief? Where's the positive energy, the drive? Why would the other two spend time with me if I'm this boring and neurotic? I wouldn't want to act this if it were just a part. If I've got to play her as a version of *me*, that'd be really lowering to the spirit.

Don't jump to conclusions, I tell myself, read on to the end. Let's see, keep an open mind, find out what's okay.

I finish it, close the script and stare out of the window, not seeing much. Ophelia in Bolton instead of Desdemona at Oxford, okay. Cressida for Helena in London, why not? We don't need historical accuracy, we need authenticity, the right feel. Anna sings *Blueberry Hill* instead of Dee, okay, at least the scene is there. So she's living with a boring man, okay, why not? Don is now Henry 'Hyper' Huggins, as Howard said, a piano-player, maniacally genial when not catatonic because he's composing. His Master Gruppenplan is there. Why wasn't I chuckling and gasping, unable to turn the pages fast enough? Howard's remembered all the little stories I told him—Di singing *Blueberry Hill* at The Casserole, Gaye with her one-liners and her penchant for the best quality olive oil, my mother as the Widow undermining me with acid comparisons to the others. Don's song *Little Ladies* is in there, transmogrified into the name of the group. We're now The Little Ladies instead of Rock Bottom. Not as witty or funny or apt.

It hasn't caught the spirit, the life, the sheer energy of the group. He's used us as character cut-outs and gone off in another direction. Technically it's about us, but the feel is all wrong. I imagine trying to get inside Anna, slide my arms into her coat. I shrivel and curl up even thinking about it. It's exactly, identically, the kind of part I've come to dread, the nicely-brought-up middle-class girl with no warmth or fire. Howard has taken on board my frustration with this stereotype—Celia in *The Philanthropist* a perfect example—and is reinforcing it. The whole reason for Rock Bottom is to escape from all that into rock and pop, where the energy lies, where it's more real and physical and fun.

I'd better think about this. Within Rock Bottom, my character is vastly different from myself, but it's exciting to play. All of us are projecting something more dangerous, cooler, more highly charged, sexual, exaggerated. Unconventional and wild, not stuck in a stereotype, but an archetype, women in charge of their own destiny, striding through life, towering over the ordinary, commanding the audience with passion and humour and generosity. Wacky. Don got it in the first week:

> *Boy you're a big girl now, yes you are*
> *And everywhere you go you're a bright shining star.*

There's nothing of that in here. Anna is a small woman. Her soul is narrow, she's afraid all the time. She's *mean*.

This is not okay, not okay at all. What should I do? GB's in Birmingham doing *Trinity Tales*, Di's doing some film or other, *Percy's Progress* or *Eskimo Nell*, I lose track. Never mind. There's always the phone.

'Annie! Hi! You sound a bit low. What's wrong? Having a ball up here. Did I tell you I'm playing the Wife of Bath? It's hilarious. Fab company, too. Peter's in it.'

'Peter?'

'Peter Benson. I told you. And Bill Maynard's being hilarious, the old bugger.'

'Did you read the script yet?'

'Ah, that's why you're depressed. It'll be fine, Annie.'

'I don't see how.'

'Pretty tacky, really, isn't it? I expected rather more of Howard, frankly, darling. You said *Verité* was good, didn't you?'

'It was fine. This isn't.'

'Well hey, it's television, a script's just a blueprint, we can do things with it.'

'I don't know what. I don't see how we can agree to do this. We'd have been better off with Brian Degas. He got it right.'

'Well, I don't know if he's back from the States or I could have a quick word.'

'What do we do?'

'Say yes, of course.'

'I don't know. I found it really depressing.'

'Don't worry, Annie, it'll all come right in rehearsal. Don't rock the boat now. Wait till we get our hands on it. We'll rewrite it on the hoof, add some jokes, it'll be fine.'

'But the feel's all—'

'Annie, darling, stop worrying, just say yes. We can call someone else in, another scriptwriter, maybe Alan Plater might fancy—'

'I think we should tell them we're unhappy now so they can change it. They've got to get the spirit right.'

'Don't be silly. We say yes and go in there and change it in rehearsal. It'll be fun.'

'You think so?'

'I know so. Don't whatever you do put the mockers on it. Just go with it. Change it later.'

'You sound like Miss Adelaide.'

'Who?'

'You know. *Guys and Dolls*. Marry the man today—'

We sing the next line together. 'And change his ways tomorrow!'

I'm mildly reassured. It goes against my instincts not to be up front about this, start the discussion now before Howard's gone too far down the line for radical rethinking. He's already in such a blind panic he can hardly speak.

Perhaps Gaye's right. Say nothing. Accept. Work with it.

Don sends a formal letter of acceptance to Thames saying we want to do the show. He's called to a meeting about merchandising, which goes fine, then another. After the second one, he comes home hardly able to speak. It takes quite a while before he can tell me what happened.

'Verity. She was in a foul mood. Hungover, I think. Late. Rude. Lost her temper right away. Called me a liar. Said she didn't trust me. Said if I don't get Di out of *Little Night Music* by tomorrow, the deal's off, she'll recast. I offered to call Di. Screamed at me, she did, when I told her Di couldn't come to the phone, she was in a meeting with her social worker about Jaymie. Said she didn't give a shit about Di or her kid. Stormed out. I got twenty-four hours.'

'This is madness. Didn't Peter Bailey say he'd try to help? And Toby Robertson? Intercede for us?'

'Yeah. But no point till *Night Music*'s opened. They've got the dress rehearsal tomorrow, they're all going mad at Pilbrow's office getting ready for the first night. How could I speak to anybody right now?'

'It's not even your job. It's for them to do. Thames, I mean. Why doesn't she just—'

Don slams out of the room and locks himself in the music room. I know better than to disturb him in this state.

May, 1975

'Howard? It's Annie. Annabel.'

'Oh. Hi. I'm really busy right now—'

'Howard, we haven't spoken for weeks. I need to speak to you. Please.'

'Okay.'

'We've heard they're not using us. My agent says they're going to recast.'

'Annie, I can't discuss this right now. I'm frantic trying to get the scripts in. Frantic.'

'I can't believe you're saying this. I'm really disappointed, Howard.'

'Disappointed?'

'Yes. Rock Bottom are in trouble here. We don't know why, you presumably do. It's gone so far down the line we've only got one remedy left. I thought you should know.'

'Remedy?'

'Yes. Nobody at Thames will talk to us, nobody will deal with us in any way. I'm ringing you to say we're going to take a writ out against the series going ahead.'

'I should take a writ out against you!' Howard's voice rises. 'This whole thing is ruining my peace of mind. How can I write with these threats hanging over my head? I've tried and tried to get on with it. You people just won't let me work. I think I'm going crazy.'

'Howard, if you go to Thames now and say you can't write

unless you know you're writing for us, they'll get it organised in ten minutes.'

Up go the decibels. My phone ear's already hurting. I swap it over.

'I don't write for you. I don't write for anyone. I write for me. And you've blown it, you guys. Don is a liar and a cheat. So is Larry Fenton. You guys have really screwed it.'

'Howard, this is ridiculous. Don may be all kinds of things but he's not a liar. Or a cheat.'

'Oh really? Didn't he promise to get Di out of her contract? Didn't he?'

'Howard, calm down. It's not up to him to release her, even if he could. *Night Music*'s nothing to do with him. It has to be Verity to—'

'Then he's a liar. He promised. He cheated me out of the music publishing on *King Kong*. Him and his fucking mentor. Larry has corrupted him. He's not who I thought he was.'

'What on earth are you talking about? Have you spoken to Larry? This is rubbish, Howard.'

'And it's total insanity for Don to claim Rock Bottom is his— or yours.'

I take a breath. Stop.

'What?'

'This series has nothing to do with Rock Bottom. It comes directly from *King Kong*.'

I'm so amazed I burst into laughter. 'Nothing to do with Rock Bottom? How can you say that? It's *all* Rock Bottom. It's got Rock Bottom stamped all over it. All through it, like a stick of rock. You know it's ours.'

'I won't listen to this. You're a crazy woman. This is my series. *I* took it to Thames, *I* sold them the idea, *I*'m writing it.'

'Yeah, you took it to Thames but you asked our permission first, didn't you? At the lunch you were going to pay for and didn't?'

'I have less than three months to complete a whole television series. So I will thank you to get off the phone and let me write.'

'Well, if that's your attitude, the only thing I can say is we'll see you in court. It'll make a nice final episode, won't it?'

'What?'

'Court, Howard. See you in court.'

I bang the phone down hard.

And shake for an hour afterwards.

The extended honeymoon is well and truly over.

9

Rock and a Hard Place

May, 1975

There are only two lawyers' firms I know of who specialise in show business—Harbottle & Lewis and Wright, Webb, Syrett & Sons. I go to Wright, Webb, Syrett because of Oscar.

Oscar Beuselinck. Short, heavy-jowled, bespectacled, I don't think he can ever have looked young. There were plenty of budding lawyers at Oxford. They claimed it was a dull subject to read, endless facts and dates and cases to memorise. Most of them found time to make films, do theatre, play sport and socialise, unlike the scientists, who had no time at all. Several of them were brilliant actors who could have gone on to have a career in theatre. Mostly they didn't—how sensible—and became solicitors and barristers within a stable profession that, if they worked reasonably hard, could promise them a lifetime of rewards.

I'd never met a lawyer like Oscar, though, till *Hair!* He was truly a one-off. He represented all the producers, Michael Butler, Robert Stigwood et al. I wouldn't have come across him if he hadn't been Paul Nicholas's father. Paul was the star of the show. This dual position allowed Oscar to throw his considerable weight around, something he much enjoyed, and also to get to know all of us in the tribe. He hung around the theatre often enough for us to call him Grandad and he took all of us under his wing. He bought us drinks, lent money, gave advice, solved

141

problems. If any of us were in trouble, Oscar was there, bustling about, meddling in it, sorting it. When he heard I was leaving the show and going to Paris to do it there for six months, he called me in. Blunt, Oscar was. A bit direct. Crude. Sometimes bloody rude. And so kind.

'How you getting to Paris? You got a decent place to stay? Your car good enough to get you there and back?'

'I haven't got a car, Oscar.'

He affected huge astonishment. 'Not got a car? How're you getting there?'

'Train, I suppose.'

'Getting home after the show on the fucking Metro, then? Can't have that. Got a sodding driving licence, at least?'

'Yes, Oscar.'

'All right. You'll be hearing from me. Bye.'

The week before I left the London company, I got a little note from Oscar, with a registration number on it and a key attached. 'Red and white Ford Anglia parked outside your front door. Drive safely. O.'

He wouldn't let me pay. Didn't want anything in return. No wonder we all called him Grandad.

Oscar listens and frowns and twiddles his thumbs and spins his pen as Don and I explain the situation. He barks orders down the intercom for coffee and minions. He paces up and down and stares out of the window at Soho Square, just getting its spring green. He harrumphs and grunts and bellows questions.

'Bastards! From now on I represent you, do you hear? They'll hear from me, I promise you.'

He bangs his fist on his ornate leather-topped desk. It seems to be used to this treatment.

'Oscar. I want to stop them going ahead. Doing the series. Now.'

'Just gimme the paperwork. Everything you have that proves it's yours. We'll sort them out.'

Don and I look at each other.

'There isn't much. Any, really.'

Oscar stares. 'Agreement? Outline of the idea? Contract between you? What did you send to Thames in the first place?'

'Nothing. Just the agreement they drew up last October.'

'Ah, that's what we need. Hand it over.'

I fumble for it in my handbag.

'It acknowledges it's your idea, then?'

'I don't think it does, not specifically. It gives us right of first refusal to do the series. Nothing about who owns what.'

He shakes his head. 'That's difficult, then.' Reads. 'Show it to a lawyer, did you, before signing this?'

'No.'

He shakes his head again.

'How can we stop them, Oscar?'

'Tricky. You got no proof, you got no copyright.'

'They're about to start rehearsals. They've cast the leads already. We have to stop them going into the studio to record. Can't we do that? They mustn't, mustn't be allowed to record it. We'll lose everything.'

'Take out an injunction against them, you mean?'

'Yes. That's it. An injunction. Now. Then they'll have to sort things out, won't they?'

I know I'm desperate, clutching at straws. They haven't spoken to us in weeks.

Oscar nods. 'Better get counsel's opinion on this. See what kind of precedents there are. No copyright. It's unusual, see?'

Don and I look at each other again. 'How much will that cost—counsel's opinion?'

'Don't you worry your pretty little head about that just yet. We need it and fast. Grandad'll take care of it for now.'

He yells down the intercom at his poor secretary, swigs his coffee, bustles us out of the door.

'You'll be hearing from me within the week.'

It's harder for Don. I know Oscar, I feel at home in his office, with its employees' three-piece suits and good haircuts, Oxford was full of them. Don, weighed down by an outsize chip on his shoulder and burdened by guilt, is grim and morose. I'm frightened, certainly. But more than anything, I'm so fuelled by anger I can drive this bit, I can drive it all by myself if I have to.

I've started another episode of *Crown Court* when Oscar calls with the time and date of the meeting with counsel. I'll be in Manchester recording the show. Can't afford to wait around for me, time is too pressing. The girls aren't around. Don's been party to all the Thames meetings and discussions; he may be the youngest and least experienced, but he's had to shoulder so much responsibility for Rock Bottom already, he'll be fine alone.

'Make sure you tell him...'

'Don't forget the conversation with Ronnie Beck when Howard went crazy and...'

'Take that agreement with Thames, won't you?'

Don looks weary. 'I'll do my best,' he says, and that's it. He's taking this very hard, blaming himself, I can tell. I'm burning up with determination, desperate to halt their progress. I loathe and despise them. Rock Bottom is ours. And they're trying to take it away.

When I call from the Manchester studio, Don doesn't answer. There's no answer an hour later, or at midnight. He'll be in the pub or the gutter by now. Does that mean hope or despair, I wonder?

When I get home the next day, he's in his music-room as usual, sitting at the piano, with his Beethoven scowl. That could mean anything—a chord progression he's not sure about, a hangover (though he rarely gets those) or bad news. I make us both a cup of Nescafe and perch on the windowsill till he's ready to take a break.

'Sorry,' he mutters, grabbing his pen, 'just got to finish this bit. Promised I'd get it to Carl yesterday.'

'Okay. Hello to you, too.'

At this, he looks up and sees me. The frown vanishes, just for an instant.

'Hi. With you in a minute. Promise.'

By the time the minute is up, I've finished my coffee and his is cold. He leaps from the piano stool, stretches his back, kisses me, stares out of the window at the grey sky.

'Bin here since six,' he says. 'There's another one done, ready for the copyist. Fifteen-piece arrangements, these are.'

'Had any breakfast yet?'

'Dunno. Dunno if there's anything here.'

'I've looked, there isn't. I'll shop later.'

'Might as well get a sarnie down the pub then.'

He grabs his jacket, fags and keys and off we go across the road to the Three Stars, a good twenty yards away. I sometimes wondered if he'd taken the flat because of it. He spends a lot of time there. More, recently. We take our usual corner table and I wait till he's had half a pint, two sandwiches and a packet of crisps before I ask the verdict.

'Verdict? How d'you mean?'

'Counsel. Nicholas Strauss. What he said.'

'Oh.' His face shuts down. The rest of the pint disappears. 'Not good.'

'What do you mean, not good?'

'He says we can't. Take an injunction out.'

'But Oscar said—'

'He sent us for counsel's opinion, didn't he? Can't have bin too sure.'

'What's the problem? Is there another way round this? What did he suggest? What were his reasons?'

Don rubs the heel of his hand across his eyebrows and sighs. 'I knew you'd be like this. Calm down. I can explain.'

'Okay. Okay. Yes, please. I'll shut up.'

'Look. Erm. He said… it's *possible* to take out an injunction against them going into the studio.'

'I knew it! I knew it!'

'Hold on. Not finished yet. Legally, it can be done. He said if we're found to be wrong—'

'How could we be? We know it's all true.'

'Hold on, I said. We got to be able to prove it. They're innocent till proved guilty, right? Like everyone else. So we got to prove our case. He said it'd be hard. Nothing on paper, have we?'

'I suppose not, but—'

'It'd be difficult to get everything ready in time.'

'Rubbish. We could do it in a day if we—'

'*And* he said if we lose, if they don't accept our story, it could be very expensive. Very.'

My heart shrivels. 'Did he say how expensive?'

'Big bit of machinery to stop, a television series, he said. Costs of delaying it very high. Contracts run out, studio bookings get screwed. They'd charge us the works for all that.'

'How much, Don?'

He takes a deep breath. 'Two hundred and fifty thousand quid. Maybe more.'

I see. Now I see. Between us all, we could raise maybe two hundred, once Granada have paid up. Two hundred thousand is a joke. Ironic to be doing *Crown Court*, just at this particular moment. I buy us another drink and some more crisps while I try to think.

'That's two hundred and fifty thou plus legal fees. Theirs and ours. Cheers.'

I gulp my pineapple juice. Magically, my head clears. 'Well, look, even if the worst happens, the very worst, what are they going to do? Send us to prison? We can sell everything we own.'

'We don't own anything, Annie. That wicker chair of yours? Our bed?'

It's true. The only thing we have of any value is Don's grand piano. Don's always been nervous of the bailiffs. The minute he got the piano, he put it in his dad's name, just in case.

'So what's the worst they can do?'

He wipes the beer froth from his moustache and puts the empty glass hard down on the ironwork table. 'I might be bankrupted.'

'What would that entail?'

He rocks his chair forward and back, forward and back. 'They take away your bank account. That's what they do. They take away your cheque book. You can't get any money unless people pay cash. Nobody'll do that. Could be two years. I'm not risking it, Annie. I'm not.'

I know Don too well. He's slow to make decisions. He'll lie awake all night making his mind up. And once it's made, he'll never, ever, change it.

'I'll have to do it on my own, then,' I say.

'Don't be daft. How could you?'

He's right. My courage ebbs away. This is a joint venture, Don's and mine, we do things together. If he can't face taking such a risk, what's the point in arguing?

The sleek liner that is Thames Television's new drama series sails serenely on.

June, 1975

Down we go, drowning in isolation; the few snippets of news never from Thames or Howard, not since 'See you in court!' My darling friend from LAMDA, Phil Sayer, turns down a part in the series out of loyalty to us without even telling me, I hear it from someone else. Tony Borer, a designer working for Thames, does the same thing. Other fragments aren't so pleasant. Our friend Julie Covington (small, dark, feisty, great voice) is cast as Dee. Hmm. Bit close to home. Then Rula Lenska as Q. Never heard of her. Rumour says she's a Hungarian countess, very aristocratic, tall with red hair. *Jesus*. Then Charlotte Cornwell is cast as Anna. Blonde, middle-class, does Shakespeare, I'm told.

They're casting *lookalikes*? With similar backgrounds? I can't believe it.

If Thames is a liner, it towers over our fragile little skiff, threatening to annihilate us, smash us into fragments. How can we continue as Rock Bottom if they take our look, one of the cornerstones of our appeal? Take our backgrounds? Take our whole story? We have no chance if they do that. Our boat is sinking fast.

One day in Soho, I bump into Julie.

'I hear you're in the Rock Bottom Series?'

'It's called *Rock Follies* now. I'm sorry, Annie, but it's a great job.'

'No need to apologise. Not your fault, we all know that. Painful, that's all.'

'We're not happy either, any of us. They're trying to sign us up so they can manage us as a group.'

'What? What do you mean? Who? Who's trying to sign you up?'

'Dunno. Andrew Brown, Howard, Jenne Casarotto. They want us to be a group as well as do the series. Tried to get us to sign a contract with them. Of course we refused. I complained.'

Oh Christ. I call Oscar.

'We can get them on that, don't worry,' storms Oscar. 'We'll issue a writ. NOW!'

'Against whom?'

'All of them! Schuman, Thames, Brown, Howard's bloody agent.'

'Oscar, Julie wasn't quite clear about exactly who it was.'

'We'll find out. I'll get someone digging right away.'

Don and I go in to see the draft writ he's had drawn up.

'Oscar, we have to talk about money,' I say. 'We haven't got any.'

'I know, I know. None of you bloody artists ever have. Except my son, who's just a money machine. All in hand. Don't give it a thought. We've got to move on this. I need all of you in here double quick, no fucking about. Who are the others? Di

Langton? Lovely. Gaye who? Oh. Fine. You'll all apply for Legal Aid right now.'

'Legal Aid?'

'Of course. If we can present a good enough case, Legal Aid'll fund the whole thing.'

'That's great. I didn't realise—'

'It's not fast, I can promise you that. But if they think you've got a case, we can get the bastards into court. So get 'em in, okay? And I want every agreement, every contract, everything to do with the group. You name it, I want it. By tomorrow morning, first thing.'

'We haven't got much, Oscar,' I say.

'What do you mean?'

'Nothing much written down,' mutters Don. 'Not as such.'

'Not as such? Not as such?' shouts Oscar, in *Witness for the Prosecution* mode today. 'You've got contracts, agreements, record deals, publishing.'

'W-we haven't got much. Nothing that says we own the idea. Done on handshake mostly. With friends.'

Oscar frowns, thrusting his jowly face across the desk, looming over Don. Lucky we're sitting, he'd be glaring at his navel otherwise. 'You trying to tell me we got nothing to go on?'

'Oscar,' I say, before he turns into his favourite character of hectoring solicitor from *Inadmissible Evidence* (which he swears is based on him anyway), 'Oscar darling, don't bully Don. We tell you the truth, you do what you can for us. Okay?'

He subsides and sinks back into his chair. 'You look like a nice young man. I know this lovely lady. If she trusts you, I trust you. I'll get you someone good to look after you.'

He yells into the intercom. 'Sally! Send in Mark Wemborn. NOW!'

'He's in a meeting, Oscar,' says a bright voice.

'Get him out. I want him in here this minute.'

'Yes, Oscar.'

Poor Mark. Poor Sally. I wouldn't want to work for Oscar. Not that Sally sounded upset.

A knock on the door. A kind-looking youngish man with a pink face puts his head round the door. 'Want me, Oscar?'

'Of course I bloody want you. Why do you think I asked? What took you so long? Who the fuck employs you?'

Mark smiles, closes the door. He doesn't seem upset either.

'These two young people have been ripped off, with two others. I want you to draw up their case. And they have to have Legal Aid. Sort it, will you.'

Mark raises his eyebrows. 'Legal Aid, Oscar?'

'You heard. We're getting them Legal Aid so they can sue the bastards.'

He comes out from behind his desk, grasps Don's hand, mutters something in his ear, gives me a smacking kiss. 'Now get out, I've got work to do.'

Outside, Mark sighs and runs a hand through his thinning hair. 'Right. I'll find a room.'

He wanders off.

'What did he say to you, Don?'

'Oh. He said, "You're a lucky bastard".'

I laugh. 'His bark's worse than his bite.'

Don scratches his chin. 'As long as he bites them, not us, I don't really care.'

Summer, 1975

Legal Aid. Form upon form to fill in. Pages of essential information in very small type. Minute details of income over decades. Wading through the bureaucracy is like the worst school exam for which you haven't revised. Worse still, all four of us have to do it or we can't proceed.

'Annie, what do they mean our accounts for last year? Is it Rock Bottom's accounts?'

'We haven't got any. They mean our own.'

'But I haven't done this year's yet. Don't they know about Schedule D?'

'I don't know what they know.'

'Christ! I'm sending this straight to my accountant.'

'Good idea. Call Di and suggest that, will you? Might speed things up a bit.'

'If Di has an accountant, I'll start shopping at Marks and Spencer.'

'I thought you already did.'

'Watch it, my girl. You're so sharp you'll cut yourself, as my grandmother used to say.'

Phone Di. No answer. Next day, phone again. No answer. There's a kind of rhythm to this. Phone Di…

Don grinds his teeth and goes into the office for Larry's help.

I grind my teeth by myself.

People are beginning to divide up into sheep and goats: those with us, those against us. When Straker has a party at his flat, both are there, mostly ours. Straker's friend Torquil (not part of the controversy, so neutral) and I start chatting. He's young and handsome and just starting out in the music business. David Toguri, definitely one of ours, comes up and kisses me. Dear David, who worked so hard to make our concerts such a success. It's great to see him.

'This is a wonderful choreographer,' I tell Torquil. 'He helped create Rock Bottom, my group.'

I have to mention us all the time, I always do. David shakes hands with him and beams at me. 'You gotta congratulate me! I got a great job.'

'Terrific. Congratulations! You going to tell me what?'

'I got the job of choreographing *Rock Follies*!'

I feel dizzy. The floor comes rushing up to meet me.

'Excuse me,' I mutter and turn away.

'You all right?' asks Torquil. 'Annie?'

'Just get me out of here, will you?'

He puts an arm round me. The nearest door opens onto the garden. With Torquil's help, I stumble out into a paved garden, bare except for a forest of empty champagne bottles lined up against the fence. Nothing else. Paving slabs and champagne bottles, a strange landscape. It'll do. Torquil walks me up and down for an hour or so till I can face going back. Why I don't scream the place down, hit David, burst into tears, I've no idea. The blow struck deep, too deep for dramatics. Back in, I pretend nothing's happened.

David's one of theirs now.

Denis Main Wilson calls. 'Should go through the agents but what the hell!'

'Dear Denis, what the hell, indeed. How lovely to hear from you.'

'Got a little idea for you. Your group is rocking along, you might be too busy.'

'Ah. I'd love to say we are. What's the idea?'

'I've been looking around for something to get to grips with since *Till Death Us Do Part*. Something interesting. It's become impossible at the Beeb now, harder and harder to get things off the ground with all the grey men in grey suits. Bureaucracy! I detest it.'

'And have you found anything yet?'

'Nothing they're giving a green light to, the idiots. Not a creative spark between them. Anyway, they're letting me do a pilot, if you please. It's very, very funny, written by Ronnie Wolfe and Ronnie Chesney—'

They did *The Rag Trade*, a work of comic genius. Denis produced it, along with The Goons, Tony Hancock, Eric Sykes and *Till Death Us Do Part*. We're talking giants here.

'Oh my God, Denis. What is it? Tell me quick!'

'It's for a re-run of *The Rag Trade*. Thought you three'd be perfect casting.'

I can see us instantly—GB as Miriam Karlin, blowing her whistle and yelling 'Everybody Out!' me as Sheila Hancock aiding and abetting, Di as Barbara Windsor.

'I think I have an idea about how you'd cast us!'

'Yes, darling! Might suit Rock Bottom, don't you think?'

We both dissolve into laughter. It's so perfect, I can't imagine why I hadn't thought of it myself.

'Will you ask your girls? And of course I'll get onto the agents. Just thought I'd tell you first.'

Oh, bless him. It might be the only thing we do this year, possibly the only thing we ever do. Unless the Beeb decide to go ahead with the whole series. Oh! I put the receiver down and the implications start to hit me, along with insane hope. We could be in direct competition with our other selves in *Rock Follies*. Maybe RCA will renew our recording deal, maybe we can add songs to *The Rag Trade*? Maybe, maybe, maybe. At the very least, we'll get to work together again. I write the conversation down in my diary, along with dates and times and names. This care and attention comes too late to save us from Thames, but now I leave nothing to chance.

GB and Di say yes, they're both free that week. We're on. When the script arrives, I devour it in minutes. It's perfect, funny all the way through, feed, gag, feed, gag and we are so right for it I could cheer. No wonder they call Denis a genius. We'll have a ball with this.

So it's a touch unnerving when Denis turns to me at the end of the first day's rehearsal.

'Darling, I have a cassette here of the signature tune. You'll like it, I promise you, it's Alex Welsh and his band, super stuff. We have to record the vocals for it on Wednesday. Be a love and write some lyrics for it, would you? Bring 'em into rehearsal tomorrow and I'll get a pianist in.'

Tomorrow? He wants them tomorrow?

'Of course,' I say with more confidence than I feel. 'I'll have a go, Denis.'

'Thanks, darling.' He gets to his feet and stretches. 'Lovely day's work today. You're all marvellous.'

'Denis says we're all marvellous,' I tell Don when I get home.

'*Mar*vellous! *Mar*vellous!' we chant in our best Kiwi.

After an evening of feverish lyric-writing, I crawl into bed at three am. Alex has written a catchy little tune which doesn't want me to sleep and I don't, but it's all done. The next day the girls swing into it with me as if they already know it and Denis is pleased with the recording. So am I. He gave it to me to do and he likes what I wrote. *Mar*vellous! Maybe Rock Bottom is in with another chance. Maybe *The Rag Trade* will put us back where we ought to be. Maybe.

The pilot's done and will go to the big cheese, Billy Cotton Junior, Head of BBC Light Entertainment. Denis is a legend, it's hard to see them turning him down.

'See?' he says in the bar afterwards. 'Trust Denis. I told you to wait another two beats on that line. Got another laugh, didn't you?'

'You're a genius, Denis, you were so right. D'you think there's any chance of them picking it up as a series?'

'Oh, darling, who knows?' he replies, downing a triple scotch. 'I told you. They're all grey men now, I'd never have got anything off the ground with these buggers in charge. The Beeb used to be an exciting place to work. Room for experiment. Now they're all' (in tones of deep disgust) '*accountants*.'

At the beginning of August, Wright, Webb, Syrett & Sons issue a writ against Thames. Reports start trickling in about their reaction. An actress friend calls me. She was at a dinner party with Verity Lambert who, when the subject came up said, according to Susie, 'Huh! Three little actresses. What can they do against the might of EMI?'

I give Susie's name to Mark Wemborn to interview her as a

possible witness, along with a long list of others. He never gets round to it.

December, 1975

Not a good year, 1975, so far. Not my best. *The Rag Trade* came to nothing, Billy Cotton Junior thought it too vulgar for the BBC, Denis was right. A dead end. It's hard to see how 1976 is going to be any better. Don and I go through the motions. The flautist and his singer girlfriend have finally given in and moved out. No more finishing my orange juice without replacing it. No more queuing for the bathroom. No more snide remarks from Sally because she's a trained singer and earns nothing, while I'm not and I do. It ought to be wonderful having the place to ourselves at last.

It's not wonderful. The heart of our relationship has shrunk to a wizened pea. The valves don't work properly, blood isn't pumping though with any vigour, the arteries are blocked.

'You in for dinner?'

'Dunno.'

'Fancy a drink this evening?'

'Mmm? Dunno.'

'Gaye's show opens next week. Shall we go?'

'Erm, don't know yet. Got to finish the music for Geoff's film. Up against it right now.'

'Can I come to the recording?'

'Er, probably not. Studio's small.'

'But I thought you—'

'See ya.'

Front door shuts. He's gone.

How will we get through Christmas with no concerts to plan or songs to write, no producers to meet or recording contracts to puzzle over? Without the phone calls to make and the rehearsal rooms to book and choreography to practise and costumes to clean and the girls to keep on board and the songs to try out and the people to gather in and feed and surround ourselves with? What will we do?

The whole of 1975 has been horrible, but none of it quite sinks in till now. Looking back at it from the dreary wasteland of December's nothing, it isn't good. Don with his rock arrangements for a new musical *Pilgrim* and going out on tour with it, me with my first directing job, both of us ending up at the Edinburgh Festival with our respective shows. Did I mind we hardly saw each other, never spent a night together, while we were there? Had we already drifted so far apart I didn't expect anything? Of course I expected it. It hurts I didn't get it.

I stumble through being out of work and having no money. I go to the launderette, I shop at the North End Road market, I make meals Don doesn't come home to. I can't remember the last time we went to The Casserole. Di's working, Gaye's racketing around, Rock Bottom has disappeared into a dark hole. Until we get Legal Aid, I can't even get going on preparing the case. No money: no lawyers. And all the while, all year, I know Thames have been making the series. *Our* series. It's supposed to start screening early in the New Year. What'll I do then?

Jean Diamond rings. An agent who's always supportive, always kind.

'Darling, a lovely bit of news. The Bristol Old Vic have asked for you, a straight offer, no auditioning, three plays, five months' work. Isn't that wonderful? Annabel? Are you there?'

'Oh, Jean. Yes, wonderful.' I try to sound excited. 'When does it start?'

'January. Richard Cottrell sends his love and hopes you'll accept. He's longing for you to join them. Very charming. Old friend?'

'Yes. Very old friend, from Oxford days.' I clutch the phone tight. I can't turn this down, even for Don. Five months' work— and I'll get paid a bit. This is the break I need, but...

'Are you all right, darling? I thought you'd be thrilled.'

'I'm fine, Jean, really, just a bit surprised. It's been a while, hasn't it.'

'Wait till you hear the plays. And the parts.'

'Oh yes, tell me.' I don't sound very enthusiastic even to myself.

Jean reels them off. 'Lika in *The Promise*, Regina in *Ghosts*, the Countess in *Flea in Her Ear*. What do you think of that? Just what you need, I'd say.'

'Perfect. Just what I need. Great, Jean. Thanks.'

There. It's done. I shall get through 1976, the first half anyhow, in rep in Bristol, back to acting again. Far away from London when *Rock Follies* goes out. Good. Far away from Don, too. Not so good. But we're not so good anyway, so maybe...

If Thames slammed the door on Rock Bottom last April, this job ensures the door is locked and barred.

I concede defeat.

10

At Rock Bottom

Bristol Old Vic Theatre, Tuesday February 24, 1976

The first episode of *Rock Follies* goes out tonight. I don't mention it. I learn my lines. I don't watch.

Green Room, Wednesday morning, February 25

Actors dump coats and gloves and scripts to dive for the coffee and biscuits, chatter, hug and joke. In walks my friend Richard Cottrell, head of the theatre, eyes alight, a spring in his step and the stammer which only vanishes when he sings.

'H-hallo, darlings. Good m-m-morning. Did you see *Rock Follies* last night? Wasn't it s-splendid. S-s-such strong characterisation. Our own Charlotte p-p-playing the lead. I've never seen television drama like it. So t-t-true to life!'

True to life? I want to yell. *Of course it's true to life. It is life. Our life. They stole it, for Chrissakes.*

'Didn't see it, I'm afraid,' is what I mumble. I cross to the coffee machine.

'You all right?' asks Sheila Reid, peering at me. I nod and pour myself some coffee.

After rehearsals I call Don. He sounds catatonic. I've never heard him so low. He doesn't want to talk.

'Darling, this is so horrible. I can't bear being so far away.

The whole thing's a farce, I can't believe what's happening.'

He mumbles something.

'Don't give up, please, Don, it's not over yet. Oscar will think of something. *We'll* think of something.'

'Mmm.'

'I'll come home next weekend if we're not rehearsing Saturday. I'll hitch a lift.'

More mumbling.

'I didn't catch that. Don?'

'Joan Shenton says call her. Bye.'

The phone clicks down at the other end.

He sounds desperate. I can't do anything this far away.

I had a more urgent phone call to make before Joan. It took a while to make. No phone in my digs, a very public one at the theatre, needing coins aplenty, Bristol to London's not cheap. I put it off. When I summoned the courage, she didn't answer me straightaway.

'Gaye? Are you still there?'

'Of course.'

'Gaye?' I croak, muffling the mouthpiece with my hand. This isn't for anyone in the company. 'I said I hate being so far away. Especially now.'

'Christ, there's a man across the road exposing himself.'

'I just don't think he's coping.'

'Oh no, it's a bag of onions. Pity.'

'Do me a favour, would you?'

'What?'

'You drive right past his door every day. Could you just pop in and have a cuppa with him? I hate him sounding so—so *desperate*. If he even answers the phone, which he doesn't much.'

'He's probably out enjoying himself.' A thump, followed by a clatter. 'Stop it, Smudge, stop it! Damn cat just jumped onto my knee and knocked the phone out of my hand. Sorry, darling, got it back now. Funny how he barges in just when I'm trying to do something! Always my mascara or the olive oil or the phone. Oh yes, did I tell you I got that telly? I'm off again soon. Three weeks this time. I don't suppose you could look after the cats while I'm—no, you're in Bristol, aren't you. Silly me. Look, darling, I'm just about to—'

'GB, *please.*'

'What, darling? How's it going, by the way? *Flea In Her Ear*! Lucky you, I love farce. How's the company? You've got Billy there, haven't you. And gorgeous Sheila Reid. Oh and a tongue down the throat for Harold Innocent. What a bastard. Funny, though.'

I have one last go. My voice echoes down the backstage corridor. 'Please, GB, *please* go and see him. I can't get home till after we've opened. Don's your friend as well. You've always got on so well with him. I think he might be having a bit of a breakdown, I'm really worried about him.'

A miaow from Smudge, and a sharp bark from Gaye—at me, not Smudge: 'Well, if he's heading for a breakdown, he'd better take himself to the loony bin and sort it out. Not my problem. Bye.'

Click. She's hung up on me, too.

I'll have to wait till the weekend.

When I get home, Don's still miserable, the kitchen's a mess and the fridge empty, apart from some very old bacon and a slice of white bread with green mould on it. I take him out to the pub for an early lunch.

'Got some good news,' I tell him when he's wolfed down a toasted cheese and ham.

'Oh yeah?'

'Yes. You remember Joan Shenton ringing? I spoke to her.'

'Joan who?'

'We roomed next to each other at Oxford. She's a journalist, married to Jack Crawshaw, the producer of *This Is Your Life.*'

'Oh.'

'I haven't seen her since Oxford. She rang to say she and Jack watched *Rock Follies*—'

Don groans and sinks his face into his beer.

'No, wait, it's okay. She said she was shocked. She recognised me right away *and* my mother *and* our relationship. She said it was unmistakeable. She knew nothing about Rock Bottom, Don, but she saw the connection at once. She'll be a witness for us. Only thing is, she says we'll have to subpoena her.'

Don looks up at this. 'Why?'

'Because,' I say in triumph, 'She works for Thames Television!'

This gets a faint, brief smile. He's back with me again, just for a moment.

'The minute this job's over, in May, we'll go to Oscar again and get things moving.'

'Get what moving?'

'Suing Thames. And Howard. We're going to do it. I'm not letting this go, Don. I'm not.'

'RCA are,' he says, draining his glass.

I freeze. 'What?'

'They're sorry, but what's the point? At best you'll just look like copies of the *Rock Follies* girls. It couldn't work. They couldn't sell us now. They've pulled the plugs on the album.'

I hadn't foreseen that. Of course. No wonder Don's morose. So am I now. We sit in silence till the pub shuts for the afternoon.

Oh, it's so successful, *Rock Follies*. The critics love it. The public love it. Three girls, all actresses, all completely different, struggling to make a rock group of their own in the treacherous world of show business. Backstage stories, meaty parts for three gorgeous girls, rock music, fun costumes—like Abba but English and with a strong story line. Of course they like it. They release an album of the music. Top of the charts, goes platinum, *Rock Follies* rocks. The series bought by the States for release there, the three replacement girls all established as stars. Julie Covington outclasses the other two according to all the reviews, which I torture myself by reading. She's nominated for a Bafta. All three of them have now got top-line careers ahead. Another series announced. Our entire Master Gruppenplan, in fact.

1976 isn't turning out to be my best year either and we're not even halfway through yet.

West Kensington Mansions W14, June, 1976

> Dear Diary,
> Back from Bristol. Atmosphere very strange here. Don wrapped up in himself. It doesn't feel much like home. Five months is too long to be away. How do I pick up the pieces?

Of course I can't. The elephant in the room is Rock Bottom. Not that's it's an elephant now. Once it was, a hungry, obsessive young elephant, demanding our time, money, thoughts, dreams, energy. Two demented blackbirds trying to feed an elephantine cuckoo. Now there's just space, the nest is deserted and we're exhausted. We don't know what to say to each other. Don doesn't look me in the eye. Jane McCulloch, Toby Robertson's wife, has me over. We sit in her garden and I pour out my heart. She's very sympathetic. Don worked on *Pilgrim* for Toby and we're all close friends.

I last out three weeks, waiting for things to change and then give up. Stay calm and adult and friendly, I tell myself, it'll all come right.

'Maybe we need a bit of time apart, Don.'

Excuse me, haven't we just had five months apart?

'Something's not working, is it? Maybe I should go back to Westbourne Terrace for a little bit and give you some room? We could speak in a few days. What do you think?'

A silent nod. Not a rush across the room to fold me in his arms. Not an acknowledgement of how cold he's been. No apology. No reconciliation.

He'll miss me when I'm gone.

You fool, you were gone all this year. You were in Bristol for the last five—shut up. Make it easy for him.

I repack my case.

'I'll leave it to you. Take your time, Don. When you're ready to talk, give me a call.'

Head back to my own long-neglected flat, in a sort of dream. A fool's paradise.

He'll realise his mistake. He'll call and tell me he can't live without me. It'll be all right in a few days. Or a few weeks.

No, it isn't. It isn't all right at all. It's *my* mistake, not his. He doesn't want me back. He's with someone else.

Jane McCulloch. She's left Toby for him.

It's all over, as the song says.

In every way.

Westbourne Terrace, London W2, July, 1976

The recording contract with RCA was gone, the television series was gone, the dream of making it was gone. The cosy, hopeful little nest with Don at West Kensington Mansions, Beaumont Crescent, W14, that, too, was gone. Morning after morning I woke to vomit-coloured walls, not-quite-matching mustard John Lewis sheets, ochre shutters through which droned endless traffic to and from the Westway, and wondered where I was, who I was. Ugly word, ochre—dull, flat, stale and unprofitable. Hideous colour, too. This had been my home once? Who chose vomit colour for a bedroom? For anywhere.

As if she didn't know. As if she didn't remember exactly how and when that paint was applied and by whom. Not her choice. She let all her lovers walk over her, choose holidays, wallpaper, restaurants. She let her friends do the same.

'Can't meet tonight after all, Annie. Something's come up.'

'What? You promised.'

'Oh shut up, darling, don't whinge. You'd do the same. Can't talk about it now.'

Got a better offer, then, have you? One day I'll say it. Scream it. *Just a stop-gap for you, am I—if nothing better comes up? Is that what you think? You use me, you borrow my money and never give it back, you pretend I'm your best friend and then never speak to me for weeks. You have no loyalty or respect, you drop me in it time after time and I crawl around in the mud saying 'love me love me' like a pathetic spaniel.* One day. One day...

It never lasted more than a morning. By the time I'd showered and cleaned my teeth and done last night's washing-up and made my bed and dried my hair and put on my make-up and dressed myself nicely as if there were nothing wrong, I could look at myself in the mirror and a normal human being stared back. I could get through the day, go for interviews, answer the phone, cook people meals, be gaiety itself with the people who still spoke to me.

The night was another matter. In the dark, the skin of *normal* sloughed off, leaving the slug beneath.

Abba have a hit with their new single, *Dancing Queen*. It sounds very like *Tambourine Queen*. It could have been us having the hit. We were ahead of our time, way ahead. We might have...we could have...our songs were... I mourn and keep it to myself.

The heatwave summer of '76 brings weeks and weeks of sunshine. I get a job in a new play about Belfast, *Spokesong*, at the King's Head, Islington. It's a hit. A wonderful part for me, the wonderful Niall Buggy to play opposite, no money, but everyone—*everyone*—comes to see it.

Not Don, not Di, not Howard. Everyone else. It runs and runs. If Dan Crawford hadn't been so desperate to transfer it, it could still be running. It lasts from August 1976 till the following March and then goes into the West End, with my name in lights outside the Vaudeville Theatre. With both my names so long, I never thought anyone would pay for that, but they do.

It should be alphabetical billing, but Buggy, ever a gentleman, insists on my name going first:

Annabel Leventon
Niall Buggy
in
Spokesong

June, 1977

Rock Follies of 77! scream the headlines. The next series. Platinum album assured, stellar careers for all three golden girls of television, Rula, Charlotte and Julie, instead of Gaye, me and Di.

I make sure I don't see any of it.

While I'm in *Spokesong* I also direct a play for the American Repertory Theater, in a tiny fringe theatre on the Edgware Road, which sells out and gets great reviews. I'm invited to New York to direct it there, when *Spokesong* closes. I'll be working at Joe Papp's famous Public Theater, where *Hair!* first took shape. That's thrilling.

The day I arrive in New York, 7/7/77, there's a city-wide blackout. A month later, Elvis Presley dies. The city mourns and so do I.

I do my directing job as well as I can second time around, with half the cast new to me. Joe Papp comes to the first performance, says it won't transfer to Broadway, it's not a strong enough piece. I am too British to ask if I might run one of his theatres instead, though I'd like to stay forever. So in September I come home. The day I get back, I'm offered a job as assistant director on a new musical about Elvis. His story, to be told entirely through his music. The director is the legendary Jack Good, who worked with Elvis, Tina Turner and Manhattan Transfer, and brought rock'n'roll to British television with *Six-Five-Special* and

Oh Boy! I meet Jack and adore him at once. A grammar-school boy who makes it to Oxford and then into rock. We have plenty in common. I say yes.

I help devise the script, I copy out the lyrics, I cast it and direct it with Jack. We need three Elvises, a young one, another one for the rock'n'roll and army years, and one for his triumphant return to form in Las Vegas in 1968. Jack brings in P. J. Proby as the older Elvis. I discover Shakin' Stevens, unknown and brilliant, playing the Greyhound pub to three men and a boy one evening, just up the road from Don's flat. I get him in—Shaky, that is, not Don—and he's just as superb at nine-thirty the following morning, stone cold sober. Jack books him right away. We also need two rock bands. I bring in Fumble, the rock'n'roll revival band from the show Rock Bottom did for RCA in December, 1974.

We need a girl singer for the only featured female part. *Elvis* is a male-dominated show, being rock'n'roll. I ask Elaine Paige in to meet Jack. She's had a lean time of it recently, but she shows up looking bandbox fresh, as she always does, her voice in terrific shape. She ought to give lessons in being ready when the call comes. She sings *Yesterday* and makes Jack weep. He calls her down to the stalls and walks her out of the theatre, arm round her, saying, 'You are too good for this show, my dear. It would be a waste of your talents. Something better is just around the corner. We wouldn't do you justice. Wait and see.'

In the middle of all this happy Elvis involvement, they ask me to audition for *Evita*, the new Andrew Lloyd Webber show. I know how magnificent a part it is—Julie Covington, fresh from her success in *Rock Follies*, made the album, which was a huge hit. She's turned down playing it on stage. They'd probably ask Di, since she does every musical in the West End, but she's in *A Chorus Line*. I handed out programmes as a celebrity usherette for Michael White when it first opened. I even auditioned for it, but in *A Chorus Line* dancing comes before singing or acting and I didn't have a hope. *Evita* is different, a hugely demanding singing role and the plum acting part of the decade for a woman, one of the greatest in the twentieth century.

Getting *Elvis* on is just too hectic. There isn't time. I tell my agent I can't get there.

Three months later, Elaine Paige gets the title role.

1978

Elvis gets the Olivier Award for Musical of the Year. I'm surrounded by musicians, dancers, singers and old chums. I'm free as a bird—to enjoy it all, every last scrap. And I do, I enjoy it all. Still on my mission to bring music and theatre closer together, I become the show's lynchpin when Jack Good goes back to the States.

Nobody knows my heart is broken, I'm the life and soul of the company. But when I get home, there's nothing. The ball gown turns to rags.

The group gone, Don gone. I cry myself to sleep every night.

Westbourne Terrace, January, 1979

Talk about drowning my sorrows. By the end of January, as well as looking after *Elvis* (in the theatre twice-weekly to see the show and give notes, run understudy rehearsals and replacement cast auditions, organise company calls to keep the show in good shape) I have four other jobs running simultaneously: rehearsing a play at Hampstead Theatre, directing Sunday night rock'n'roll concerts at the Astoria with the *Elvis* company, Freddie Fingers Carr, Alvin Stardust and Joe Brown and in Norwich in my time off (ha!) filming a television play for Anglia with Judi Dench. Once the Hampstead play is on, I play in the evenings, then run to the Astoria and sit up all night doing the lighting for the Sunday concerts.

One evening after the Hampstead show, I meet someone. His

name is Johnny. He's been to all the shows I've done in the last five years, he tells me, and asks me out. I haven't the time or the energy, I'm still in mourning for Don, I'm exhausted from all the work. Yet somehow I find myself in Soho watching *The Deer Hunter* with him.

The court case has to wait. Not that anything's happening, we're becalmed, not a breath of wind, a ripple of movement. Those big lists of witnesses waiting to be interviewed—nothing. I've handed in every document they could conceivably need—all too few of them—my diaries, the song lyrics, the publishing contracts for *It's All Over, Horoscope, Tambourine Queen, Boy You're a Big Girl Now, Piano-player, Ragtime Piano Joe, We Were*, the contract Rock Bottom made together, our agreement with Don, the defunct recording contract. There isn't anything else.

And nothing from Wright, Webb, Syrett & Sons, solicitors to the stars, either. Nothing from Legal Aid. Di never filled her forms in, or never sent them back, or who knows what. Anyway we have to start again, all of us, apparently. If I don't drive it, no-one else does. Right now, I'm too busy. And too tired.

Did I say four other jobs? That's only three. Another one looms, the biggest of them all, the lead in a BBC costume drama set in Cornwall, *Penmarric*. It's eight months' non-stop work. Moving the court case forward is about to become impossible, it'll have to go on the back burner again, I need a little space to manage my life. *Have* a life, even. Between checking up on *Elvis, Penmarric* rehearsals at Acton, recording episodes at the BBC TV Centre in White City and filming in six-week blocks in Cornwall, I get married to Johnny. There's no time to find anything to wear, so I borrow one of my beautiful costumes as a bridal gown and they give me a Saturday afternoon off at the end of July. We'll have one night's honeymoon before I start back on the Monday.

The night before my wedding, GB and Doug Fisher (my Oxford boyfriend) take me out to dinner at Langan's, turn up the next day, help me butter the bread, make the smoked salmon sandwiches, fill the bath with ice for the champagne, collect the hired glasses, get the flat ready for the reception, come as the only non-family guests and do the buttling at the reception afterwards. Angels of mercy.

Chelsea, October, 1979

Penmarric goes out in the BBC's big costume drama slot. Unfortunately, it's too like *Poldark*, the hit series only a few years before, so it gets discounted. Bang go any hopes of reviving my television career. Or any career. It was fun, though, I enjoyed making it, made lots of friends, got my picture on the front cover of the *Radio Times*, interviews, photos, newspaper coverage. Then nothing.

Still nothing on the court case, either. After the flurry of work and marriage and settling in to Johnny's little Chelsea house, I need some time to recover before I focus on the case—or lack of it. I call Wright, Webb to see what—if anything—is going on. It turns out that the last clown in charge has actually left the firm without telling me and with nothing achieved. The huge list of possible witnesses? None of them contacted.

'That's it,' I say to Johnny one evening. 'That's it. I'm beating my head against a very large brick wall. Even the lawyers can't be bothered. The girls, I understand. Well, I don't, but I've got used to it. But the lawyers are being paid to sort this out, for God's sake. What am I to do?'

Johnny listens. 'I can't tell you that, girl. It's up to you. What do you want? You better think about it. It's making you miserable.'

It is. It's making me very miserable. And frustrated. I want to enjoy my new life, I want to be able to get on with it without this ugly, useless cloud always over my head, threatening my happiness. And it won't go away. It won't get better.

I call Oscar.

'Oscar, nobody told me David P. has left. He didn't bother to let me know. He didn't bother to do very much about Rock Bottom either. In two years, has he done anything at all?'

Oscar sidesteps. 'How's your love life, darling? How's that husband of yours? Is he behaving? All going well?'

'I'm not calling because of Johnny, Oscar. I'm calling to tell you I've had enough. You've been very kind. We've taken the case as far as it can go, I'm tired of trying to roll this particular boulder uphill without anyone helping, it's time I started to have a life. I'm going to let it go.'

There's a short pause. Then the bellow of a bull down the phone.

'Don't you even think of it. This case has legs, I'm telling you. There's no way you're stopping now. We're nearly there, I swear to you.'

'Oscar, with all due respect, that's total bullshit. Have a look at the file. There's nothing in it. No movement on any front. It's been four years. And nothing's happened. I quit.'

More bellowing. 'I'm not accepting this. It's outrageous. You get yourself in here first thing tomorrow, I'll have someone for you so brilliant you won't see his backside for dust, he'll move so fast.'

'I can't go through all that again. I can't face the disappointment. How many brilliant employees have you given me so far? Three? What have they done? Nothing, Oscar. *You* may be brilliant. But you're you, they're not. I'm quitting.'

'Great. Ten-thirty tomorrow morning, then. And don't be bloody late. We'll get this case off its arse in no time. Any of the others want to bother, they're welcome. They're bloody useless, if you ask me. But you better be here. You'll see.'

He hangs up. Shit.

I wanted it to be over. I wanted a bit of peace and quiet.

I wanted—oh, to hell with it, I'll go in.

One more meeting. That's all.

11

Fight Back

Wright, Webb, Syrett & Sons, 10 Soho Square, London W1, January, 1980

Oscar's office is all bustle. Coffee, biscuits, Oscar all over me, zooming about at a hundred miles an hour, shouting, flinging his arms about, pretending to talk on the phone, slamming the receiver down, working himself up into a lather of activity. To impress me, I presume. It's a great performance, but overdone. Oscar isn't subtle, never was. He likes everyone to think he's the crudest shyster lawyer in show-biz. He was very embarrassed when I saw him at the Festival Hall once with the Russian Ambassador, listening to Victoria Postnikova play Tchaikovsky. Tried to pretend he didn't see me, slunk back in the box like a criminal. He doesn't like anyone to think he's cultured. Or shy. He certainly doesn't give any impression of that this morning. He's impossible. I give in and laugh.

'Okay, Oscar. I'm here. You can calm down. What rubbish have you got lined up for me?'

He pats the best chair. 'Park your lovely arse in that, dear. I have a surprise for you. You're going to be a very, very happy girl.'

'Oh yes? I can't wait.'

Thick finger slams on intercom. 'Sally! Get Keith in here double quick.'

He must have had this all organised. The door opens

immediately. I remember the last two times, when pleasant grey mice slunk in, eyes down, subservient, dwarfed by Oscar's shenanigans. It's hardly worth looking round. I finish my coffee.

'Miss Leventon, I want you to meet Keith Schilling. Keith, this stunning armful, who I have lusted after for more years than I care to mention, is not only a superb actress and singer, she also happens to be my most important client. I want you to take her case in hand and bloody well get on with it. It is from now on your top priority. Do I make myself fucking clear?'

Keith glances at me, unsmiling, shakes my hand and sits down. 'This the *Rock Follies* case, Oscar?'

'Rock Bottom case, you fool. Yes, it bloody well is. Why do you think I dragged you in here?'

Keith says nothing for a minute. He appears to be thinking deeply. I watch with some interest. He's behaving completely differently from anyone else on this. He's blond, solidly built, serious. And all of twenty-three.

Oscar is swift to catch my thought. 'You may think he's young, but let me tell you, this is the brightest brain in London. If anyone can get this off the ground for you, it's Keith.'

Keith looks at me.

'Shall we get on with it, then?' he asks, still unsmiling. 'Got a room across the way. We can start now.'

He gets up and opens the door for me. It looks like he means business.

He does mean business. My life takes another enormous turn, this time for the better. Keith Schilling is on the case.

From now on, we travel forward, witnesses are interviewed, events listed chronologically, checked time and again with me and Don till Keith is satisfied, witness statements in order, letters copied and filed, diary entries—pathetic though they are—copied, receipts for recordings and costumes, dates of meetings with Brian Degas, Jack Rosenthal, Thames, recording sessions, press cuttings, publishers, draft contracts for recordings, proof of song publishing, restaurant names for lunches with Howard, anything and everything that could give us credibility is hunted down with ferocious ruthlessness, scraps of paper seized upon, chance remarks delved into, till there is a scenario of every single thing that happened from our point of view, backed up by every scrap of evidence we can come up with.

It's pitiful but it's the best we can do. There are huge gaps, because we don't know what happened between Howard, Verity Lambert, Thames and Andrew Brown, we can only guess. Some things we may discover in court. All I can be totally sure of is that I have given Keith every tiny bit of useful information I can think of. He does the rest. It takes a long time, months and months, but slowly, bit by bit, the wheels grind forward, Legal Aid is reinstated.

June, 1981

Long before they start talking about court, I get a dream part, one of the two I've always wanted to play, Beatrice in *Much Ado About Nothing*, at the Open Air Theatre in Regents Park. Balm to my bruised soul, and a gift for a comedienne, she's witty, stylish and vulnerable, the antithesis of the grim compiler of facts I've become since Keith came on board. I grab her and embrace her. She dances with me through the whole summer. Light relief, literally. One evening (one of the dry ones, when we're not rained off) I'm standing in the wings waiting to go on for the party scene, when I overhear a couple of actors talking. You can do that at Regents Park, the audience can barely hear you when you're onstage, let alone off.

'Don who?' one of them asks.

'Don Fraser, the composer,' replies the other. 'Went off with Toby Robertson's wife Jane, leaving a most lovely girlfriend, by all accounts. Stupid bastard.'

The music strikes up. As we sweep on stage, I say over my

shoulder, 'That girlfriend—it was me!' and feel absurdly cheered.

Months pass. Bit by bit, Keith puts our case together. Oscar was right, he can do it. Almost before we know it, a date is set to go into court. June 14th, 1982. It's a civil case, which means no jury. The presiding judge hasn't been announced yet, we won't know who it is until the week before. And according to Oscar and Keith this is an important, even crucial, factor. His word will, literally, be law.

For the last seven years, everyone in the business has urged me to abandon the case—you haven't a chance of winning, actors are punished if they sue a television or film company, they blacklist you and tell everyone, you're cutting off your nose to spite your face, it'll do more harm than good, you'll never work in television again, it's not worth fighting them, it happens all the time, they rip everyone off, you're no different, get used to it, let it go, move on.

Of course they're right, I can see that, I just *can't* let it go. It's not just that Rock Bottom meant—*means*—too much to me, it's more than that. If it were just Thames stealing it, I might have said we were naive and stupid, it's big business, they took us for a ride and we let them. But because of Howard, it's betrayal of two things beyond price—friendship and trust. Writers, designers, directors, performers, we're all on the same side, we have to stick together. It's one of the invisible bonds that unite us in an insecure world. And Howard wasn't just a writer, he was my friend. I trusted him and he betrayed that trust. I can't move on, I want it sorted. Something else niggles away at me, but I don't quite know what.

I resign myself to having no future in television.

Oscar's office, Soho Square, London, May, 1982

Low, backless, squashy seats humble the mere visitor, cut her down to size. Reception files her perfect nails, makes little notes, nods to the doorman. A slim, wiry man signs in, sits at the far end of the squashy seating, picks up a newspaper from the neat pile—*Variety, The Economist, The Telegraph*—on the glass coffee-table in front of him, crackles it into place and glances over his reading glasses in my direction. Beautiful suit, sober tie, perfect white shirt. He holds his look, catches my eye and twinkles, not in the least cowed by the surroundings. Then turns back to his paper, his face creased in private amusement.

In comes Oscar, bustling, frowning, making waves, pushing the walls back with his furious, theatrical energy. Struts straight across to the suit, grabs his hand, pats him on the shoulder, glaring round to make sure he has everyone's attention. Then he comes over to hug me, drag me over and introduce me to our senior barrister, the elusive John Wilmers, QC. Oscar told me his nickname weeks ago. The Animal. I don't want a brute representing us. I don't want brute force annihilating the opposition, I want steadfast intelligence and clarity and persistence and honesty. More than anything, I want him to believe me. To believe *in* me.

Mr Wilmers QC doesn't look anything like an animal. He ignores Oscar's bluster, gets to his feet, holds my hand and looks right inside me. In that instant, I know I can trust him. With him on my side, Thames Television, with its open contempt for us, dwindles in size. John Wilmers is up to anything.

A month before we're due in court, Keith prints up a version of my statement and sends it to me for final comments. It looks quite different typed out, it has a kind of authority now. Sixty-eight pages, nineteen sections, each section with a title and page number on the index page. This is what efficiency looks like. This is what I'd been missing till Keith came along—what lawyers bill so handsomely for and is frequently absent—care and attention throughout. I'm getting it now.

As a summary of the last decade or so, it makes gripping reading. Between the lines, between the statements of fact and the explanations of conversations and meetings and broken promises, lie pain and hope and joy and frustration and exhilaration and despair. I wonder if anyone else will ever see it and understand.

One morning I wake to find myself sitting bolt upright. A woman shouting 'Murder!' I'm sure of it. Johnny's gone to work, there's nobody in the street. Perhaps it was a dream? I've not been sleeping well for days. Hardly surprising, given what's coming up soon. I sit on the edge of the bed, my feet on the rough fringe of the rug. Then things get clearer. Shocking and very clear. The woman's voice was mine. It *was* a dream. It's more than a dream, it's a memory. Me waking up from the anaesthetic shouting 'Murder!' A nurse pushing me back, saying 'It's not us, it's you done it, dear.'

Don's not going to like it. I'm not going to like saying it. The lawyers may think it'll do more harm than good, but it's the piece of the jigsaw that's been missing all along for me. I'm going to have to tell them, maybe even tell the court. The only person I'd ever told was my sister. My pitiful, shameful secret. Don's and mine, really. All those years ago, in West Kensington Mansions, in April, 1973, when I was thirty-one.

On my thirty-first birthday, we couldn't afford to go out to celebrate. We had nothing, we owned nothing. Don had his beloved and only possession, his piano, in his father's name, in case the bailiffs ever came round. He shared the flat with two other musicians, both of whom owned a musical instrument, one a flute, the other a clarinet. That was all we had.

I couldn't think why, but I was unaccountably happy that day. In the afternoon, I had an appointment with the GP. Nothing important. I knew I couldn't be pregnant, we'd been to a family planning doctor and done everything she said. This was just to establish why my period was late, in case anything was going on.

'I'll meet you in the pub in half an hour,' I told Don. 'I'm just popping in to get the results. Bound to be negative. Just double-checking.'

Half an hour later, I skip into the pub, inches off the pavement, stuttering. Don gets me a glass of wine and listens to my ecstatic burbling.

'Oh, Don, Don, you're never going to believe this. You'll never believe what's happened. Oh God, I'm shocked, I'm on air, I—what a birthday present! We ought to get champagne. The Casserole tonight, even if I go into the red. I don't care. I don't care about anything. This is amazing. That GP—I—I went in and he looked up my notes and came round his desk and shook my hand and said, "Congratulations!" "What?" I asked. I didn't get it. "You're going to be a mother," he said. I burst into tears. So did he! I was so touched. Got a Kleenex? I'm doing it again. Sorry, sorry, I'll stop in a minute. I'm just so flabbergasted. So—so—oh, fuck, I'm happy. We're going to have a baby! Cheers! I suppose I shouldn't be drinking this, should I? Oh God, I'm on top of the world, this is so amazing.'

'Annie.'

'Yes, darling. Aren't we lucky? Isn't this the best thing that's ever—'

'Annie. Listen.'

It takes a few goes to get my attention. 'Yes?'

'Having this baby,' he says. He's gentle. Kind. 'I can't go ahead with it.'

It takes a while to sink in. Slowly, slowly, euphoria seeps away through the soles of my feet, draining through the pub floorboards. Then I rally. I don't believe him. It's so perfect: we love each other, we've been together two years, so we didn't plan it, it's here anyway. The next right thing. Right?

I go on not believing him for some weeks. We live on the fourth floor, without a lift? I'll leave the pram downstairs. Plenty of people have babies and nothing in the bank. Even composers have families and carry on composing—look at Bach. Etc, etc. Don, six years younger than me, and far from being professionally established, is convinced it would be a disaster for him. Even if we sold all our tape recorders, microphones, drums, table and chairs, that would last us about two minutes with another mouth to feed. He's terrified he'll have to teach, or something equally unfulfilling, to keep a roof over our heads. In vain I cite Elgar, one of Don's heroes, who taught till he was forty-four before being recognised as a genius. Don sounds reasonable but this has nothing to do with reason or logic. He's just not ready. He can't—won't—*can't* go through with it. It's a simple choice for him—either I leave him and have the baby by myself or do what he wants and stay.

Of course I think about going, leaving him, having the baby on my own. But why would I do that? It's a product of our relationship, not a substitute for it. It's *our* baby, to be shared, or we shouldn't have it. If the timing's wrong for Don then I have to take that into consideration. It wouldn't be fair on the baby either. Not fair on anyone. I hold out as long as I can.

Abortion in the Seventies was free, legal and safe. After twelve weeks, the legal limit, I gave in and had an abortion. The effect was dreadful. Not physically, but emotionally. I couldn't recover. A huge void opened up between us. Bereft and shocked, I went away for a week by myself and did a lot of thinking. *We'll have another when the time is right for both of us, I mustn't let myself get bitter, it's up to me to be positive.*

Blot it out, forget it, get over it.

Convert it into something creative, something you can do together.

Hurl yourself into filling the gap.

Pick yourself up…

And somehow, except for waking crying most nights, I succeeded. I'd told nobody except my sister, the subject never came up again between me and Don. I blanked the episode out. It remained buried for nine years. Till now, just before we were due in court. And what did I replace that baby with? A three-woman rock group.

All the years I'd been fine-tuning the case and I never saw it till now—the very root of Rock Bottom, the real reason we started. It underpinned everything, the emotional trigger for the group and my hopes for it—and the part I would most like to leave out.

This nasty little memory has been well concealed. The imminence of the court case must have pushed it up from its burial ground: Rock Bottom's reason for existence is down to me. Because of the baby, *my* baby, Don's and mine, the baby I wanted so badly and didn't have. Nobody but Don, my sister and the abortion clinic ever knew about it. Rock Bottom was born of that loss, specifically created to heal the wound. Of course, I see it now. It's why I gave up so much to keep the group going: the girl lead in a new musical, *Billy*, because it would be on try-out in Manchester for eight weeks when our single was coming out; a leading role in a Granada series, because it would take me away for six months at another crucial time for Rock Bottom—our first concert. It cost me my agents and severely dented my career and my bank balance at a crucial time. But I put all my creative money on Rock Bottom. My baby.

Termination. Abortion. Brutal words for a brutal process. I'd just remembered it. And why it mattered. I call Don.

'Don't say that. Much rather you didn't say that,' he mutters.

I so understand.

I call Keith. 'This feels important, Keith. But if we can leave it out, it'd be a big relief.'

'I'll speak to Wilmers.'

Word comes back. It is important. It'll go in.

Friday before the High Court, June, 1982

High summer in the Middle Temple gardens, deep green, lush, confident trees and elegant lawns. Don, Gaye and I sit quietly for once. Mr Wilmers QC, fiddles with his pen and glances out of the window.

'Unfortunate Miss Langton can't be here,' he remarks.

We leap to her defence: she's on tour/she's in Bristol/her car broke down/two shows yesterday/extra rehearsals, etc., etc.

'I assume she will deign to drop in on Monday. Does she comprehend the nature of the High Court? As a plaintiff, she is of key importance. As also is the question of her reliability.'

GB: Oh, Di'll be there, don't worry about that. Miss a court appearance? No way, José, she loves all that.

Annie: We're never quite sure about Di appearing, actually. Once she missed a recording session, we never knew exactly—

GB: *(cutting in)* Annie, darling, you know perfectly well that wasn't her fault. She told me afterward precisely why—

Annie: *(cutting in)* She did? You never told me.

Mr Wilmers is sharp. 'I can't be responsible for the damage done by her non-appearance. Mr Justice Hirst has only recently been appointed. He is therefore something of an unknown quantity. As a barrister, he had the reputation of being, how can I put it—somewhat passionate about things. Convey that information to Miss Langton, would you?'

We nod assent. *Passionate? That mean he's a drama queen? A bully? Oh shit.*

Over his reading glasses, Mr W aims a piercing look at each of us in turn. 'Now then. Don, this doesn't apply to you, you look fine. A really crucial matter, which you being actresses will readily appreciate.'

He's being deliberately pompous, I can tell, he's getting us used to how they talk in court. Or else he's laying it on very thick. I suppress a desire to giggle.

'I refer of course to your appearance.'

Instantly, we stiffen.

'A court is very different from theatre. Very different from a pop concert. You are bringing this action yourselves. It is vital you wear the kind of sober outfits that show how serious you are. Outrageous appearance is out, jeans are out, showing lots of flesh, out. Do I make myself clear? I need you to look like responsible adults in an adult world. Actresses understand how costume indicates character. May I rely on you to show up on Monday very, very differently from the way you look today?'

We look at each other. What's wrong with the way we look? GB's small waist is neatly cinched in with a wide belt, her usual assortment of chains dangle fetchingly, clinking just a bit when she laughs, which is now, a great cackle. I frown. What's in my wardrobe more sober and serious than today's outfit: a tight black pencil skirt with a long slit at the front so I can cross my legs (£4 from the North End Road market in 1971). Cleavage, yes, maybe my shirt could be buttoned a little higher, but it's clean. Red suits me, always has. And the ankle-strap sandals are cool and show my long legs off rather well.

Mr Wilmers twinkles. 'No need to get bolshie, girls. Just make sure you clean up your act, look like—'

GB cracks up. 'Sober citizens? That's hilarious! We're a rock group, darling.'

The twinkle fades. 'Not in court you're not. Think about it, please. And tell Miss Langton.'

He gets up. The meeting's over.

We uncross our legs, collect our handbags and follow Don to the door.

'One more thing,' Wilmers says abruptly. 'Miss Leventon, do you actually *own* a bra?'

Outside, Don slopes off and GB and I collapse in laughter.

'Oh, Annie, did you see his face? He couldn't look at you. Do you *own* a bra?'

I wipe tears from my eyes. 'I'm not sure I do, *actually*.'

Our mirth redoubles. 'You better fucking well get one, darling, if you want to be allowed in. What a shriek!'

'Who's going to tell Di-Di? She won't want to look like a sober citizen.'

GB is firm. 'Tough, darling. I'll tell her. You'd better run to Janet Reger's first thing and invest in some undies. The judge sounds a bit dodgy, don't you think? I hope he's not a complete bastard.'

'We'll find out on Monday, won't we?'

'Christ. Monday. We're almost there, Annie.'

'Christ. We are.'

At Temple Station we hug.

'Monday, then.'

'Monday. Shall we get there early and have breakfast?'

I swallow. 'If I can eat anything. I feel sick now.'

'Rubbish, darling. You'll be fine. Let's meet in whatever caff is nearest the courts, there are bound to be hundreds all down Fleet Street. Meet you outside the High Court and we'll find the ones the lawyers use. Keith'll tell us. Eight-thirty, okay?'

'We won't recognise each other, not if we're dressed right.'

'Take no notice, Bird's Egg. Dress as you please. Some would say you look too sober now.'

It's true. I'm in my version of sober now to meet Wilmers.

'Won't do, Annie. You've been warned.'

'Unless Mr Justice Thingammybob likes birds.'

'That sort of passionate, you mean? Let's hope so. Byee.'

Next day, I go to the Kings Road and buy three frocks. I haven't worn frocks for years. Sweet, conventional little summer day-dresses, one flowered, one yellow, one sky-blue. Demure, maybe a bit fetching. Totally unlike me. But with the new bra and the new court shoes (court shoes ha ha) I'm indistinguishable from your average office worker.

Is that being a sober citizen? I have no idea.

12

High Court

Fraser and Others versus Thames and Others. Queen's Bench Division. Before Mr Justice Hirst. Court 12, 10 am, June 14, 1982

People hate Mondays. Mondays mean back to the daily grind after relaxing and dropping the routine and enjoying themselves and socialising and staying up late on Saturday night and having a nice lie-in on Sunday and eating too much at Sunday lunch. Mondays mean back to the office, the school, the place You Have To Be: the loss of freedom.

I love my work. I long for it. It may be short-lived, badly paid, *un*paid. It's frequently inadequate, unchallenging or frustrating. And I love it. Even in a long run, although Sunday off is crucial, I don't much enjoy it. It breaks the rhythm, divorces me for too long. So Monday is usually my favourite.

This Monday makes me shiver. Getting my contact lenses in takes twice the normal time. My mascara wand wobbles so much I have to wipe black off my eyelids and start again. I can't light my cigarette. Don and I are silent as we prepare for battle, the biggest battle of our lives, which we—*don't be stupid*. I don't know if Don is silent or not. He's not here, not with me anymore. Long gone. Six years gone. He's with Jane now, I'm married to Johnny. *Stop it.*

It *is* the biggest battle of our lives, though, Don's as much as mine, even if we haven't spoken for seven years except in conference at lawyers' offices and chambers. And Gaye's. And Di's. This is the real thing. A High Court judge will decide our fate. And I'm all on my own this morning.

After buying my sober dresses, court shoes, handbag, after reading all my notes for the hundredth time, my fate now passes out of my hands and into the lawyers'. I hope they bloody well do their job. I've seen them in chambers with their tomes and piles of files tied in pink (not red) tape, safe in their little lairs, protected by their clerks, their salaries, their protocol, their *knowledge*. I've met them in Wright, Webb, Syrett & Sons, 10 Soho Square, London W1 and fought their inattention, their sloppiness and distinct lack of care and attention throughout. Argued, cajoled, despaired: Nick's extreme caution, Mark's vagueness, Oscar's scenes, the general indolence, failure to get witness statements, the failure to grasp the essentials of the story, the sheer lack of interest. Till two years ago, when Keith Schilling arrived and became my team mate. A brutal midwife, he dragged and chopped and shaped a sequence of events out of me that made sense to us both.

Now to the climax of this grand opera. Act Three: the High Court. No wonder I'm shivering in bright morning sunshine as I walk down Kingsway, from Holborn Station past the Catholic Church and the Office of Births, Marriages and Deaths, round the curve of the Aldwych to the beginning of Fleet Street and on the left, the stern stone arch of the High Court this Monday, June 14th, 1982, to meet my fate. *Our* fate.

Gaye shrieks at my nice little dress. 'Darling, what have you come as?'

She's glamorous in black Jean Muir or something similar. With her chains clanking and glittering as always, hair freshly done, she looks a million dollars. We gather in the cafe that will be study and meeting-place for the next few weeks: Keith, Gaye, Don, Don's girlfriend Jane. And me—ex-girlfriend, very ex. Six years ex. Don and Jane whisper together. I hope it's not about my dress.

'Where's Di?' asks Keith abruptly.

'Yes. Where the hell is she?' I say, alarm bells ringing again.

Keith looks furious. 'You think she's still in Bristol?'

Don is brief and grim. 'She'll be sleeping. In her hotel.'

We find a phone and call the hotel. She is. She's still there. Not to be disturbed, apparently. Gaye and I are horror-struck. It's nearly nine-thirty am.

'Jane'll drive to Bristol and fetch her,' says Don.

Might as well be grateful for her help. We need it.

We collect our wits, wipe the coffee off our upper lips, reapply lipstick and march across the road to the lofty carved entrance of the High Court. Court Twelve, it says on the notice board halfway down the huge marbled hallway. *Fraser and Others v. Thames and Others. To be heard by Mr Justice Hirst.* Jesus! Off to find Court 12. Up stairs, round corners, up more stairs. A long corridor. At the far end, closed doors on the right. We're early—some of us.

We've been there all of two seconds when I see Howard Schuman walking towards us. May, 1975, to June, 1982. My maths is hopeless, but that's seven years, surely? Seven years from my last words to him on the phone, 'See you in court!' to us here outside Court 12, waiting for the double doors to open and admit us. Barristers in wigs and robes and bundles of papers chat to each other. Of course they do, they all know each other, this is a kind of club. They're probably friends, certainly colleagues.

Howard and I know each other. *Knew* each other. Once colleagues, certainly friends. Have I ever in my whole life blanked anyone? Prue Vosper at school once blanked me for some imagined insult. It wasn't pleasant. Am I going to do it now? I don't care about Andrew Brown, with his vacant grin and bouncy walk, I don't give a toss about Verity Lambert, she's a businesswoman, no better than she should be. But Howard, my one-time friend, Howard, who wrote one of the best parts I've ever had on television, Howard whom I trusted.

That's what it is. I trusted him. That's why I've fought for over seven years. *Get a grip, Annie.* It's because of him we're here, instead of touring the States with platinum albums coming out of our ears, the female Rolling Stones and the female Marx Brothers rolled into one. I don't have to make eye contact, be polite, pretend it's a fucking cocktail party. This is serious stuff. No acting today, it's the real thing. I blank him.

And Andrew Brown and Verity Lambert. They don't deserve recognition.

I stand tall. The double doors swing open and we're inside, sitting on the front bench, Gaye, Don and me. Howard and the others on the same bench, but to our right, so we don't have to look at them at all. It smells of wood polish in here, the same one they used at St Anne's College in Oxford. That's oddly comforting. Keith is behind us, John Wilmers and the junior barrister, Nick Strauss, behind him. A perfect hierarchy of position. They have all the advantages, the lawyers, this is their world, their costumes and wigs, their ceremony. That's a shock. I'd thought as plaintiffs we'd be central. Far from it. I see now we're just extras.

The majesty of the court is awe-inspiring, as it's meant to be. They know exactly how to make you feel small, insignificant and lowly. It's not a large hall, just a medium-sized room with wood-panelled walls and polished floors. They don't want you to be that comfortable either. Hard wooden benches for all, though I bet the judge will have cushions for his august rear-end behind that bench. It's called a bench, but it's more of a massive desk, imposing, solid, hard-angled and, like everything else here, totally masculine, the law declaring its severity and strength in every joint of wood. It resembles a small theatre, with its benches for the plaintiffs, the defendants and the lawyers raked up from front to back so the judge can be all-seeing and all-seen. I find that oddly comforting, too.

We, the plaintiffs, on the left-hand side, will be under his lordship's right nostril when he sits down. Behind us, Keith is preoccupied, serious as always, focussed. He's prepared this case, organised it, worried over it, laid it all out. Now he'll be judged on it. He's only twenty-five, just twenty-six perhaps. Young to have all this responsibility. The same age as Don in 1975, facing those bastards at Thames. Another little shiver.

'All right, Annie?'

'Yes,' I whisper back. 'Excited.'

'Me, too. What larks, Pip!'

Here in the High Court my greatest ally is Gaye. The gap between me and Don is too big. Too much left unsaid, never to be said. Keith has to run the show, Wilmers, our senior barrister, is the headmaster, Nick Strauss at his right hand, taking minuscule notes.

'Not headmaster,' says GB, 'Head of English.'

'What does that make Nick?'

'Deputy head, of course.'

'And Keith?'

'Head boy,' we say together and crack up. We're not even prefects. Never were. Thank God for GB. She takes the terror out of any situation with her irrepressible sense of humour, her lightning wit.

'All Rise.'

'Here comes God,' I mutter, feeling like a naughty schoolgirl, not a sober citizen. Or a plaintiff.

Round-faced, rosy-cheeked, bespectacled, a little stout, maybe fifty-five, in scarlet as well as black, Mr Justice Hirst bustles to his place. Younger and healthier than I was expecting, not some dried-up elderly stick. He might even have a sense of humour. He looks uncannily like my brother Patrick. I like him at once.

'You've pulled,' GB whispers as we wait for the command to sit.

'What?'

She can't mean Hirst. He's not even looking at us, he's busy adjusting his robe, his reading glasses, his pen.

'Idiot. The sidekick. He fancies you!' she hisses.

To Hirst's right is a beautiful man in a beautiful suit with beautifully cut silver hair. He's looking our way. Who's that?

Mr Hirst sits. I get my notebook and pen ready. Gaye scribbles a note and passes it to Keith on the bench behind. He frowns, leans forward and mutters in her ear.

'The judge's clerk,' GB whispers. 'Gordon Something. The Angel Gabriel, I think. Right hand of God. Yours, anyway, Annie. You're in there.'

'What about you?'

'Not decided. You get first pick today. Where the fuck's Di?'

Where indeed.

We sit. On our right, the defendants sit. A hush steals up from my bones, my sinews. A tightening of muscle, a stiffening of the spine, a cold chill on my scalp. On my upper lip, a tiny vibration jumps and tingles and settles. Here we are, at last.

For at least the first hour, I sit stiff as a board, ramrod straight, breath constricted, till I calm down enough to take a little notice of what's going on around me. Wilmers is on his feet, laying out our case. This isn't theatrical, this bit. Calm, dry, reasonable, the sound of his voice is soothing. It's hard to concentrate for long. I have my notebook ready in case there's something missing or wrongly placed, or there's any little detail that strikes the wrong note. Odd to hear it from another angle, this story I've lived through and replayed so many times since, trying to find the key, the key to the mystery of what went wrong and why. Keith and I have spent two years going backwards and forwards for clues. There's still so much we don't know, can't know, till they give evidence. They're on the dark side of the moon.

'Help me, Obi-Wan Kenobi. You're my only hope,' I write and pass it to GB, with a little doodle of Carrie Fisher with her hair in earphones.

'Harman's gone over to the dark side,' she whispers. 'Unless he's a wookie.'

We glance at Defence Counsel. He's fussing and frowning and muttering to cohorts and taking notes. When he leans forward to write, his outsize wig flops forward with him and settles over an eyebrow. He pushes it back and scratches his head every time.

'What frightful wigs,' murmurs GB. 'They must have got them as a job lot in a market somewhere. Smithfield, maybe.'

Mr Justice Hirst (or David, as GB already calls him) has the more flamboyant one, befitting a judge. What colour can his hair be underneath those grey frizzy corkscrew curls? All the lawyers look like extras in a Hollywood costume extravaganza. We only need Bette Davis in a huge ball gown to sail in and we could all burst into song.

'No, darling. Errol Flynn, I think. On a rope. Or Johnny Weissmuller.'

Stifled laughter. It's a bit early in the proceedings to behave like this. Must be the tension.

By a quarter to twelve, my bottom is numb. I drift away from Wilmers and his 'I refer the court to ... I rely upon document number C961, dated January ... and with respect to the last paragraph thereof, where ... ' and watch Mr Justice Hirst listen, nod, sniff, raise his eyebrows, write and nod again. His glasses make his eyes look very big and permanently surprised. The grey horsehair curls round his plump face lend a jolly, almost inconsequential air, like a fond parent in a Jane Austen novel. However, the ferocious quality of his attention, the way his brows draw together, the set of his lips as he takes a point on board, his sharp tone as he queries something Wilmers says, all this shows me someone altogether more formidable. I start doodling again, trying to catch his look of concentration.

'What's that? A dying sheep?' hisses Gaye, looking over my shoulder at my masterpiece.

Bang!

Hirst jerks his head up, frowning.

Wilmers heard it, too. He pauses. Hirst's gaze is fixed on

something at the back of the court. I look round. The noise must have been the double doors opening. Now they close quietly, with a soft click, behind Miss Diane Langton. She stands in front of them, in a black scoop-neck dress with a very short full skirt nipped in at the waist, red embroidery on her midriff and all round the skirt as if she were about to dance the tarantella, black stockings, high heel peep-toes, cleavage forever, hair up, adorable black curls escaping from—*I don't believe this*—escaping from a saucy little pillbox hat, a lacy veil floating over her brows. And perfect Fifties makeup. The Merry Widow. She looks at the judge from under her false lashes, with a winning combination of penitence, glamour and just a breath of cheek. She gives the tiniest hint of a curtsey and lowers her gaze. The court holds its collective breath. Wilmers stares in horror. Either she ignored his dress code instructions as relayed by GB, or she's taken great pains to interpret them. The result is pure genius. Her absence was putting our case at risk, her appearance might just have won it for us.

Keith breaks the spell. He gets up and leads her down the steps to where we're sitting. She gives him a brilliant smile of thanks, sits in perfect ballet pose next to Don. And waits.

Someone else's move. She's done her bit. She's here.

13

Unravelling

June, 1982

'Here! Look at this! You're in *The Times*, you girls.'

Johnny waves a newspaper at me as I emerge from the bathroom next morning.

'Mmm? What?'

I'm not at my best first thing. My internal clock is geared to theatre time: start slow, rev up round about six pm, ready to roll from seven pm for the rest of the evening and beyond. I put my specs on and take the paper.

It's a photo of us and a short report of the case beginning. Wow. I've been so locked up in this for so many years without any feedback from the rest of the world, I look at it, bemused. We're worth a mention. How come?

At the end of the day, there's a message from my agent on the answerphone. Hampstead Theatre want me for a Clifford Odets play, *Rocket To The Moon*. Starts rehearsing in three weeks. There must be a connection between this and our photo, the last thing I would have expected. They'll have to give me time off to go into the witness box. And what about the mid-week matinee? You never have understudies in small theatres.

When the script arrives on Day Three, I'm almost too tense to read it. Two days of Wilmers laying out the bones of the case, the judge making notes, asking questions, the written evidence, such as it is, handed out, copies to everyone, the pathetic and only proof of our story: Molly Parkin's article in the *Evening Standard*; Sue Francis's review of *Rock Follies* in *Sheet Magazine* recognising the girls as us and asking why we weren't doing it; our agreement between ourselves to promote the group, our funny little biographies, Gaye's by me, mine by Di, Di's by Gaye; our diary entries to pinpoint the few, so few, conversations or meetings we ever wrote down, the letter of contract with Thames. It's pitiful.

I spend the evening reading *Rocket To The Moon*. Lovely play, nice supporting role, not too big, two great scenes, one in each act, plenty of time off stage. I should be able to be in court some of the time. And I'll have something else to concentrate on. Perfect timing, however it happened. How wonderful. I need something else to think about or I'll go mad. I'm like a bow strung too tight, I could snap at any moment.

Tomorrow Don goes into the witness box.

Poor Don. He's a terrible witness. He's so afraid of saying the wrong thing he can barely speak at all. Wilmers does his best to draw him out.

'Mr Fraser, would you tell the court in your own words how you…'

'Erm, well, I, er, i-i-it was on a Tuesday. I d-do know that. He, that is, H-H-Howard, Mr S-S-Schuman, that is, he said that i-i-if R-Rock Bottom…'

God, it's painful for him. And Wilmers. And us. The defendants giggle into their hands and smirk. If we're all like this, they're home and dry. My heart sinks.

Mr Justice Hirst, not a patient man, it seems from the huffing and puffing when something irritates him, is patient with Don. He doesn't rush him, he doesn't snap, he listens, eyes on him, pen poised, in total concentration, asks him to repeat if he hasn't caught the phrase. A gentleman.

Wilmers gets what he can out of him. Don can't speak at

lunchtime either. 'You were fine, the judge heard you, he listened to you. It's okay.' We pat him on the shoulder, an exhausted horse trembling after a big race. We crack jokes, buy cups of tea, bring him chips in the funny little canteen two floors down. Then he's back. It lasts all afternoon. Wilmers teases the story out with infinite patience and it's interminable. Forming the group, taking the idea for a television series to Jack Rosenthal, working with Howard, Andrew Brown bounding up to say 'Marvellous! Marvellous!' after our first concert, Thames merchandising meetings, *A Little Night Music*, Thames' behaviour. It goes on all day. We're all exhausted.

Tomorrow it'll be cross-examination time.

Mr Jeremiah Harman, curly horsehair wig (a little too big), billowing robe, lumbers to his feet to annihilate a defenceless, miserable Don.

'Tell me, Mr—ah—Fraser, would you say you were cut out to be a manager?'

'Er, mmm, no, not really, that is, I never ...'

'Perhaps you could explain to the court how you came to be in a position for which you say you are so eminently unsuited?'

'Objection, my lord. He didn't say that.'

'Very well, a position for which you *appear* to be eminently unsuited?'

'Er. W-we h-hadn't found the r-right m-m-manager. None of the g-g-girls could do it. I sort of h-had to ...'

'Are you seriously suggesting, Mr Fraser, that in the whole of the music industry you were unable ...'

Etc., etc. Even more painful.

Time after time, Don is steamrollered. Till Mr Hirst starts getting cross with the heavy-handed sarcastic tone and sticks up for Don. I thought judges were supposed to be strictly impartial. Not this one. It's fascinating.

'Mr–ah–Fraser, are you claiming you wrote a song called *Little Ladies* which you played to Mr Schuman in 1974, before he named his group from *Rock Follies* "The Little Ladies"?'

'Y-Yes, my lord. I remember p-p-playing it to Howard. On a Thursday. It goes *'Little ladies, Ladies who, Do what little ladies do.'*

Harman sniggers. The defendants snigger. Gaye and I clutch hands and freeze. Di, of course, isn't here. She won't be back till she has to give evidence, she's still on tour.

'Thank you, Mr Fraser. It sounds rather fun,' says Mr Hirst, writing it down.

Don goes red and holds his head a little higher.

The afternoon drags on. Jerry Harman makes Don look like an idiot or a liar when he can, Wilmers jumping up to object, Hirst's nostrils flaring in irritation.

'Mr Harman, I must request you stick to the point or we will never get home.'

'Yes, my lord.'

'And may I just say, in general terms, that a witness may be difficult to understand, indeed irritatingly hesitant, he or she may speak too quietly or be unable to express himself or herself clearly. However, this does not alter the fact that he or she may still be a perfectly credible and trustworthy witness and should be treated with respect. You may carry on, Mr Harman.'

'Yes, my lord.'

Don still takes a battering, but now he has Hirst's kindness to hang on to.

Unfortunately, Harman being told off doesn't improve his attitude. Incredulity and scorn fill his voice as he challenges Don's account of the meetings at Thames, the events during the period of *A Little Night Music* and Di's availability. He holds Don entirely to blame for the breakdown with Thames, effectively accusing him of lying.

'I put it to you that even when you received the letter from Thames written on May 12th, requiring you to confirm Miss Langton's release by the afternoon of the following day, you failed even to respond, which portrays you in a very sorry light.'

'But,' Don stammers, 'I—I was out that morning, w-working out of the office. I didn't know a letter had been sent. H-how could I—?'

Harman cuts across him. 'Oh come now, Mr Fraser. Might I suggest it was your total incompetence that resulted in the breakdown of communications between Rock Bottom and Thames, who, let it be admitted, had done everything possible, and more, to enable you to release Miss Langton from her contract.'

He gets his knuckles rapped again, but it's cruel. I know Don already blames himself, though we don't. It's hard to watch. Even with Hirst's support, Don looks defeated.

And tomorrow it'll be my turn. If they finish with him before the weekend.

They do. Friday lunchtime they release him.

At two o'clock I'll be on the witness stand.

It's a long walk from the front benches, down two polished wooden steps, across in front of the judge's bench, past the stenographer, a stern woman from Central Casting with scraped-back hair, fingers resting, wrists up, waiting for speech. Judge above me to my left, defendants on my right. Andrew, Verity, Howard. All solemn at this second, looking a bit smug after Don's performance. Two steps up, turn sharp left, here I am. I've seen so many film versions of this. Murderers, innocents, accusers, protesters. Witnesses who break down, witnesses outwitted, witnesses screwing a handkerchief into a little ball and shredding it, sobbing. Even the *Crown Court* I did last year rises up to meet me. I swallow. My mouth is very dry, my hand an ashen imprint on the dark leather of the Bible.

'Breathe!' says the voice teacher.

'Stand tall!' says the movement teacher.

I lift my chin and drop my shoulders.

I am not a witness.

I am a plaintiff, I have a cause, I will be heard.

'I swear to tell the truth, the whole truth and nothing but the truth.'

My voice is steady and clear. I've waited over seven years for this. I'm ready.

The blood beating in my ears drowns out Wilmer's earlier homily: 'Listen hard, answer the questions, don't give too much detail till I ask for more, stick to the point'.

I trust Hirst, he was kind to Don and he reminds me of my brother Patrick, who I'd trust with my life. There's Keith, there's Nick, there's Wilmers, all on my side, all there for me. Forget Harman and his mob.

From far, far below, Gaye and Don gaze up at me. Gaye winks. I'll do my best for them.

Wilmers first, to establish who I am, my background, education, credentials, experience. I've rehearsed all of that a hundred times. There's one bit I'm dreading: the new evidence. Freshly discovered. Buried for nine years. Then boom! It surfaced a week or so before the trial began. The reason for Rock Bottom's entire existence.

The baby I'd so longed for, was so ready for and got rid of, is still here, but in the form of a three-girl group—*my* group. Having it snatched away in infancy and brought up by someone else is hard to bear, impossible to accept.

That's what I'm fighting for.

Wilmers takes me through Oxford, my career, meeting Don. I know what's next.

'Miss Leventon, would you tell the court in your own words how the idea for the group Rock Bottom came into being?'

I take a deep breath.

'In April, 1973, I discovered I was pregnant.' *Pause*. 'We had no money. Don's career wasn't established. I was the principal breadwinner, we'd only been...'

I hear the wobble in my voice, feel it on my lower lip.

The judge, pen hovering over the page, turns his head.

Wilmers gives me a steady look. 'Please continue, Miss Leventon.'

The court is very quiet.

'So I agreed to have a termination.'

'I can't hear you, Miss Leventon. Would you repeat that, please?'

I clear my throat. 'Sorry. I had a termination. I terminated the pregnancy.'

'And?' Wilmers voice is calm and insistent.

'It was out of this that Rock Bottom was created, the empty space left between us, between Don and me. It had to be filled. The group was born directly out of that need. It became our baby. The one we would have had if ...'

Pause.

Tears drip on to the polished wood of the witness stand. Hirst mutters to his clerk, Gordon, who passes me a box of Kleenex.

I blow my nose loudly and wipe my eyes. Below me, as my vision clears, I see Howard, Verity and Andrew mime throwing up.

'Would you like a moment before we continue, Miss Leventon?'

'No thank you, my lord, I'm all right.'

That's the worst bit over. We continue. How Don and I dreamt up the group, how it developed, how we saw the contrast between the three of us as a bonus, highlighting it in performance till we became a sort of fictional creation of ourselves, adding anarchy and humour to and around our songs, how a television series would use and develop all that. My relationship with Howard. The glaring similarities between Rock Bottom and the three-girl group in the actual television series. Compare and contrast, like A-Level English. Our hair colour, our heights, our backgrounds, our class, our jokes. My mother as The Widow with her undermining remarks, my contact lenses, my diets, my affair with Don. The pianist being also the manager.

It's two very long days before Wilmers finishes.

Now Harman's turn. I've already decided he's a pompous old

Victorian who hasn't prepared his case very well. His treatment of Don was brutal and heavy-handed. I can expect nothing less.

'Miss, ah, Levington,' he drawls, heaving his gown into place as he lumbers to his feet. Powerful features, lopsided mouth, as if a sneer is his default mode.

'Leventon, Mr Harman. It's pronounced Leventon.'

'Miss, ah, Leventon, then.'

Can he say a sentence without 'ah'?

'Now then, Miss, ah, Leventon, I suggest we stop the acting and come to the facts, shall we?'

I bristle. Before I can think of a suitable reply, Mr Justice Hirst sits bolt upright, looking outraged. 'That was a most improper observation, Mr. Harman.'

'Much obliged, my lord,' says Harman and gives a deep bow towards the bench. His wig flies off, hitting a minion in the bench in front.

I am dumbfounded. You couldn't make this up. I daren't even think of Gaye. Harman then makes an obscure reference to my reading English at Oxford, something to do with Beowulf and Grendel, to which I make a puzzled reply, wondering where this might possibly lead. Hirst starts shuffling papers and puffing his cheeks out. Harman presumably thinks better of it and moves on.

'With regard to the show, ah, *Hair!*'

Of course. The dreaded nude scene. My heart turns over, rights itself. I knew this would be an issue.

'Isn't it, ah, correct that this show, in which you played a starring role, is not only full of blasphemy, foul language and nudity, but also is a diatribe against social values, an iconoclastic show which in essence rebels against the state?'

'Yes.'

'Wouldn't it be right to say, Miss Leventon, that you espoused—wholeheartedly—all its hippie values, if I may put it that way?'

'Yes.'

'Then I put it to you that you are anti-establishment, despite your Oxford University education. You have brought this case because Thames is a powerful company and you wish to bring it down simply because you detest authority in any form.'

Wilmers leaps up, growling. Before he can speak, I hear myself snap back with utter clarity: 'Certainly not. I loved doing *Hair!* and I also have the utmost respect for authority. Why do you think I brought this case to the highest authority in the land?'

Scribble, scribble goes the judge.

I can breathe again.

By lunchtime, I'm freewheeling. Harman is going for simple targets. I have less and less respect for him and more and more for Hirst, who gives me room to get everything off my chest.

'Miss ah Leventon, is it not the case that you knew perfectly well that Thames were unable to work round Miss Langton's schedule in *A Little Night Music*?'

'Absolutely not. I knew exactly the opposite. When we were filming Howard's play *Verité* for Thames the year before, all recording stopped when Tim Curry left for his performance of *The Rocky Horror Show*.'

The defendants whisper and mutter amongst themselves. A note goes back to Harman, who clears his throat and frowns over it. Perhaps he can't read their writing.

'Do you need some time, Mr Harman?' asks Hirst, sounding tetchy. He's quicker to get cross with Harman than I am.

'I beg your indulgence, my lord, just a second.'

'Hmm,' snorts Hirst, leaning back against his vast throne and stretching his arms above his head.

'Ah, Miss Leventon.' Harman comes in for the kill. 'Is it not the case that Tim Curry's show, *The Rocky* um *Horror Show*, was in fact playing in the Kings Road, Chelsea, not in the West End at all, unlike *A Little Night Music*?'

'Can't see that makes much difference if you're coming from Teddington.'

More shuffling and muttering from Howard and co, like a *University Challenge* team conferring. Another scrap of paper goes back.

'But,' says Harman in a triumphant tone, having peered at the note, 'Is it not also the case that Tim Curry's show began *later* than *A Little Night Music*?'

'I have no idea what time it began, only that they released Tim from the recordings to get there.'

'Come now, Miss Leventon, this is obfuscation. I put it to you that you knew perfectly well, did you not, that it would be "*Curtains*" for Tim Curry at nine o'clock.'

Heavy emphasis on curtains.

I explode into laughter. '*Curtains* for Tim Curry?'

'Perhaps you would tell the court what you find so amusing, Miss ah Leventon?'

'Sorry, it conjured up an unfortunate picture.'

'I beg your pardon?'

'Curtains for someone generally means they're brown bread.'

'I beg your pardon?'

'Brown bread. Dead.'

Gaye snorts.

'And?'

Poor Harman. He's only got the phrase a bit wrong. It's mean of me. I can't restrain myself.

'Perhaps,' I say in a friendly tone, 'Perhaps you meant it would be "curtain up" for Tim at nine o'clock. That's the phrase we use.'

It's a cheap jibe. Harman looks discomforted. He glares. 'Thank you for the enlightenment, Miss Leventon. I'm sure the court is deeply grateful.'

Wilmers frowns at me and mimes 'calm down'.

Hirst sighs. 'Perhaps this is the moment when we might take a break for lunch.'

All rise.

14

Ravelling

In the lift going down to the canteen Wilmers, who has warned us he's not allowed to tell us what to say, manages a grim, 'Don't get cocky, don't look as if you're enjoying yourself' out of the side of his mouth. He looks furious.

The truth is I *am* enjoying myself. Eight years of tension, anxiety and heartache and I'm finally letting go. I nod and try to keep a straight face.

Gaye says, 'You're brilliant, sweet girl. Woo. Does he dislike *you!*'

That startles me. 'Wilmers?'

'Jerry Harman, idiot.'

'Can't help that. He's a fool.'

I try to sober up, though.

The afternoon goes through without incident, till Harman tries to get me on confidentiality.

'Isn't it a fact, Miss Leventon, that you knew this idea was Mr Schuman's all along?'

'No. That isn't the case. Don and I told Howard about the series idea, not the other way round. Months after we'd taken it to Jack Rosenthal, asking him if he'd develop it. It had nothing to do with Howard. He wasn't even interested in it. It was only after our first concert in July, 1974, when Andrew Brown was enthusiastic, it was only after that, that Howard expressed any real interest in it.'

'Miss—ah—Leventon, you told the court you and Mr Schuman discussed each other's projects openly. This project was developed by him from his play *Censored Scenes From King Kong*, was it not?'

'Absolutely not. Rock Bottom came long before *Censored Scenes*, which was wholly different anyway. This was my project. My only one. It was always ours, not his.'

'Miss Leventon. You are an actress. Mr Schuman had projects in which you assert he promised you roles.'

'Is that a question? Sorry, yes.'

'And isn't it true that Mr Schuman came over to discuss his project *Censored Scenes From King Kong* with Mr Fraser, in which he said there was a role for you?'

'So he said.'

'Surely Miss Leventon, knowing this was something that might include you, you would have looked at the script?'

'Only if Howard had given it to me to read.'

'Oh come now, Miss—ah—Leventon, are you seriously expecting the court to believe that when Mr Schuman left the script of *Censored Scenes From King Kong* for Mr Fraser, you didn't sneak a quick look at it?'

'Absolutely not. That was between them. It was confidential. I would never have dreamt of doing such a thing. I got to know the songs, of course, because Don was composing them in the music-room. I remember them very well. I could sing them now if you like.'

'No, thank you, Miss Leventon. I don't think any of us would want that.'

'Oh I don't know,' murmurs Hirst. 'Might make for a bit of light relief.'

GB snorts. I avoid her eye.

Harman changes tack.

'Is it not a fact, Miss Leventon, that when Thames discovered Miss Langton was not available for *Rock Follies* owing to her prior engagement with *A Little Night Music*, they honoured their commitment to you to act the part of Anna Wynd?'

'I don't accept Di wasn't available.'

'Answer the question, Miss Leventon, if you would be so good.'

'Very well. Thames, after saying Di couldn't do it, offered the other parts to Gaye and me, yes.'

'And isn't it the case, Miss Leventon, that there was nothing preventing you from accepting what you have indicated would be the best job of your career?'

I am furious. Wilmers' acting notes go out of the window. All restraint vanishes.

'There was everything preventing it,' I shout, kicking the side of the box, thumping my fist hard on the polished wood. 'We were a group, for goodness' sake! It was written for us and about us. We were the whole basis for the series. Without Di, it wouldn't have been Rock Bottom. It would just have been three actresses playing parts. As it turned out to be. Just three actresses. Not a group at all.'

'I suggest to you that your attitude was simply one of stubborn pride. In turning down the part of Anna, you were cutting off your nose to spite your face, as the saying goes.'

Now I'm incandescent. 'It was precisely the opposite, it was to retrieve the situation. I believed, still do believe, they were using Di as an excuse. If they'd really wanted us to be in it, Verity would have got on the phone to Richard Pilbrow, the *Night Music* producer, and done a deal, got Di out of matinees, say, in return for doing another three months. Or six months. That's all she had to do. It was up to Verity. That's what producers *do*. She didn't do it, did she?'

Note from Howard to Harman. He glances at it, looks back at me, heavy eyebrows raised.

'Miss Leventon, I put it to you that far from being loyal to Miss Langton, you had in fact already considered replacing her when she proved unreliable.'

My anger drains away in a horrid rush. I swallow.

'That is true, yes.'

Heads rise like a flock of deer scenting danger. Judge, Wilmers, Keith. *She's going to fall into this one.*

I plunge straight in. 'Early on, Di was in two minds about the group. She worried about her solo career, she worried about earning a living. And she was unreliable. She... sometimes she failed to show up.'

'Failed to show up for what, exactly?'

'Umm. Rehearsals, mostly. Though once a demo recording session.'

Harman smiles thinly. I'm cornered.

'And how did you respond to this unreliability, Miss Leventon?'

My heart is beating like a mad thing. *Tell the truth. Tell the truth.* I tell the truth.

'Gaye and I discussed replacing her.'

Harman is triumphant. 'So, if it suited you, you would replace her. And if it suited Thames, you wouldn't!'

My mind clears. 'Absolutely not. It is true Gaye and I—and Don—discussed who we might use instead. We decided the best person would be another girl from *Hair!* who'd been my understudy. Elaine Paige.'

Harman raises his eyebrows and shrugs in exaggerated ignorance. He hasn't heard of Elaine, has no idea she became an overnight sensation in *Evita* only four years ago. Mr Justice Hirst brightens, however. He loves show-biz. He loves having Edward Fox and Sian Phillips mentioned. He's heard of rock music. Unlike the judge last year asking, 'What *is* rock music?' Hirst knows exactly who Elaine is.

'So, Miss Leventon,' purrs Harman, moving in for the kill. 'You were quite prepared to drop Miss Langton for—'

I cut in. 'No, I wasn't. We simply couldn't do it. It wouldn't have been Rock Bottom without Di. She is integral to the group, walkabouts and all, an essential part of it. Without Di, it would become something else. She is unique and irreplaceable. We realised that then. I haven't changed my view.'

Next day, it goes on. And on. Harman is just completing a particularly convoluted accusation of which I'm starting to lose track, when the double doors behind him swing open. My brother Patrick's standing there. Round head, stout, glasses, middle-aged. I stare. No, not my brother, more like Hirst's, if he has one.

'Miss Leventon. Would you care to enlighten us on this matter?'

'I'm so sorry. Would you mind repeating the question?'

'If it was a question,' murmurs Hirst.

Harman sighs dramatically and starts again. 'Miss Leventon, is it not the case that you invented this whole conversation and that in the event, you were simply...'

'Miss—ah—Leventon, wouldn't it be more accurate to say that, far from you being...'

Lunchtime.

All rise.

At the back of the court, the visitor waits, smiling. It's my friend Paul Collins, Toby Belch to my Viola at Oxford, now a lawyer, I remember. A barrister, even, maybe.

'What on earth are you doing here?' I ask, tucking my arm through his, introducing him to Gaye and Don. Nick Strauss and John Wilmers know him already.

'I work here now and again,' says Paul, with some modesty.

Over lunch he mentions Simon Hawkesworth, also in our Oxford *Twelfth Night*. One of the lords, wasn't he?

'Exactly,' says Paul. 'And now also a barrister. Based in Manchester.'

'And?'

'Got a case down here, so he's staying with me.'

I am mystified. 'That's nice. But—?'

Paul grins. 'The thing is, he was in the disrobing room yesterday and he overheard one of the barristers reporting that a witness called Annabel Leventon in Court Twelve was making mincemeat out of Jerry Harman. So I thought I'd better come and see for myself.'

Gaye leans forward, yelping with laughter. 'It's true, Annie. What a great notice. One of your best. Poor Harman can't cope at all.'

'He's an arsehole,' mutters Don.

'It must be hard,' I say, 'When your clients are not only lying but haven't conferred. He's got three conflicting versions to deal with.'

'And all lies,' says Don, grimly shovelling chips.

'And all lies,' I agree. 'He *is* an arsehole, but I don't envy him.'

Secretly, I'm hugging myself. *Mincemeat, eh?*

By mid-afternoon, Harman can't think of anything else to get me on. After a whole week in the witness box, I'm free. Gaye's turn. I step down (it's true, you do have to step down) and walk past the defendants and under Hirst's gaze. I've behaved very badly, I know. Answered them back, wept, kicked the box, yelled, made jokes. And done my best, my absolute best. I feel as if a huge boil has been lanced. I'm clean. I meet GB coming the other way. I can see she's really, really proud of me. We stop for a second, look at each other—*well done, Annie, good luck, GB*—and kiss full on the mouth.

It's Friday afternoon. Everyone's hot and tired. Not Gaye. She's superbly turned out, hair deep crimson, brilliant dark eyes, a picture of composure. Queenliness, almost. One thing nobody cannot deny, as they say in *Guys and Dolls*, GB has class.

It was GB who contacted Edward Fox and Sian Phillips as witnesses. I'd never have thought of it. They were (are) theatre and now television royalty, having played *Edward and Mrs Simpson* in a major series for Thames TV, as it happens, both starring in the West End at the same time. Resourceful, GB. Persuasive, too. They were immediately up in arms on our behalf and promised support. Nigel Hawthorne was also her idea. *Yes Minister* carries huge weight as the most successful show of the decade. If Hirst admits to watching television, we know he'll be impressed by them. Probably send Gorgeous Gordon after them for an autograph.

There's something about Gaye. Partly her grand upbringing, partly her being a child actor and knowing everybody in show business, partly her sheer size and presence. More than anything, even the decibel levels, it's her chutzpah. The only time I ever saw her crumple (apart from when lovers dump her on a fairly frequent basis) was when Don told her to shut up at Selsdon Hall, the year of the Rock Bottom concerts. I can only think of one other time when she was even temporarily disconcerted. I had a few friends round for supper one Sunday AD (After Don) in Westbourne Terrace in the late Seventies, when I was rehearsing *Spokesong*. My co-star Niall Buggy was there. He'd chosen to sit in a beautiful Twenties wheelchair I'd recently bought second-hand. There was a long anguished ring on my doorbell. I ran down the two flights to find Gaye in floods of tears, having been dumped again.

'Darling GB, I've got friends here. Don't worry, I'll march you straight into the kitchen and shut the door and you can tell me all about it.'

Hiccupping and red-eyed, she dragged herself up to the second floor. I was whisking her through the living-room to protect her from strangers, when her upbringing asserted itself: 'How d'you do? I'm Gaye Brown. Gaye with an 'e', Brown without', and shook hands all round. Duty done, we shut ourselves in the kitchen till I'd heard the latest tragedy. It took a while. Meantime, the party in the other room was going fine. Eventually Gaye said, 'I'm all right now, Annie. Thanks for mopping me up. You're an angel as always. I owe you one,' opened the kitchen door to join the others and stopped with a shriek. We all stared at her. What was the matter?

'You, you—are you—what happened?' she gasped, pointing at Buggy, who was now sitting on the sofa. She'd assumed the wheelchair was his and a miracle had occurred. Buggy roared with laughter and did a little dance to prove he was cured and gave thanks to the Lord for his deliverance. It took about three seconds for Gaye to shriek again, this time with laughter, and become best friends with him.

Apart from that, I've never seen her unable to cope. Ever.

I'm not going to today, either. She's polite, gracious and funny. The judge is charmed, Wilmers relieved. Me, too. You never know with Gaye. You never know what might come out of her mouth. Too quick by half, she can be. I feel nervous watching her. But she's on form. In the last twenty minutes of the day, she scores a bullseye.

Wilmers asks her to explain what she felt watching the first two episodes of *Rock Follies*.

'Horrible,' she says.

Hirst looks up and asks her to elaborate. She turns to him, spreads her arms out wide and says with breath-taking simplicity: 'Well, my lord, there we were—and there we weren't!'

He almost applauds. She deserves it. It's perfect. It could win the case for us. Wilmers can barely believe his luck. He beams at all and sundry. So do we.

It's the end of the most intense week of my life and I'd like to let down my hair with someone before going home. GB has a baby waiting for her, Jane takes Don off as always, the lawyers are ready to drop.

My husband has a little surprise for me. He meets me outside the court.

'Where are we going?' I ask. I'm never sure about surprises. There have been a few too many recently.

He pulls an envelope out of his inside pocket. It must be

somewhere very special, he's not wearing his grubby tracksuit. That's a surprise in itself. I open the envelope and gasp.

'Oh Johnny, how brilliant. And what perfect timing! How did you know?'

'I just thought you might like to see him,' he says. Then honesty gets the better of him. 'And I want to see him, too.'

The tickets are for Rudolf Nureyev at the Coliseum. The most beautiful man in the world, the greatest dancer of his generation.

'I met him,' I burble, flinging my arms round Johnny. 'Well, not exactly met. I saw him leaning against a pillar watching me at the first night party for *Hair!* I didn't have the courage to go up and say hallo. And I've never seen him dance. Johnny, this is marvellous!'

Johnny knows the catch phrase too.

'*Mar*vellous! *Mar*vellous!' we say as we bound to the Coliseum.

I've been tense as a wire all week, now I can let go. We have great seats, with an empty one next to me till a huge, burly, red-faced man squeezes himself down onto the red plush, taking up quite a bit of my space as well. I'm in a very jolly mood and start chatting to him. He doesn't look like your average ballet enthusiast. He turns out actually to be what he looks like, an ex-rugby player from New Zealand who happens to love ballet.

In the interval, Johnny buys me champagne and Fred as well. I invite him to dinner the next evening, thinking he and Gaye might like each other. When he shows up at our little converted shop in Mossop Street, he walks in and immediately points to a black-and-white photo of Rock Bottom framed and on the wall.

'Oh my goodness,' he says, '*Rock Follies*!'

That does it. GB and I are boggle-eyed.

'Did you tell him?' she asks.

'Not a word.'

'We should get him in as a witness!'

He'd seen *Rock Follies* in New Zealand years before and identified us at once.

It feels like a very good sign. We're looking for them.

Did I say Gaye might have won us the case last Friday? This Monday, she almost loses it.

She climbs back into the witness box to be cross-examined, elegant, stunning, fresh as a daisy after her weekend. It's impossible to believe she's a single parent with a one-year-old. Jerry Harman, amazingly, takes to her. They understand each other at once. When he asks which Election Day she had her party, she says, 'The one we lost!' He gets it at once. Tories, both of them. Toffs. They come from the same world. Don irritated him, David Hirst intimidates him, I infuriated him. Gaye charms him.

His elephantine gallantry rises to the occasion and she has an easy time of it. There isn't much left that Don and I haven't already covered. I start to relax and enjoy their exchanges. They clearly do, too.

It's Hirst who provides the flashpoint.

Harman: Miss Brown, are we to understand that you took it upon yourself to call Verity Lambert when, as you put it, things began to look sticky?

GB: Yes. I thought, why not? Someone had to break the silence. I thought the women could sort it out. We usually can, you know.

Harman: *(smiling)* Perhaps, Miss Brown, perhaps. And what was the nature of your telephonic communication?

GB: *(blinking)* What? Oh, I see. Well, I just picked up the phone and asked to speak to her. Simple.

Harman: And did she agree to speak to you?

GB: Oh yes. She was very friendly. She explained that things had gone too far to be salvaged. She said she couldn't work with Mr Fraser, who she said had been unwilling to release Di from *Night Music*.

Harman: Thank you, Miss Brown, I have no more—

Hirst: *(interrupting)* Miss Brown, did you respond to Miss Lambert's comments?

GB: Of course, my lord. We were polite to each other, naturally. Why not?

Hirst: And how did the conversation end?

GB: *(without hesitation)* Oh, I said, well, in that case, good luck with the series.

Hirst: *(stares for a second)* Thank you, Miss Brown.

Draws his brows together, looks down and scribbles furiously. That's done it. We've just lost.

GB: *(seeing me, Wilmers and Keith both horror-struck, tries to retrieve the situation)* It might not have been exactly that.

Harman: *(overriding)* So you said to Miss Lambert, good luck with the series?

He sounds incredulous. A great solid rock of gold has just crashed onto his desk.

GB: *(now confused)* Well, maybe not those exact words. Words to that effect.

She's shovelling earth onto the coffin here. I can't breathe. I look away.

Harman: *(genially)* Thank you, Miss Brown. No more questions.

All rise.

Thank God.

In the corridor outside, Keith grabs me. 'Did she really say that?' he hisses.

'I've no idea. Probably not. Who knows? Will Wilmers have to recall her?'

Keith looks furious. 'Only if she can do better than that.'

I shake my head. 'You never know with Gaye.'

If we call her back, she might say something worse.

At lunch, she's defiant.

'I don't see why that's so bad. I can't really remember what I said, anyway. They can't shoot me for it. Shall we have cottage pie again? Di, darling, here you are! I'm all done. You're on this afternoon.'

What's said cannot be unsaid. Wilmers, Keith and Nick mutter together at another table.

In the afternoon, Di takes the stand in her black Merry Widow outfit. It takes all of three seconds for me to realise that she, of all of us, is the canny one, the court-wise one. She stands beautifully, demurely, shoulder-blades squeezed back to show her tits to full advantage, her chin prettily dropped so she has to open her eyes wide. She's like Marilyn Monroe—the more make-up she wears, the more innocent and vulnerable she looks. I am full of admiration.

Nothing ruffles her composure. The judge puts his elbows on the bench and leans forward to drink her in. All the men are besotted. Except Howard. And even he forgets his angry victim pose and succumbs to her charm, as with every audience she's ever had. No wonder the management of *Windy City* (about to come in to the West End) are playing ball, allowing her to squeak in to the theatre after the half. They want her there. And we need her here.

Gaye's last remark can't be erased, but with any luck it might get buried by Di's performance. She almost curtsies again to Hirst. She catches Gordon's eye and lowers her lashes, dimpling. Might as well get 'em all on her side. Wilmers' job is made much, much easier.

'Miss Langton, please explain to the court...'

'And what did you understand by...?'

'Miss Langton, tell the court in your own words how you would describe Rock Bottom...'

'Not like any other girl group ever,' she says promptly. 'We was all lead singers for a start. And girl groups all look alike, don't they? We was all different, like—like a bag of Dolly Mixtures.'

The judge nods and writes.

Plain sailing. A hundred percent perfect.

Harman rises to cross-examine. He gets the same deferential treatment. She's sharp with it and he gets nowhere. She explains the rather complicated facts of her original contract for *Night Music* and its expiry, leaving her free to take other work. She is clarity itself explaining why she'd asked Verity Lambert at the Thames meeting if she would be free to take other work as a solo artist.

Harman harrumphs. 'I put it to you, Miss Langton, that this was a ruse. You already knew that you were under contract for the forthcoming West End show *A Little Night Music*.'

Di is completely unfazed. Her tone is gentle, earnest, friendly. 'It wasn't like that, Mr Harman, if I may say so. It was more—'

Harman cuts her off. 'Yes, thank you, Miss Langton.'

Di: (to the judge) Might I please explain, your Worship?

Wilmer winces. The judge nods, mesmerised.

Di: You see, your Honour, it was *because Night Music* had fallen through I asked the question. I had a child to support. I couldn't afford to be out of work for four months for a share of five hundred pounds, could I? I needed to know I could earn a living.

Hirst nods again.

Di: Thank you, your Honour.

She bestows a smile on him and turns back to Harman, ready to continue. I'm spellbound. We all are. Hirst scribbles.

Harman, stumped, tries a few more tacks, but she's ready for anything. He asks how well she knew Howard.

Di: Hardly at all, to start with. He was Annie's friend. I knew she thought the world of him and his writing. And he wrote the words for one of our songs with Don. *Memory Lane* it's called. All Beatles lyrics. Lovely.

Harman: *(in pompous trap-laying mode)* So you 'hardly knew' Mr Schuman, despite the fact you assert he based the character Dee in Rock Follies entirely on you.

Di: *(still unruffled, looks kindly at him)* I said to start with, Mr Harman. After the first concert, he hung around all the time.

Justice Hirst: Hung around, Miss Langton? Do you mean he spent much time with you?

Di: Yes, your Honour. He was—*(cocks her head to one side)*—how shall I put it? He was always there. Like my handbag.'

It's genius. Hirst nods and writes.

Harman: *(reduced to harassing her over small details)* You say you can't remember, Miss Langton. This is absurd. I put it to you that you don't remember because it never happened.

Di: No, really, I don't remember. I never put anything in my diary or anything else like that, so honestly there's nothing to remind me. But it doesn't mean it never happened.

Harman: This is ridiculous. You stand there and lie barefaced to this court when you—

Judge: *(furious)* Mr Harman. Miss Langton is being extremely polite to you, under trying circumstances. I would request that you treat her with the same courtesy. I expect you to give her an unreserved apology immediately.

Harman: *(ungracious)* Yes, m'lord. Miss Langton, *(voice trailing away)* my apologies.

Di: *(very gracious)* Thank you.

Towards the end of her cross-examination, Harman asks her to get one of the books from behind her to look at a document. Di, being tiny, does her best, but she drops some of the others on the floor with a clatter.

Di: *(shocked)* Oh!

Judge: *(agitated)* Won't someone please help Di?

Di: *(afterwards)* I knew he liked me, Annie, when he forgot to call me Miss Langton. I knew it was a good sign.

Was it ever. Game, set and match.

15

Witnesses

High Court, July, 1982

The fourth week of the trial. Tomorrow, rehearsals begin for *Rocket To The Moon*. My part isn't huge, but from now on, I'll have to be in Hampstead and miss out on most of our witnesses.

I catch Sue Francis, music journalist.

Harman: Are you telling the court that Miss Leventon wore long, frilled, flowered dresses and you considered her *stylish*?

Sue Francis: *(smiling, precise, definite)* Oh, yes. Laura Ashley was all the rage in the early Seventies. I believe they asked her to wear a Laura Ashley dress of her own in the play she did for Thames. I saw it. She looked delightful.

Harman: I put it to you that what you wrote in your music magazine, called, I believe, *Sheet*, on the twenty-seventh of February, 1976, had no validity whatsoever, but that you were put up to it by Mr Fraser.

Sue Francis: Oh no, I hadn't seen him for the longest time. Or Miss Leventon. I was watching *Rock Follies* and was struck by the extraordinary likeness to Rock Bottom. I couldn't believe what I was seeing. To me, it was unmistakable. It was a portrayal of them, undoubtedly. I was really surprised it wasn't them, as it was certainly their characters. That is why I wrote the piece in *Sheet*.

I manage to see Jack Rosenthal as well.

Jack: In my view, the idea Don and Annabel outlined to me for a television series was a bold and original one, quite different from the normal image of a conventional pop singer or group. The idea of three actresses, of wit and intelligence, with established careers forming a pop or rock group is striking and unusual. I understood it was to be partly based on their lives and part invention. Don and Annabel asked me to consider doing it in about November, 1973. I turned it down as I know nothing about the pop world, but I grasped immediately it could be very successful. Original ideas are what everyone wants. They form the basis of every good piece of writing.

Wilmers: When they approached you with their idea, did you regard the information as confidential?

Jack: Yes. I regarded it as their idea, which I had no right to develop in any way without them. Confidentiality as a principle is crucial in my world, or you could never pitch an idea.

Harman: Mr—ah—Rosenthal, with nothing written down, there is no way of establishing ownership of an idea, is there?

Jack: Even when it *is* written down, it's no safeguard. But the principle is understood by everyone in the business.

Hirst: Thank you, Mr Rosenthal. *(Writes.)* By the way, I very much enjoyed your play *The Evacuees*. Superb piece of writing. Very moving.

Jack: Thank you, my lord.

After that, we're into full rehearsal and I have to beg time off to catch anyone really important. Mostly it's refused. They're paying me to do a job. Gaye rings me every evening to keep me up to date.

'Annie, your mate Maureen was brilliant. She corroborated everything we said. She said she'd tried to persuade Jack to write the series. She thought it was a brilliant idea for television. She called it a journey through the entertainment jungle, or something like that.'

'That sounds great.'

'Oh, and Annie, she remembered it was her idea for you to approach Howard as writer. Once Jack turned it down.'

'Did she? Oh bless her.'

'It's going awfully well, Annie. Shame you can't be here. Di's in Plymouth this week. Don's monosyllabic and goes off with Jane all the time.'

'She's there a lot, is she?'

'Yup. It's rather dull without you.'

'The minute we've opened, I'll be back. Promise.'

'I'll tell Gordon. He's missing you.'

'Oh, shut up.'

'He's gorgeous, isn't he? I'd have a go myself if he weren't so clearly besotted with you. Going now. Love to Johnny.'

I miss nearly everything from now on—Ronnie Beck, our music publisher, Tony Edwards, my friend who runs Purple Records, Don's mentor and music publisher Larry Fenton, my darling now ex-agent Jean Diamond, who kept notes of everything and is stout in our defence, Nigel Hawthorne from *Yes Minister*. According to GB, when Nigel's finished his evidence, Gorgeous Gordon indeed catches him up in the corridor to tell him how much Hirst loves the series.

The last witness to speak on our behalf is the incredible Molly Parkin. I get the morning off at the last minute and slide in to Room 12. It's richly rewarding. Dressed as only Molly can be in ultra-extravagant haute couture, outrageous colours and a hat somewhat over one eye, possibly not intentionally, she is very clear about Rock Bottom, in her habitual loud drawl.

'I had a weekly full-page spread in the *Evening Standard*, Friday's People. I chose up-and-coming, interesting people, on their way to success, just before their careers peaked. Rock Bottom was the only interview I did where they didn't make it to the top. They should have done. I went to a concert. They were magnificent. All stars in their own right, all…'

Wilmers can't stop her. They're all spellbound by her total conviction, her startling appearance, her nasal voice.

Harman: (trying to cut her down) Miss Parkin, perhaps you could explain to the court how, in your article, you…

Parkin: (waving him aside) I know where your questions are leading and it's shameful.

Harman: Miss Parkin, I assure you I had no intention—

Parkin: Yes you did. You should be ashamed of yourself. My private life is my private life. It has nothing to do with my success as a journalist, whatever you may say.

He can't compete with her, he's not in her league.

At lunchtime I have just have time to give her a hug, careful not to dislodge the hat further, before rushing back to rehearsal.

Week Six, July, 1982

We've done presenting our case. Wilmers wrapped it up last Friday. Keith has done a terrific job, he's been meticulous. He's left nothing out. Every witness, every scrap of paper evidence, every newspaper article, photo, poster, flyer, every little note, every relevant diary entry collated and given a document number and photocopied and handed out for all to see. Even our RCA logo, a pink and red ankle-strap platform peep-toe shoe with a bow on the instep, has been displayed.

RCA came up trumps. Our A&R man, Alan Sizer, made it very clear that our hope and intention of having a television series was partly instrumental in them giving us the recording deal. He believed we wouldn't be so easy to promote without such a boost, being as different from the norm and looking as unusual as we did.

Now for the other side. Harman starts to lay out the defence. And I'm in rehearsal, I can't be there for any of it, I'm dependent on Gaye for snippets of information. She says Keith takes copious notes, sends messages flying in all directions—to Nick Strauss, to Wilmers, to Oscar's office, double-checking everything, a blond terrier worrying away at a bone as information comes up that Thames had never mentioned, documents that weren't disclosed, assertions to be verified. There are still so many gaps in our knowledge, so many meetings we knew nothing about, decisions made we can only guess at. At last we're getting their version of events, however warped.

I *have* to hear the defendants. I have to.

Robin Lefevre, my director, kindly lets me off for a few days and will focus on David Burke and Mary Maddox, the leads. And the timing's right. The morning I'm back in, Harman chooses the defendant with the highest status, Thames Television's trump card—the Head of Drama, the legendary Verity Lambert.

Her blouse is a giveaway. How demure in white satin, how severe. With the black skirt and black shiny low-heeled shoes, it's almost formal court attire without the wig and gown. Elegant, modest, covered up to the neck, yet feminine, she leaves nothing to chance. While I was in the witness box in my nice dress, trying not to look like a raffish, unreliable rock'n'roller, her outfit sneered up at me from the front bench, topped by an oval of contempt and disdain, mouth turned down at the ready, a sneer never far away. Sandwiched between her two male cohorts, both outsiders, one a New Yorker, the other Kiwi, she gave them credibility just by her proximity. They're a triptych of outraged innocence. The men have pursy little mouths, their eyes dart venom. Not so impressive. Verity is perfection. All three are right under Hirst's gaze. He had to turn his head to get my profile while I was up there. He had to pause, eyebrows twitching, pen hovering, head on one side, before I dared turn directly to him to explain something.

'Could you repeat that?' he'd murmur.

The defendants snorted and sniggered in a silent movie of repudiation, right in front of him, exaggerating their response to make sure he got it.

Now for Verity's performance. The white satin blouse has become her trademark, day after day. How many has she got, for God's sake? Does a minion wash and iron the same one? Perhaps she gets them from the wardrobe department. Maybe Thames have allotted her a budget for Court Costume. Twenty white satin blouses for the use of Ms Verity Lambert. Check.

Pale, composed, authoritative. Unlike angry, sharp, emotional me or GB's rapid-fire, unpremeditated bursts of genius or stupidity. As far as you can get from Di and her cautious charm and eyelash-flapping veracity, Verity has authority and uses it, flaunts it. It puts her on a par with David Hirst. *I am, in my own way, as august as you*, her stance proclaims. Dispassionate and wise, exposing wicked children's lies, she speaks adult to adult. If I were the judge, I'd find that compelling. *Verity*—her very name means truth.

Up in the witness box, that white blouse is her undoing. The minute she starts lying, it quivers like a highly-strung horse, you can't miss it. And there are plenty of lies. 'We never use actors for a series while they are working in the West End.' 'I never said they were free to work as individuals till we had decided to go ahead.' 'I absolutely deny...' 'That never happened.'

I know they are lies because I know the truth. I know they are lies because I was there. The blouse certainly knows. 'Here comes a biggie', it announces, an elegant white jelly flashing warning signals round the court. It's so obvious, I could laugh.

Then I get a grip. That's just my point of view. *I* know why it's shimmering, she's telling another lie. But to the judge, who doesn't know, it could be seen as truthful conviction as she nobly defends herself.

Wilmers asks her about the Stella Richman situation, where

Thames agreed to share royalties in the series. Ever polite, he makes it sound almost inconsequential. Verity stays calm. She explains how she'd spoken to them, told them Thames wanted to develop the series. Wilmers asks her to explain why in Brightwell's confirmation letter he mentions the series to be written by Howard Schuman, entitled the ROCK BOTTOM series.

'Oh,' says Verity, 'I may have mentioned in conversation with him that I liked the name Rock Bottom as a possible title.'

'Stella Richman also uses the name Rock Bottom in internal notes. Did that also come from you?'

'I suppose it must have done.'

'And Thames use that title in their negotiations with Stella Richman Ltd, do they not?'

'Yes. I liked the name.'

Clever Verity. Very clever. But the blouse shimmers, so I know. Originally the series was called *Rock Bottom*, not *Rock Follies*, because of us.

Then Andrew Brown. Tall, brown-haired, eager. Not much gravitas, but Verity had enough for all three of them. With Andrew in the witness box, I begin to get John Wilmers' measure. There wasn't much he could do against Verity, she was so well defended. Andrew's another matter. I get the impression he's not used to lying. He looks very uncomfortable, an overgrown schoolboy caught out, trying to avoid punishment. He all but flinches when Wilmers, sniffing a falsehood, pursues it like a polite bloodhound, flushing it out for all to see.

I feel bad for him. The contrast between his evidence now and his exuberant '*Mar*vellous! *Mar*vellous!' after the first concert is extraordinary. We enjoyed doing it in our best Kiwi accents. Don was best. He'd had it first-hand, this gawky beaming Thumper bounding up to him on the pavement outside the theatre. '*Mar*vellous, *mar*vellous! This could be great television. I'd like to talk to a few people about you, how d'you feel about that?'

We all remember Don's parody of him, falling about and

using it ourselves. Not the kind of thing we'd forget, because of the accent and the enthusiasm. Though apparently Andrew has.

'So are you saying, Mr Brown, that you did *not* speak to Mr Fraser after the first Rock Bottom concert of July 14th, 1974?'

'Er. That's right. I didn't speak to him.'

'Do you deny saying to Mr Fraser after the July concert that you thought the group were marvellous and would make marvellous television?'

Andrew stammers and twists his neck about. 'I, uh, didn't see Mr Fraser.'

'Nor Miss Leventon?'

'Um. Not after the show, I didn't see them then, no...'

'Perhaps you would tell the court what you actually did after the concert was over?'

'Ah. Yes. Well, I came out of the theatre...'

'Through the foyer?'

'Yes.'

'And you failed to speak either to Mr Fraser or Miss Leventon, who were there, despite the fact you had enjoyed the show?'

'Um, I don't exactly remember, I don't think I saw them,' mutters Andrew, sweat beading his forehead.

Wilmers raises an eyebrow and looks down at his notes.

'I'd like to move on to a later date, when the girls who replaced Rock Bottom were offered the leading roles in *Rock Follies*. Was it your idea to sign them up to you as manager in order to promote them as a group separately from the television series?'

Andrew shifts position from side to side, his hands clutching the stand. More sweat pops out.

'Please answer the question, Mr Brown. Was this your idea?'

No answer.

'Mr Brown, I put it to you that it was your idea, along with Mr Schuman, to promote the Little Ladies as a group beyond the *Rock Follies* series, with the intention of profiting from this arrangement.'

Andrew looks up to the ceiling as if asking for a miracle from on high. A big tear rolls down his face. 'Ah, no. N-not my idea, not exactly, not as such…'

'So you went along with an idea of someone else's?'

'Well, I…'

'Will you tell the court whose idea it was, if not yours?'

Andrew swallows and looks down at his feet. 'I don't exactly recall.'

'Do you agree that you were party to an attempt to form and promote a group similar to Rock Bottom?'

'Umm, well, I, er, yes.'

'Thank you, Mr Brown.'

My lower back twinges. The wooden benches are too hard, the tension of sitting day after day watching people twist themselves into knots is starting to bite. Wilmers makes all his points. They're right and true and fair, but I stop breathing each time and so my back starts hurting. I'm grateful for *Rocket To The Moon*, where I have to throw all this away and focus on my job. It's a big relief.

Keeps me sane.

My director Robin, bless him, can manage without me for another day. I come in for Howard's turn. All these weeks I've not looked in his direction, except from the witness box, when he was right under my nose and I couldn't avoid him. He climbs up there with his nice tweed jacket and his glasses, slightly receding hairline and cuddly New York persona. Intelligence, warmth, humour. I got used to all that being part of my daily life, I liked swapping stories over the phone: 'I've written a song about horoscopes, Howard.' 'Yeah? How's it go? Oh, that's neat. Did Don play you our new song?' 'I can sing it to you now, if you like: *The lights are going out all over Europe, We'll have to muddle through as best we can.*' 'Hey, you know it already!' 'Easy. I love it.' 'Love yours, too.'

A mutual appreciation society, we were. It's hard to believe now. He looks serious, solemn, righteous, even. And as tense as I am. Harman leads him through his version of events. So many discrepancies between his and Verity's evidence, so many between his and mine. When he's asked about the origin of the idea for *Rock Follies*, he says it came directly from the Duck Sisters in his play *Censored Scenes from King Kong*. Julie Covington and Beth Porter as two cabaret singers? Hardly rock. Hardly a three-girl group. When he claims he told us he'd met Verity in May and was bringing her to the first concert to audition us, I am furious. We had no idea she was there, we had no idea he'd already met her.

It's very odd. Everything he says is wrong, but he says it with such conviction. Then he starts asserting things that must be true, he proves them from diary entries: a meeting with Verity Lambert in May, 1974, before our first concert, meetings in August to develop the plan of a six-part drama series, each part an hour long, the promise of a commission to write the first script. I'm stunned. He never told me any of this. He knew it all before we met him for lunch, he'd already pitched the idea to Thames without my knowledge. His version of the lunch with Rock Bottom at La Tavernetta is a complete joke. He'd handed in his pilot script at the beginning of December? No way, he told me he hadn't finished it. Everything he says is wrong.

I send notes via Keith to Wilmers on the points he makes: not true, that's a lie, that can't be true. He absolutely denies Don's evidence about being shown a typed list of Howard's various working projects, including a TV series called *Rock Bottom*. He invents a conversation he and I are supposed to have had, when I asked for his help because Thames wanted to get rid of us. When he offered to stand up to them and refuse to continue writing, I said it would be no use. He says I showed symptoms of 'classic, self-destructive paranoia'.

Keith sends me a note. 'Any truth in this?'

'Of course not!' I send back in wrath. This is the last straw.

GB writes, 'Large brandy at lunchtime. My treat!'

I may need more than that.

When Wilmers gets up to cross-examine, things change. Challenged on his assertion about the first pilot script, Howard stands by it. He handed it in to Thames at the beginning on December, Verity didn't like it and wanted re-writes. He re-wrote it and handed in the second draft in early January.

It's not true. It can't be. He would have told me.

'Why wasn't this first draft entered as evidence?' asks Wilmers.

'I threw it away after they turned it down,' he replies.

Wilmers queries this again, glances at my shocked, disbelieving face, shrugs and continues his questions.

The next day, Howard arrives waving a script. He says it's the original first draft.

'Where did you find it?'

'In the bottom drawer of my bedside table,' says Howard, defiantly.

I'd always believed he betrayed me only at the last minute to save his series. I was so wrong, he appears to have lied to me over everything to do with Thames. If his first draft had been turned down and he had to re-do it, that explains why he wasn't talking to me then. I really, really want to see it.

When asked about the lunch with Rock Bottom, he denies it was in order to celebrate his success with Thames and the prospect of the girls getting good parts in it.

'But your counsel cross-examined all the plaintiffs on this meeting, based on those facts.'

'Oh,' says Howard. 'That was a bad mistake on Mr Harman's part.'

'Really?' asks Wilmers, in an interested tone. 'And you never corrected him even when he pressed all of them separately, in cross-examination, to accept this version of events?'

'I really meant the lunch was to ask the girls if they were

committed already to Mr Degas and the BBC or whether they'd like to play characters in my series.'

'So it wasn't a celebration?'

'No.'

Hirst intervenes. 'Are you saying your counsel used this line of cross-examination without having established the truth of it with you? Are you suggesting he made it up himself?'

'No, no. It was all a dreadful misunderstanding.'

Hirst stares at him for a long moment, then glances at Harman. I follow his gaze. Harman looks flushed and his brows are drawn together but he says nothing.

Wilmers goes on to the comparisons between us and the main characters in *Rock Follies,* as described by Howard:

1) Anna Wynd: blonde, wears contact lenses, always dieting, a serious dramatic actress, widowed mother who makes acid remarks about Anna's inadequacies, Anna's own insecurities about her talent compared with the other two.

2) Q: tall, red-haired, upper-crust, a penchant for self-indulgent hedonistic boyfriends, her insistence on the best olive oil, her one-liners.

3) Dee: 'a hefty, dark-haired cockney', the best singer of the three.

To every single comparison between Rock Bottom and the *Rock Follies* girls, Howard has an immediate, definite, rock-solid answer, proving the character of each girl is taken, not from our group, despite his close contact with us (which he calls nebulous) but from any number of other actresses: Eleanor Bron, Anna Massey, Beth Porter. In fact every actress he's ever met has unknowingly contributed to the *Rock Follies* girls' characters except the three who were actually living the life he portrayed in the series. None of it came from his imagination, he says. Equally none of it came from me, the actress who played the lead in his first TV play and with whom he spent so much time during this period.

The more he's asked, the more sparkling the recollection he has for all the non-Rock Bottom actresses who provided him with data.

Methinks the lady doth protest too much, I write and pass along to GB.

Bastard! she writes back.

He's digging his own grave. If he said it was all his own invention, it'd be more plausible. If he just said, 'yes, I based it all on them and so what? It's my observation and my idea to exploit it for television' he might get away with it. It's his word against ours. He saw us on stage, he saw us in rehearsal, he wrote for us, he saw us in the recording studio. Effectively we gave him all the background, the flesh of the idea. Anyone in that position could use it. It would be blatant copying but who could have stopped him? If he would just admit it and assert only that the idea of using it for television is his, he might succeed.

But he won't. He refutes the lot. It's wholly his: the concept, the storyline, the characters, the heights, hair colour, class, background, singing styles, sense of humour, politics—all his.

As the questions continue, his attitude develops from an earnest sincerity with total recall to outraged innocence. He clutches the box, his body tense, crying out against slander: 'This is my work. It's all I have. I'm a creative writer. You are telling me I have no talent. My creativity is on the line here. You say I haven't written this. What do I have? Only my writing talent! You're denying my talent.'

Impassioned stuff. How does he do that? The only explanation I can come up with it that he really believes his own lies. He has to or he'd fall apart.

I'm glad to be getting back to rehearsal tomorrow.

16

Recall

High Court, July, 1982

Beth Porter comes in as a witness. I can't work out why, she was never part of any of this. I asked Julie Covington if she would come and speak for us but she refused, saying she didn't want to take sides. That I could understand, she was in such a difficult position. But Beth? Very odd. She's American, a friend of Howard's and in *Verité* with me and Tim Curry. I've known her slightly for years. I don't understand what she can have to say. I'm in the last week of rehearsals, so GB will tell me all later.

'What on earth was she doing there, GB? What did she have to say?'

'Nothing really. She said she and Howard talked about his idea—ha ha!—ages before us.'

'That's it?'

'When she was doing *Censored Scenes from King Kong*, I think. Is that what it's called?'

'But that came after *Verité*, and *Verité* came after we'd formed Rock Bum. And after Don's Master Gruppenplan.'

'All bullshit, darling. And guess who they've got coming tomorrow? Margaret Matheson!'

'Who's that?'

'She's only Head of Drama for Central Television.'

'Oh, shit. I suppose she's going to say they never work round actors' theatre schedules.'

'I can't get in tomorrow, darling. Will you be there?'

'For some of it, I hope. If I get off in time.'

'Give me the gory details, won't you, Bird's Egg? I don't want to miss any of this charming little soap.'

Nor do I. This part of it must be nearly over. Their defence doesn't seem that strong to me. Except for Verity. She's enough all by herself.

Margaret Matheson is another high-ranking woman of authority, formidable, right outside the picture, with no reason to lie. She states with conviction she would never employ an actor in a lead role if they had ongoing theatre commitments. I believe her. Someone as calm and adult and competent as Margaret Matheson carries weight.

Their whole case now seems to rest on this: if Di hadn't done *Night Music*, there wouldn't have been a problem. It makes no sense given the way they behaved, but it makes me shiver. I feel as if we're balancing on a very narrow ledge with an angry sea pounding beneath us.

Wilmers gets to his feet. He squeezes admissions out of her: she's more draconian than other TV executives on this; she concedes that in practice it's fairly normal to work round leading actors' schedules. She also agrees it's standard practice for a television company to negotiate a deal with the theatre producer in order to release the actor.

That's the best he can get out of her. It's quite a lot.

I lunch with Nick Strauss.

'When's John going?' I ask. I know he's committed elsewhere at some point.

'Too soon,' snaps Nick, glaring down at his lunch. 'We won't complete before the summer recess.'

'When is that?'

'From the end of July till October.'

I'm aghast. 'But that's next week! Two whole months?'

'Yes. John will be in Hong Kong when we start again. I'll have to do the closing speech.'

Nick's been on the case as junior barrister ever since Don was sent to him by Oscar. Nick was the one who gave us counsel's opinion on taking out an injunction against Thames before they recorded the first series. Of everyone, he knows most about the case, he's been advising us since we began. According to Keith, who should know, Nick's the one whose painstaking preparation of the law has made the case possible. He's not junior, that's a technical term, he hasn't decided to take silk yet. However, he knows and I know that he's not Wilmers.

I put my knife and fork down. Lunch has suddenly lost its taste.

I miss everything else till after *Rocket To The Moon* opens at Hampstead. The day I'm back, they pull in a surprise witness, Judy Raines. Keith raises his eyebrows at me. I write: *Close friend of Howard's. Wrote the lyrics to one of our songs, Dirty Rat. Vaguely friendly once. No idea why she's here.* He reads my note and passes it to Wilmers.

She's small and neat and American and not so friendly now. Naturally we haven't seen each other since the split, she's here to champion Howard, she never knew our side. On the stand, she's modest and self-effacing. Everything she says is delivered as if the truth is being squeezed unwillingly out of her, only because she cannot tell a lie. First she talks about bringing her lyrics to Don and that Rock Bottom performed a song they wrote together. Then she mentions a lunch she and I had which I don't recall. In a charming, throaty whisper, with downward glances and a little puckering of the mouth, she delivers poison.

'I'm sorry to say Miss Leventon was very bitter about Howard. She said she would have no mercy for him. She also told me another person she'd really fallen out with was her brother, who she never speaks to. She sort of implied it was a pattern.'

What? This is so silly it can't be harmful.

'She spoke to a theatre manager at the Oxford Playhouse and tried to claim my lyrics as hers.'

My God. She's here to call me a thief?

Finally she delivers her real message.

'I met her once by chance. On the street, near my apartment.'

'And where do you live, Miss ah, Raines?'

'Oh. I live right by Harley Street.'

'And what conversation took place on this occasion, Miss Raines?' trumpets Harman, leaning forward in anticipation.

'Oh,' she murmurs, a worried frown on her face, 'we weren't able to talk for long. You see, she had an appointment.'

'An appointment? What kind of an appointment?'

Her voice sinks further. 'I'm sorry to say she told me she was seeing a psychiatrist.'

There. She's landed it. She's trying to nail me as some kind of lunatic.

All rise.

Keith pulls me out into the corridor. I feel winded.

'How much of this is true?' he demands.

'It's bullshit about my brother. It's bullshit about stealing her lyrics.'

'And?'

'It's true I met her on my way to see a therapist.'

We look at each other. Most middle-class English people of Hirst's generation are suspicious of anything to do with psychiatry. In 1975, it wasn't something you could talk about. Even now, in 1982, it's just the kind of smear that could destroy Hirst's belief in me. My credibility could simply drain away.

'John will probably have to recall you.'

I swallow hard. 'I'll have to take the stand again?'

Keith looks grim. 'I'll talk to him.'

Wilmers says, yes, I'll have to defend myself against this. Now I'm shaking in my nice court shoes. This is no fun. If Hirst thinks I belong in a funny farm, we could lose the case. I hadn't thought this would come up. It wasn't as if I'd ever been to a doctor, I'd never seen a psychiatrist or been inside a mental institution. I'd had problems and found myself a therapist to talk to. In the Seventies, therapy was just beginning to be accepted. I found a lovely woman who just happened to see her clients in Devonshire Street, in rooms above the Jungian Society. Judy just happened to live across the road.

Hirst has been wonderful so far, much more modern than any of us could have hoped. This might be a bridge too far. I tell Johnny.

'For cryin' out loud, they're calling you mad? They're crazy!' he yells, making us both laugh. 'I'll come to court with you. About time you let me.'

'Johnny, it's so kind of you, but I'll be in even more of a state if you're there.'

'Rubbish. I'm coming. I'll wear my best jacket, promise.'

I'd known GB for nearly twenty years so I'm familiar with loose cannons. Another one in court would be too much, even if he behaves himself and doesn't explode, which is unlikely. In the end, I go alone on the Tube to Holborn, so I can spend a few minutes in the Kingsway church.

Last week, with a tube and bus strike on, I had to borrow Johnny's newspaper delivery bike, no brakes, flat tyres and a great, unwieldy metal basket in the front for the papers. London seems quite flat till you're on a bike. Negotiating Hyde Park Corner and Piccadilly in rush hour was a challenge, so I made it easier on myself by going down Birdcage Walk past Buckingham Palace, through Admiralty Arch and along the Strand. If the Strand isn't flat enough, the Aldwych is like Everest. I was pink and breathless when I arrived at the High Court gates, nearly crashing into a large black Daimler in the process. The occupant, also pink—it was still a heatwave—turned and looked, eyebrows shooting up above his specs. For a moment, I didn't recognise him. Then I saw who it was: David Hirst without his wig. I brushed hair out of my eyes and gave him a little smile as he swept silently past and found myself giggling as I locked the bike to the railings—inside the courtyard, after a bit of argy-bargy with the gate-keeper. I think he gave me permission because he saw Hirst giving me a discreet but regal flutter of the fingers as he went past. So much for the sober citizen Wilmers had hoped for, I was now a delivery boy.

Today it's calm and cool in St Anselm and St Cecilia's. Just being here reduces my worries to dry autumn leaves floating to the floor. It's a Catholic church, but I don't suppose they mind a non-believer for a change. I have quite a little conversation with Him/Her while I'm there.

I list what's on the plus side:

1) I'm telling the truth.

2) I trust the judge. He must have formed a solid opinion of me by now, for better or worse.

3) *Help!*

He looks serenely over my head as I sit in the rear stalls—sorry, pews. This isn't a suffering Jesus, thank goodness, it's a contemplative one. Unless it's St Anselm? Whoever it is, it works. My breathing gets deeper and slower, my pulse steadies and gives up trying to burst out of my skin.

I'd better go. I'd like to stay and hide.

'Thank You, whoever You are. I'll do my best,' I promise Him.

Wilmers gets to his feet, gives me a long steady look. In him I trust. *Please don't let Hirst think I'm mad.*

'Miss Leventon, do you recall a lunch with Miss Raines?'

'Yes.'

'Did you tell her at this lunch you would show no mercy to Mr Schuman?'

'Not at all. I told her I was mystified by the situation and wished to repair the rift between Howard and me.'

'Is it true you have fallen out with your brother?'

'Certainly not. I've always been extremely close to both my brothers.'

'Thank you. Could you clarify the incident regarding the Oxford Playhouse Theatre and Miss Raines' songs?'

'Yes. I knew she was a lyricist, Rock Bottom sang one of her songs, *Dirty Rat*, for which Don wrote the music. There was another one, also by them, *Get Your Mind Off Morning*, which I've sung solo. The conversation with the Oxford Playhouse was in connection with a revue they'd asked me to compile and direct. I put her name forward as a possible lyricist. I thought I was doing her a favour.'

'I now turn to the meeting Miss Raines refers to that took place in Devonshire Place, some time in 1975. Did that chance meeting take place?'

I pause.

'Yes.'

'Would you elaborate, please?'

'I bumped into her one day near her flat.'

'And what were you doing in Devonshire Place?'

'I had an appointment with a therapist.'

There. It's said. I wait for a thunderbolt to strike.

'In what context?'

'I had some problems I needed help with. I was recommended to a therapist called Norah Moore, whose rooms were above the Jungian Society premises. I saw her once or twice a week for a while till I'd resolved the issues and understood myself better.'

'Were you referred by your GP?'

'No.'

'Were you in psychological distress?'

I hesitate. 'More mental conflict, I think, about my career.'

'Did you go of your own free will?'

'Yes, it was entirely my idea.'

'Thank you, Miss Leventon.'

So far, so bearable. John has the nicest, steadiest voice and gaze. I don't dare look at Hirst. Up sweeps Harman to eat me alive. He ignores the irrelevant bits and goes straight for the jugular.

'I put it to you, Miss—ah—Leventon, that, far from being the stable personality you choose to adopt in this court, you are in fact a paranoid schizophrenic with—'

A sudden bark of laughter interrupts him. It's Johnny in the public gallery, his face a picture of incredulity.

'Quiet, please,' mutters Hirst, peering at the newcomer. I catch Gaye's eye. She's got a hand over her mouth. I can't tell if it's surprise or consternation. She knows Johnny's laugh, that's for sure.

'I repeat, Miss—ah—Leventon, that you are a paranoid schizophrenic, with delusions of having dreamt up *Rock Follies* yourself, delusions so powerful that your fellow group members came to believe you as well.'

'I'm sorry, Mr Harman,' I reply, 'I can't really offer an opinion on that. If I were that deluded, I wouldn't know about it, would I? As for Gaye and Don and Di, you'll have to ask them, since it was originally Don's idea to make a television series based on the three of us. I've never deluded myself about that, why would I want to lay claim to it now?'

'I'll ask the questions, if you don't mind,' snaps Harman.

There's a pause while he shuffles papers.

'No more questions.'

Someone titters. It's not me. I just want to be released.

August, 1982

The court's in recess. Two whole months before we start again. Hirst has been so intelligent, so human, so focussed. Nothing has passed him by. We're in safe hands. I know it doesn't mean he can find for us, the law isn't like that. He might believe every word we say and still we might not win because of a technicality or precedent. I want to write and tell him how grateful I am that he's heard me, whether he finds for us or not. I want to thank him.

Keith is horrified. I mustn't make contact of any kind.

'I know that, Keith,' I say. 'I wouldn't do it, really. Just wish I could.'

The summer, looking like a big blank, turns out to be eventful. John Wilmers goes to Hong Kong or wherever he's booked, and won't be back. Nick Strauss is preparing to take over and can't discuss anything, he's going to have to do the summing up. *Windy City* finds a theatre in the West End and comes in to town, so Di'll be able to sit in court sometimes now she's not on the road. She's still commuting from home in Hampshire, quite far enough if you're doing eight shows a week. But there's a chance of seeing her a little more.

Best of all, *Rocket To The Moon* opens to rave reviews at Hampstead Theatre. There's talk of a West End transfer, which then becomes fact. The Apollo Theatre in Shaftesbury Avenue might be my second home for the autumn and even longer. That's tempting enough. Then my agent calls.

'The Royal Court have asked for you. It's a new play, *Carol, Sue and Bob Too*. Interested?'

I've never worked at the Royal Court. Naturally it conflicts with the West End transfer. I waver between the two. Hampstead are offering me good money, while the Royal Court is prestigious. A new play is always interesting. It's for their Young Writers' Festival. I don't know which to choose.

One night after the show, Harold Pinter, on the board of Hampstead Theatre, tries to get me to commit to the transfer. He's as awe-inspiring as they get. It's hard to take in what he says, something like: 'I hear you're not sure about going in with this. You must. This is a great team, you're essential to it, a crucial part of its success. I urge you to accept.'

I admire his plays so much, I'm flattered by his attention

and make a fool of myself trying to make him laugh. He's not in merry mood, he wants to convince me to stay. He keeps jokes for his plays, I suppose. I keep trying till Antonia Fraser bears down upon us, giving me a gracious smile tinged with a hint of menace, and wafts him away.

What a lovely dilemma to have—West End or Royal Court.

Kate, my agent, thinks I should do the Royal Court. 'Everyone's been to see you at Hampstead. You got great reviews. No point going to the West End just for the sake of it.'

'I suppose you're right,' I say, with some reluctance. I don't like crossing agents, it can be too painful.

'More prestigious to go straight on to the Royal Court.'

She doesn't know how stressed I am. Or how poor.

'Of course,' she adds as an afterthought, 'you might really need the money.'

I do. I really do. This case has been a long, long haul. My back's playing up after weeks of sitting rigid with tension on a hard wooden bench listening as intently as I've ever listened in my whole life. I'm tired. I'd like to take things easier for a little, do a part I already know well and earn some proper money for a change.

'Well,' she says, a day or two later, 'Your hesitation has been very productive. Hampstead have upped the money and offered to put your name in lights.'

'Goodness. Have they? You sure?'

'Yes. Above the title, same size as Mary and David and just below them. They must want you very badly, darling.'

They must. I decide to go to the Apollo. A little bit of security at this point would be so, so welcome.

I haven't been in the West End for nearly three years, five if I don't count *Elvis*. Since that was rock'n'roll in a converted cinema, I'm not really sure if I should, the Olivier Award for the show doesn't prove anything. Since *Spokesong* at the Vaudeville, then. Five years since I had a dressing-room of my own and my name up in lights. The Apollo is a beautiful, small Edwardian theatre, deep red plush seats, absurd decoration all over the auditorium, only eight hundred seats. The acoustics are perfect, it won't be much of a stretch expanding *Rocket To The Moon* from the little two-hundred-seat portacabin on the Finchley Road to this exquisite jewel.

I walk round from the stage door to the front of the theatre.

Annabel Leventon in lights above the title, just as they promised. And spelt right. Wow.

In complete contrast to the front of house, backstage is a proper working environment, neither glamorous nor posh. The stage-door keeper in a cramped, stuffy apology for a cupboard, dingy, cracked ceramic tiles on the floor leading to staircases up to the dressing-rooms and down to the stage. I look at the dressing-room list. Strict hierarchy prevails in the theatre, like the army, so I'm surprised to find that the two adjoining dressing-rooms on the ground floor have been given to Mary Maddox and me. We keep the door open between us. In no time it turns into the after-show party room. Deep red plush here too with worn red carpet, real furniture in both rooms—a bed, a dressing table, a basin, a fridge. What luxury after the narrow corridor for the whole company at Hampstead, a flimsy curtain between men and women. Mary and I settle in to enjoy the run, however short or long it might be.

October, 1982

We're still running in October, when court resumes. Counsels to sum up, then the judge to pronounce judgement. This bit is technical, with case after case cited, for and against, on both breach of contract and breach of confidence. I try to listen, but Harman isn't an easy man to listen to. On our side, Nick Strauss comes into his own. Here's where his competence, dedication and hard work shine. He knows the case backwards and has prepared in awesome detail, but he speaks very quietly, clearing his throat and looking miserable when Hirst rather irritably asks him to speak up.

GB and I, now sitting further back in the court as we're no longer about to go into the witness box, listen for hours to what sounds like gobbledegook: Copinger and Skone-James on copyright, paragraph xxx, Moore v Edwards (1903), Sutton Vane v Famous Film Co Ltd (1928), Gilbert against Star Newspapers 1894).

'Sounds like the cast of an Ealing Comedy,' GB hisses.

'Or a *Carry On* film.'

We start casting it: Sid James as the hero Sutton Vane, Jim Dale as Skone-James the cook, Kenneth Williams as Moore V. Edwards, Di as Barbara Windsor. Keith turns round, frowning, to find us crying with laughter.

We grip hands enough to hurt and get our faces straight.

Gilbert v Star, 1898, turns out to be W. S. Gilbert of Gilbert and Sullivan fame.

'Gilbert O'Sullivan!' I write. We grit our teeth. Mustn't get hysterical and upset Keith. Or anyone else for that matter, especially Hirst. But once we've tuned in to absurdity, it's hard to take it seriously.

Ex parte injunction, communication of information, theatrical profession, law of confidence. The words in between get lost, the meaning beyond us. The law has taken over. Hour after hour, first one then the other gets up, hitches a gown, adjusts a wig, and reads from copious notes. Confidential information … relating to plot of opera … rely upon Prince Albert v Strange, (1849).

'Prince Albert's v. v strange, Queen Victoria says,' I write. Off we go, helpless again.

My ears prick up when Jeremiah Harman cites an Australian case: a film producer, an idea for a television series, the idea used by defendants, injunction taken out.

'Just what I tried to do,' I whisper to GB.

The judge found in favour of the plaintiff.

'That what he said? In favour of the plaintiff?'

'Not sure. I think so,' GB mutters.

I drop a note to Keith. *Yes*, he writes back.

Now we lean forward, no jokes, trying to piece it together. Snatches of phrases: information of a confidential … something … something … communicated … in circumstances … importing … unauthorized … use of … cases cited … Harman reads it all out interminably, till finally he says something that brings us right down with a bump. 'The material included … a substantial written submission.'

Just what we didn't do. Nothing at all was what we wrote.

'It's not the point,' says Keith, in the break. 'Written submissions constitute copyright. Confidence is something else. You know that by now.'

When Nick gets up, he cites just as many cases as Harman. Maybe more. It feels endless. I start to long for my rest before the show. He talks about the same Australian case, and also a whole list of others—Saltman, Marshall, Seager ('Pete Seeger?' we mutter), Copydex, Cocoa.

It takes over two days for all the submissions to be delivered.

Hirst will now retire to consider his judgement. He gathers his files and papers together, puts his pens away, looks up.

'I should like to draw attention,' he says in a precise, deliberate voice, 'to the exemplary way in which this case has been drawn up. The solicitor in charge should take note of how grateful I am for his excellent work.'

Keith's face burns a deep red. He drops his head to hide it. Reverts to his real age all of a sudden. I'd forgotten he's only twenty-five.

All rise.

Hirst gets up and walks out. No particular climax, it not being theatre.

We crowd round Keith, patting his shoulder, teasing him.

'Do you have any idea,' asks Nick, 'how rare that is? Praise from a High Court judge? It's unheard of. Keith has done exceptional work.'

We insist on buying him a drink.

'How long before the judgement?' I ask.

'How long is a piece of string?' Keith counters. 'When Hirst's good and ready.'

It could be days, weeks or months?

'Yes.'

I go to the Apollo Theatre in a thoughtful mood.

17

Judgement Day

October, 1982

It could be the title of a thriller. *Waiting For Judgement.* If it weren't for *Rocket To The Moon*, I'd be biting my nails to the quick, spring-cleaning the house twice a day, walking the dog till her paws drop off. As it is, I do all of that a bit. Theatre keeps me semi-sane, requiring me to focus my nervous energy on the play for three hours a night, six on matinee days.

Oh, my God! Matinee days. Suppose David Hirst delivers his verdict on a matinee day?

I talk to Madeline Cemm, the understudy.

'Do you think you're ready to go on?'

She snorts. 'Don't be silly. I'm covering you *and* Mary. I've had no input at all. We never do. Mary's part is huge, I hardly know where to start. The company manager's given us the basic moves, that's all.'

'How would it be,' I say cautiously, 'How would it be if I worked with you so you know exactly what I do and why?'

I explain about the judgement.

'Then if they give me permission to take the day off, you'd be ready to go on for me?'

If they give permission. *If* it falls on a Thursday. If, if...

Madeline seizes the offer. I come in a couple of hours early every day and rehearse her till she's sure of every scene and I can

247

see she'll be able to carry it. Luckily she's an excellent actress. Then I go to the management and propose my plan.

'It's just in case,' I say. 'We don't know when or for how long. The solicitors think it could be a whole day. Or even two. And one of them might be a Thursday.'

'Ah,' they reply, 'but what if she's not up to it? It could ruin the show.'

'She's more than up to it,' I reply in perfect truth. 'I've worked with her every day till she is!'

It's a most unusual situation. There's no precedent. They think about it, then agree. Just the afternoon, though, I'll have to be back for the evening show, whatever state I'm in. I promise.

I warn the actors. 'It's so unlikely. But just in case. Would you mind?'

'Go for it,' they say.

In the dressing-room, Mary teases me. 'Talk about braces and belt, Annabel. You do believe in crossing your t's and dotting your i's, don't you? I've never known anyone so cautious.'

'I might as well have all options covered. It means too much,' I say. 'I expect you think I'm daft.'

'Oh no, darling,' she says, giving me a little hug. 'I'd want to be there myself. You are so funny, that's all. You make me laugh.'

'My life's ambition,' I say, 'making people laugh.'

Day after day of suspended animation. One morning, Johnny comes running, a copy of *The Times* in his hand.

'Annie! Look! Isn't this your mate?'

It's a photo of Verity Lambert, dark and smiling and strong, a woman at the top of her game. She's just been made Business Woman of the Year.

My mate…

Next day, Keith rings.

'Judgement. It's tomorrow.'

Matinee day. I knew it. I call the management and they release me for the day.

'Don't forget the evening show! You're not wriggling out of that,' the cast remind me in the evening, dropping good luck cards in to my dressing-room as they leave: 'Good luck. We'll be thinking of you. *Merde*. Fingers crossed for a triumph. Whichever way it goes, we're proud of you.' Hugs from everyone, even the stage-door keeper. Peter Kelly brings a little bunch of flowers, Mary puts a bottle in the fridge.

'For tomorrow,' she says. 'To celebrate. Or help you drown your sorrows.'

I'm overwhelmed.

Thursday, October 21, 1982

In a dream, I walk the dog.

'I'll do that,' says Johnny.

It's more than generous, he's been up working since three am.

I shake my head. 'It's okay. I'm awake.'

'I bet you are.'

Hyde Park is full of dry leaves hurtling in the breeze, squirrels out in force. Smudge charges in pursuit of both. Yellows and browns and russets, crisp against the clear, clean blue of a perfect autumn morning, the Serpentine a deeper blue beneath. I hunch against the morning chill. Frost-edged leaves crunch underfoot. It's my sister's birthday, I realise, too late to send a card. Damn. Too wrapped up in myself, as usual. I kick piles of leaves, throw bread for the ducks, race Smudge up to the statue of *Physical Energy* and back, part of the real world for an hour. It's a little misty, maybe my contact lenses. I blink and squeeze and yawn to make tears come and clean them, but my eyes stay stinging and blurred.

Along Kingsway, grey wisps float in front of my face as I hurry past St Anselm and St Cecilia. No time to look in today, I need to clean my lenses again. That'll take some time. Maybe I don't want to see too clearly. Today we'll know the worst. At least it'll be over, one way or the other.

'Don't expect too much,' Keith warns me. 'There's no knowing what conclusion he's reached.'

'Can't you tell at all?'

'No.'

Through the stone arch, down the hallway, up the stairs, along the corridor. My footsteps echo, chiming sharp against the tiled floor, then the stone stairs, then the polished wood, cutting through the hush of conversations in corners, snatches of voices in reply. Black gowns swish past, like exam day at Oxford, or Dickens's *Bleak House*. My heart gallops, sucking my breath in gulps, battering against my ribs. Small details leap out at me: Don's grown his moustache back, his hairline has receded, he's going grey. Nick is pale. He gives me a wintry smile and a peck on the cheek. Keith looks grim. That's normal, I remind myself, it doesn't mean bad news. Not necessarily. Our small band stays close together near the double doors. GB is resplendent. All her chains gleam and jangle, her auburn hair freshly cut and shaped and glossy, the kohl round her eyes making them piercing and dark. Don wears his C & A blazer with a white shirt and tie and proper trousers with a crease. Scuffed shoes, though. No sign of Di.

'She'll show up. Probably just in time for the verdict. After her matinee.'

Poor Di. She didn't get the time off, then.

The double doors swing open majestically. We file in and take our places. The same smell of wood polish hits me. My back remembers the unforgiving wooden bench.

'Why the fuck did we never bring cushions?' Gaye murmurs. 'What idiots.'

Why didn't I leave time for a quiet moment with St Anselm and St Cecilia on my way here?

All rise!

Mr Justice Hirst, in his scarlet and black, his big glasses and his portly tummy, bustles across to his bench. Gordon stands respectfully to the side in his perfect grey suit and immaculate silver hair, looking self-deprecating and at the same time, somehow noble. Gaye nudges me sharply in the ribs.

'Last chance to pull, duckie. Better get on with it.'

I have my notebook and pen. I know there's no need. I just want to retain some of what he says.

Hirst settles himself, opens his folder, checks he has water, looks solemnly round the whole room. Someone stumbles onto the visitors' bench. Hirst watches and waits for silence and attention.

From our bench, he has it. The most complete attention.

Finally, satisfied, he looks down at his file and begins to speak.

'In this action, the plaintiffs claim damages and other relief against the first defendants for breach of contract, and against all three defendants for breach of confidence. The present trial is limited to issues of liability.'

I put my pen down and clasp my hands together in my lap. Pretend I'm at school and teacher's reading a nice story. Once upon a time...

It's so clear. First he outlines the basis of the case: origination and development of, rights in relation to... *Rock Follies*.

Then he names the four plaintiffs and the group we formed, Rock Bottom.

He gives a brief sketch of each of us, our background, our education, up to Don and me living together, the abortion a small, dry fact mentioned in passing.

He gives an equally succinct sketch of Thames, Verity, Howard and Andrew and outlines the conflicts of fact to be resolved after hearing evidence over eight weeks. Numerous, deep, contentious and bitter conflicts, he calls them. So precise. It doesn't point in any direction, for or against us, but it is so accurate. It pierces the struggling butterfly straight through the heart.

Now we're pinned fast, he gives us a framework of the facts and the issues at stake. Equally forensic: abortion, distress, new focus, all-girl group, Don composer, me, GB and Di as performers, name of group, aims and objectives—the Master Gruppenplan. We used to do this in 'A' level English: *summarise the plot of the novel, outline the main characters and themes. Discuss. Hand in by Tuesday*. He would have come top of the class. I see him as a sixth-former at Watford Girls' Grammar School, in a navy pleated skirt and yellow-and-navy striped tie, and want to tell Gaye.

I'm aware of my hands relaxing their iron clasp, my heart rate quietened from a tumultuous clamour to a steady beat, loud but not intrusive. My eyes have cleared. I feel GB's back, ramrod next to mine. This man has total command: the extent to which the idea was formulated, its degree of novelty, the nature and format of the projected series are in dispute. He lays bare the spine of it with a scientist's detached clarity: *Verité*, our meeting with Howard, Jack and Maureen, Howard as possible writer, demos, Polydor, RCA. Then the meetings between Verity, Andrew and Howard, the first Rock Bottom concert, with Verity attending 'to audition' us three girls, all through the crucial meetings, the lunch with Howard, his commission for the pilot, the meeting with Thames to discuss the idea, the letter of agreement, the dispute as to its meaning, the agreement between Thames and Stella Richman Ltd to share royalties, the pilot script, the option renewed, *A Little Night Music*, the breakdown, the three replacement actresses, the success of *Rock Follies*. The 'remarkable circumstances' under which Andrew and Howard and Howard's agent Jenne Casarotto tried to sign the new actresses up to manage them as a group outside *Rock Follies*. The main characters—Anna, Q, Dee and Henry Hyper Huggins and their relation to us, if any. Incidents in the plot, ditto. The origin of the idea. The possible breach of contract with Thames, the case in confidence, the denial. The writ.

All laid out clean, ordered, clear, waiting to be dissected.

Hirst pauses, picks up his glass of water, glances at the clock, drinks. Gordon leans forward to refill his glass. He's been going for over an hour, steady, measured, noncommittal. I have no idea what his views are. I can't tell which side, if any, he favours over the other. If it weren't so scary, I'd be fascinated. I *am* fascinated.

GB nudges me. 'Okay, Annie?'

I nod and squeeze her hand. 'Okay.'

Out of all he's said so far, one phrase leaps out at me: the 're-markable circumstances' of Howard and Andrew trying to manage the three new girls as a group. A tiny indicator of his view. But it might only relate to that one small incident. He might disapprove of that and still find for them in everything else. He might believe us totally or in part, and not be able to find for us because of how the law stands. The atmosphere in court is cool, aloof. No need for you to get excited, it implies, we've seen them all come and go, bigger, meatier and more complex. You just sit there and wait till he delivers.

Hirst takes another sip and starts again.

'It will be seen that... following issues... to be decided: who had the original idea? Who knew its authorship? The Rock Bottom contract and its reinstatement, the *Little Night Music* problem, how much of the Rock Bottom idea was in *Rock Follies*? ... My findings of fact turn on credibility of witnesses.'

Oh dear. Here we go. It's crunch time. Me and my jokes and rudeness to Harman, my paranoid schizophrenia, Don's stuttering, Gaye's big mouth, Di's showgirl performance.

'Plaintiffs impressive and convincing.'

Oh. I sit a little taller.

'Particularly Miss Leventon, the most powerful character and key witness... honesty of purpose and high quality of...' something-or-other.

GB elbows me. 'Best review you'll ever have,' she writes and shoves it under my nose.

My cheeks burn. I should have had my pen ready. Those are words to treasure.

Too late. He passes on, stately as a galleon: Howard and Andrew are 'unimpressive and untrustworthy', Verity 'unconvincing'.

I can't resist. 'And Businesswoman of the Year!' I scribble to GB.

'Now for my detailed findings.' About our idea for a series, based on our lives and careers, the interrelationships of our distinct characters, both biographical and fictional, about us individually and together…

I can't write and listen. I send a note to Keith: 'You doing notes?' He writes back, 'We'll get a copy of the whole thing.'

Hirst quotes Di's graphic reference to us as 'a bag of Dolly Mixtures' to show the differences in our characters and qualities. I manage to get that down, Di'll be pleased to know he quoted her. He talks about Jack Rosenthal and Maureen Lipman as 'most impressive witnesses', Jack calling our idea very original with a clear and specific format, part fact and part fiction, the originality being that of 'three established actresses with talents and interesting private lives' forming a pop group, creating a different image from their off-stage selves. I get that down all right.

He quotes Maureen saying the idea was excellent and totally original, not so much the jungle of the entertainment world but our journey *through* the jungle. I get that down, too. He mentions two other witnesses in the entertainment industry, Alan Sizer from RCA and my pal Tony Edwards of Purple Records, both of whom confirm the originality of the idea. All of them had heard the idea from Don and/or me. Hirst accepts their evidence. I know it doesn't mean we'll win, but it's so lovely to hear I could pinch myself. GB does it for me.

He says we *did* come up with the idea for a TV series, 'original and well-formed', with the unusual feature of a three-girl rock group where each girl was an established actress of 'wit and intelligence' with a life of her own.

GB nudges me as I write 'intelligence'. It comes out as 'integence'.

'That's it, then, isn't it?' she mutters.

Sharp-eared, Hirst glances up.

'Can't tell yet,' I write.

He continues through Howard's evidence—the idea for a three-girl rock group deriving from the Duck Sisters in *King Kong*, (*just two of them who don't sing rock and aren't actresses??*) plus Shirley from *Verité* as the third, (*a school teacher who doesn't sing, dance or act?*) the Busby Berkeley movies the springboard for making it a rock group (*since when were Busby Berkeley movies about rock?*).

I'm getting angry again when I hear, cutting through the red mist, 'I do not accept this evidence.'

Did I hear that right?

Same thing regarding his view of the close friendship we claim with Howard through this period, which Howard rejected as nebulous. The picture portrayed by us is more accurate, and as for the lunch when I talked to Howard about writing the series, Hirst has 'no hesitation' in accepting my version: I told Howard, not the other way round. On point after point he prefers our version—the 'marvellous, marvellous!' conversation with Andrew after the first concert, Howard getting upset when Brian Degas might ruin his plan, Don's evidence about Howard's list with the *Rock Bottom* series on it, our version of the lunch we all had with Howard, giving him permission to pitch the idea on our behalf. He believes all three defendants, Verity, Andrew and Howard, knew perfectly well it was our idea at the latest by July 7th, 1974. He accepts our version of the meeting at Thames with Verity, he refers to the wording of the Thames contract letter supporting it: 'if we *decide against*' doing the series. When he gets to Harman's submission about my being a paranoid schizophrenic obsessed with the series being my idea and how I'd convinced the girls, he brushes it aside as out of character.

By now, my back may be aching and my writing wrist locked, but this overwhelming support, time after time, is like a glass of brandy on an empty stomach. After this, I tell myself, it doesn't matter if he has to rule against us on everything. He believed me.

And he believes Don's version of the meeting with Howard when Howard outlined the four main characters as based on us. He believes him on the option renewal, on the asking for the script; he believes our version of the dinner with Howard about the script not arriving and *A Little Night Music*, that I never mentioned Di faking pregnancy to get out of the show. He believes my version of the meeting with Andrew, Don's version of the rows over *A Little Night Music*. There isn't a single point where he doesn't believe us. So far.

He calls Don thoroughly business-like in the Thames merchandising meetings, when the series was called *Rock Bottom*, that we had the rights to the name and that the merchandising arrangements were not those you'd make with mere actors. He accepts Don's version of Verity giving him an ultimatum to get Di out of *A Little Night Music* within a week. 'I accept Mr Fraser's account…I reject Miss Sadler's account…' Howard's evidence about me asking for help and then rejecting it ('classic self-destructive paranoia') is dismissed. He accepts Don's vivid account of the abuse hurled at him by Verity, Verity wanting the breakdown, Judy Raines motivated by ill-will.

He uses the word 'remarkable' again, about Howard and Andrew's plan to manage the three new girls as a group and how it places them both in a very poor light.

Then he says that completes the chronological sequence of events.

Lunch.

Tension stays high through the break. I don't speak to anyone much, I keep my head down. I think we all do. He has nothing good to say about any of them and nothing but good about us and still we don't know what he's going to rule. To have our hopes raised so high by everything he says and know we still may not win, makes it hard to eat, let alone talk. He hasn't even got to breach of contract or breach of confidence yet. That's what counts, I know. That's what we sued about, not whether we're good witnesses. We can still lose on every count. Maybe he's being nice about us because he knows he's got bad news and he's sweetening the pill. I give up any pretence of eating.

When Oscar shows up in the canteen, I'm surprised.

'What are you doing here?' I ask. 'We haven't seen you for weeks.'

He acts offended. 'You think I wouldn't get myself here for the result of a lifetime? This is our moment, my girl, don't you forget it!'

Of course it's only bravado, which is what Oscar does best, but so welcome I hug him.

The afternoon is more of the same. Hirst's precise vowels and clean sentences apply dry logic and common sense to the most convoluted details, stripping them of emotion, reducing complications down to their essence. The *Little Night Music* sequence of events and the rights and wrongs, then the use, if any, of our idea within *Rock Follies*. I hear him talking but not much sinks in. The bench keeps me upright or I think I'd fall over. All I catch of Di and *A Little Night Music* is that he's sympathetic to Don trying to sort things out in an impossible situation and Verity could, and should, have taken a hand to resolve it, but 'was not averse to a breakdown'. Don's efforts were 'summarily cut off' on May 12. I don't hear him draw a conclusion. Perhaps in my foggy state I missed it. I glance at Gaye. She looks glazed, too. I can't see beyond her to Don, but he'll be relieved by what he's heard.

Hirst moves on. Was the plaintiff's idea used in *Rock Follies*? Much praise for Howard's originality as a writer, his creativity, his imagination. The witnesses who recognised Rock Bottom in *Rock Follies*, Gaye's remark 'there we were and there we weren't'.

My brain re-engages at this, in time to hear him say, unequivocally, he sees the *Rock Follies* series, especially the first two episodes, as substantially based on Rock Bottom and our experiences.

All along the bench there's a stirring. Oscar fidgets importantly. Behind me, I glance back at Nick. He's leaning forward, his wig slightly awry, staring intently at Hirst. Keith sits still, dogged as ever. Hirst takes a breath, then a sip of water. I can't breathe.

'Consequently, I hold that *Rock Follies did* use the plaintiffs' idea. I now proceed to consider ... '

Oh, my God. He said something definite. Didn't he? I look at Gaye, her cheekbones shining, her eyes mischievous. Hope is clearly sparkling. Wrong, wrong, I want to say. Too soon. We don't know yet. She's in no doubt, though.

'The claim in contract,' Hirst says.

I never really understood this one anyway. Was the Thames letter a contract or not? Did it include Don or was it just the girls? Was the option renewed or not? Did they really offer us the parts or not? It's always been convoluted.

Not for Hirst. He unpicks it like a lace-maker, delicate, measured, detailed. Don as joint owner of the idea: was he party to the agreement on October 4? The course of the conversation, the understanding of the parties, terms of the letter, viewed in the light of... principles of law. Now he turns technical. All those cases referred to by Nick and Harman are picked over: Tudor Marine, Bickerton and Burrell, Rayner and Grote. When he mentions Schmaltz and Avery, it's almost too much. I bite my lip and look down, avoiding Gaye's eye. More, much more, of the same intricate details as to the rights and wrongs of the contract and its breakdown. Now we are speeding towards conclusion.

'I reject Mr Harman's contention.'

Mr Fraser 'doing his utmost to resolve ... '

Thames also at fault: 'I hold that the following breaches of contract were committed by Thames.'

'The use of the plaintiffs' idea a breach ... wrongful repudiation by Thames... to recast, make and screen the two series with new actresses... breaches of contract.'

What? Did he say all that? Does it mean we...? I touch Gaye's hand. It's freezing.

'The Claim in Confidence,' he continues.

Trite law, copyright, more cases, a well-known jockey, the Copyright Act of 1911. When Sutton Vane and Copydex, Prince Albert and Strange are mentioned again, they're old friends, we no longer need to laugh, we're on the home stretch, like the jockey. The lawyer in Hirst is addressing other lawyers, arguing for and against points in law that aren't yet clearly established. He pays particular attention to both sides' submissions, careful to appreciate every detail and nuance. The claim in confidence is clearly much more complex than the contract issue and there is no precedent for it. Of course he has to be careful. It's the issue Oscar seized on when we first went to see him, the one he thought was the really interesting part, the newsworthy part. The contract was thrown in later for good measure. No wonder he's in today. It was his idea really, all those years ago, breach of confidence.

'Never been done before,' he'd said, puffing his chest out. 'We'll get 'em on that. You'll see.'

By the sound of it, we won't. Reams and reams of cases and comparisons and arguments sifted through and analysed, Hirst pulling out a tiny fact here, an inference there, little morsels of information and deduction, like Sherlock Homes. Nobody can ever deduce what Holmes deduces. I'm Doctor Watson, way behind and struggling to catch up.

'What is an obligation of confidence?' I think he asks. Then answers it by relying upon three principles, or elements, agreed by both counsel, apparently, that:

1) The information is of a confidential nature,

2) It is communicated in circumstances importing an obligation of confidence,

3) Unauthorised use of the information will be to the detriment of the person who had communicated it in the first place.

He talks about the special twist, or slant, to an idea, its germ, the springboard for it. No reason in principle why an idea shouldn't qualify for protection under the law, if it meets certain criteria. It must be sufficiently developed as a concept to be attractive as a television programme, and must have some significant element of originality, the twist or slant.

He notes that every witness from television or theatre, on both sides, agreed it was morally wrong in their business to make use of someone's idea without permission. He states in the clearest voice that my communicating the idea to Howard on January 22, 1974, was clearly in confidence, and was in the nature of a professional occasion, we were jointly concerned commercially in the possible use of the idea, each having our separate role as actress and writer. Gaye and I grip hands.

'I hold that Mr Schuman owed an obligation of confidence in relation to the plaintiffs' idea.

'Mr Brown knew from Mr Schuman the idea was the plaintiffs' and imparted in confidence.

'He is therefore fixed with an obligation of confidence.'

Miss Lambert knew. 'Thames also are fixed with an obligation of confidence.'

Then he gathers himself together, sits upright and declares for all to hear:

'I hold that Mr Schuman was in breach of confidence...

'I hold that Mr Brown was in breach of confidence...

'I hold that Thames were in breach of confidence in using the idea, in making and screening the two *Rock Follies* series.

'There will be judgment for all four plaintiffs against Thames on their claim in contract.

'On the claim in confidence there will be judgment for all four plaintiffs against all three defendants.'

All rise.

For the last time, we stand for Mr Justice Hirst. Gordon ushers him out with a small nod to us and a hint of a smile. In a daze, we pick up jackets and handbags, notebooks and files, shake hands, kiss, hug, walk out through the double doors, along the corridor, down the stairs and along the big tiled hall past the disrobing rooms and the huge information board and out into the late afternoon sun angling straight into our eyes and a barrage of microphones thrust under our noses.

'You've made history, how does it feel?'

'What a victory, give us a smile!'

'Congratulations, girls. What's it like beating the big boys?'

How did they know? What are we to say? Keith, dear Keith, (or Oscar) has thought of that. He hands us a simple paragraph to read out: 'ordeal … years of heartbreak … relief … vindication'.

We are quite unable to formulate a sentence for ourselves. Di slides in beside us, all dressed up, fresh from her matinee.

'I'll kill you, Annie,' she hisses, smiling brilliantly for the cameras, 'How d'you get off your show? Don't have to ask the result, do I? One look at your faces!'

Posing for a stills camera always unnerves me. Ask me to smile and I'll freeze. Today, I can't stop, they can take as many as they like. I just wish I'd realised this might happen, I could have dressed better, got my hair done, made more of an effort. We line up in order as always, Di, me and Gaye. Then the four of us, we insist. Di, me, Gaye and Don, still in order of height. Our smiles are huge and genuine.

When I get to the Apollo that evening, there are messages of congratulation waiting. The show goes by in a dream. When the curtain comes down, the cast open a bottle of champagne on stage, David Burke leads a round of applause. 'You've done it. You've done it for everyone. It's a victory for all of us.'

I join Gaye, Di, Don, Jane, Keith, John Wilmers, Nick Strauss, Oscar, Niall Buggy, Susi Wooldridge, Johnny and I don't know who else, in Joe Allen, at a long table right down the middle of the restaurant. Maybe the others have been there all evening, I'm too confused to know. A feast with wine and song, breaking the rule that customers, however starry, are not allowed to sing. We sing at the tops of our voices, very loudly and very badly, with Don at the piano fumbling through songs we haven't even tried for eight years, till far into the night.

We won. We won. WE WON.

18

Aftermath

Relief, first of all, cascading, flooding relief. A High Court judge believed us. Keith says Thames can still challenge the ruling, we have to wait and see. If it goes through, there'll be another trial, this time for damages. Another judge in another trial altogether will decide how much we get in compensation. Gaye goes to Cornwall for three weeks with her boy Charley. I get the most wonderful, generous, funny letter from her. Her writing is so like her—spelling, punctuation, use of words, all unlike anyone else's. Huge, flowing writing, lots of exclamation marks, almost illegible, and, more than anything else, unmistakeable, uncompromising, take-it-or-leave-it *style*.

> *Dearest Annie, ...*
> *....well-----'It sure is great' ----I still cannot quite*
> *believe it is all over - at least the biggest part! I*
> *just wanted to write & say how great you've been*
> *& without your constant nagging and total belief*
> *we'd never have gotten thru it - the last two years*
> *have been easier but all those years of wilderness*
> *one never quite realised the enormity of what*
> *we were doing quite - and certainly not the*
> *importance of it all - looking back on the whole*
> *episode of Thames and V. L. it seemed all over before*
> *it began - I think mainly because of the fact that I*

was away during the actual saga - May 5th and
12th & didn't quite grasp the implications ----

I am so proud of us - & feel so confident now as
a person - as does Don & I trust you do - Die (sic) I
haven't doubted ever - but I was amazed to hear her
on Tuesday pm before the verdict say 'I'm scared doll'
and mean it - she's a canny one you know - doesn't
let much out to be seen - but in fact thinks about
things a great deal.

Suddenly - I realise we are now celebritys (sic)
amongst others - interesting eh? --and quite right! -

.... Take great care 'Miss Star Witness'! Lots of love,
Gaye B xx

I store it away as a treasured possession, along with letters of support and congratulations from Pamela Hay in Richard Pilbrow's *Little Night Music* office, Harry Waistnage, our designer friend, Joe Waters at the BBC and my ex-agent, witness and friend, Jean Diamond.

Slowly, slowly, the adrenalin drains away, leaving a very tired person with just enough energy to do *Rocket To The Moon* and walk the dog and not much else. When the show finally closes, I just walk the dog. Mary Maddox has a much deserved nomination as Actress of the Year. So has Julia MacKenzie for Miss Adelaide in *Guys and Dolls*, the other part I always wanted to play. For which I was shortlisted. It was between me and Julia. Julia got the part. Now she gets the award.

Johnny lets me heal in my own time. Linda La Plante and I meet in Hyde Park with our dogs. Hers is an enormous poodle called Harold. Our conversation eases day by day from the trials—past and future—of Rock Bottom, to the trials of fertility, IVF and even adoption. And show business for light relief.

'Always irritated me that Howard called it *The* Show Business,' I tell her.

'Pretentious rubbish, darling,' she says. Then she tells me of

an idea she's developing for television about a police detective—
a woman. 'Great part for you,' she says.

The judgement is registered very late. Thames are given time
to challenge it.

'Hard to see how they can,' Keith tells me. 'It can only be a
legal technicality.'

We keep our fingers crossed and our heads down.

The deadline comes and goes without incident, so we're free
to apply for a date for the next trial.

We have a choice: do we take the first available date with
whichever judge might be chosen, or do we wait till Mr Justice
Hirst is free? Di's show is running, so she's okay for money,
Don's earning, GB says she can cope, I know I can. Now the
trial's over, all I want to do is get pregnant. At nearly forty-one,
I'm being a bit optimistic, but Gaye did it at the same age, so who
knows?

We decide to play safe and wait for David Hirst, however
long that might take.

A date is fixed for June, 1983, a year after the first trial almost
to the day. This time it's about money, our characters are not
in question. A week before it's due, we're summoned into Mr
Wilmers' chambers. Or John as we now call him. He's become a
friend as well as a colleague.

He twinkles at us as we sit down.

'What I want for all you girls, and Don, is for you to be able
to buy a house each. After tax. That's my objective.'

I'm in the middle as usual, Gaye on my left, Di on my right,
with Don at the end. We do it without even noticing.

'There is an offer on the table, finally. A proper one,' says John.

'Left it a bit late, haven't they?'

'Now then, Annie,' says Gaye, 'Don't get on your high horse.'

John winks at me. Gaye has no malice, she knows me too
well. They both know I've been in fighting mode so long I can't
just stop. Not a week before court begins.

'It's all right, Annie, love,' says Di, patting my arm. 'Let's just find out what they're offering, why don't we? Might as well.'

Hmm. They're bastards. And their lawyers. They'll be up to something. Don looks at his nails. Very quiet, is Don.

'Okay. Sorry, all. Didn't mean to stop you, John.'

'Perfectly understood, m'dear. Shall I continue?'

We nod assent, obedient children all in a row. In here we're not much more than that.

'Keith and I have been working for weeks now to save you going into court again.'

I jump in. 'But—'

'I know, Annabel, you've waited nearly a year for this. You held out for Hirst to hear this part as well. But you know the law is a blunt instrument. Things can go wrong. I don't want you to risk not getting the best deal. Settlement out of court is sometimes the best option. Listen to what's on offer, you can always refuse. However, in this instance, I am strongly advising you to accept. I don't believe the offer will improve. And it could be withdrawn completely.'

He raises his eyebrows and looks round for comprehension from each one of us in turn. I remind myself John's here to protect us and nod agreement. I trust him, I just don't want to be cheated again by Thames, or their lawyers.

'We have argued this on the basis of a) what you would have earned had you done both the *Rock Follies* series; b) what you earned as individuals while they were making the series; and c) compensation for loss of enhancement of career.'

He pauses, waits for comments. We've heard most of this in some form already.

'What you would have earned doing the series includes your fees as actresses, royalties from the albums, repeat fees on your performances, song-writing royalties. And fees for the composition of the music.'

Silence.

'What you *did* earn during the period they made Series One and Series Two will be deducted from this.'

Di stirs. 'You mean I got to hand back my money from *Little Night Music* and *Rag Trade*?'

Wilmers shakes his head. 'No, Di. They can't take any of that away. You earned it and were paid for it, weren't you?'

'Yeah, I was.'

'So don't worry. It's safe. But they'll only give you earnings from *Rock Follies* that go over what you earned then. Not as well.'

'Excuse me,' Di protests. 'That's not fair, John. I know I've been lucky, I've had loads of work, always have. Why should I be—'

'Better let me finish, Di. Then you'll see the whole picture.'

Di blows out her cheeks and subsides with reluctance. It's my turn to pat *her* arm. This isn't much fun, I'm with her on that.

'Right. Let's go on.'

Wilmers looks at his notes. His desk is large and mahogany and covered with papers, files, blotting paper and photos of his wife and children. Behind him, the trees in the Middle Temple courtyard are fully green, their swaying branches celebrating the beginning of summer.

'The first amount on offer is for breach of contract. Next point: loss of enhancement of career. We have fought long and hard for this. We regard these two series of *Rock Follies* as the greatest opportunity of your careers, collectively and as individuals. Simply getting performance fees is wholly inadequate. *Rock Follies*, or as it was originally called, *Rock Bottom*, would have established you to at least the same level as it did the three girls who replaced you and almost certainly much, much higher, as you are the originals, a group already operating together and well on the way to success. The opportunities from the exposure that would have arisen for you, as individuals and also as a group, were denied you. This is where we have negotiated so hard. It is a loss you share equally. Compensation for this is therefore to be shared equally.'

Silence again. Don shifts in his seat and says nothing. Even with Di between us I can feel his tension, I know him too well. 'Let it go, Annie,' advises Gaye every so often, when I can't bear the proximity, 'there's now't you can do, darling. Just get on with your life.'

Everyone says it. Move on, let go. I try.

'So now we come to the nub of it.'

Wilmers shuffles papers, clears his throat, fixes us with his most piercing gaze.

'This is what Thames are offering.'

We suck in our collective breath. Gaye squeezes my hand. I squeeze back. Di's eyelashes quiver with shock. *How* much??? All our legal costs paid? I can't begin to take it in. Before we get over-excited, however, Wilmers, has more to say.

'They say it is to be divided as follows: Di, because of her greater earnings during this period and because she didn't contribute to the song-writing, gets the smaller portion. Gaye gets more, as she earned less than Di and made a contribution to the song-writing. Annabel, because you made a larger contribution in terms of song-writing and earned less than either of the other two from your acting during the period in question, you get more still. And Don, although you would have earned no fees for acting, obviously, you would have expected to make a major contribution in terms of composing and song-writing, so you are offered the lion's share.'

My God, does he have our entire attention now. When he tells us the individual amounts, I feel my blood draining away from my head. I try to work it out. Don's been offered over a third? No, more, my maths is rubbish. Closer to a half. Almost twice my figure, well over double Di's.

'No, no, no!' someone yells. 'We're supposed to be equal. We agreed it. We put it in writing. We said everything that came to us as a group would be shared equally between us. This is divide and rule. I'm not having it. It sucks. It's horrible.'

Gaye and Di have to hold me down. I'm shaking with fury. I

can't stop. 'They can't do this to us. If we all stick together, we can go back into court. David Hirst will look after us as he did last year. I won't have this!'

Wilmers waits while I blow my nose and hurl the Kleenex into the waste basket.

'What does anyone else think?'

We'd never thought about the money. At least I never did. I wanted justice. GB and Di flounder. Now money's on the table, and in large amounts, they're clearly torn. We held out so long. It'll drive a wedge between us. It's unfair.

Don clears his throat, raises a nicotined forefinger: 'Um. Can I say something?'

The hubbub dies away.

'Um, we never said we'd share composing or acting fees. Or royalties for song-writing. Only what we'd contributed, song by song. I'm going to accept.'

I raise my head and turn very slowly to look him in the face, for the first time in seven years. He doesn't look back.

I think I'm about to be sick. 'Then we'll go on without you.'

Even to my ears it sounds pathetic.

Wilmers is practical. 'Don has made his decision. Perhaps the three of you would like to retire to consider what is best for you?'

His sympathetic tone almost undoes me.

On the staircase outside his rooms, we argue.

'Annie's right. It's unfair.'

'Never mind unfair. I've got bills to pay. I need a new car, Charley needs new shoes, I haven't paid the nanny in six weeks.'

'I could kill him. If we all stick together, we could—'

'Annie, Wilmers says we couldn't. He said—'

'Since when have you taken any notice of what he says? Don's betrayed us.'

I brush my hand over my eyes.

Di pats my arm again. 'Must be hard for you, Annie, havin'

him do that. But maybe this is the best we can do. I don't want to go back to court, and that's God's truth. I don't want to go through all that again. Maybe lose what we got.'

Nor do I. We'd look like damn fools, just the three of us. How could we ever be taken seriously as a partnership when one quarter of it has taken the bait? The strength of our whole case has just been destroyed.

'Got it, girls!' Gaye suddenly exclaims.

We shush her, they'll hear her through the door. She ignores us. 'This'll do it! We take what they offer. Say yes, thank you, stash the lolly in the bank and make Don pay for the party!'

'What party?'

'*Our* party—to celebrate winning. We'll take L'Escargot. Elena can shut it for the night. We'll invite everyone who's helped us.'

I blow my nose again. 'All the witnesses? And the lawyers? And—and—everyone?'

'That's right, Annie, darling. A stonking great party.'

'And that's how we can thank everyone?'

'You bet. Invite Howard if you want.'

'Fuck that! Are you crazy?'

We laugh, a team again.

I'm restored. 'Okay, girls, let's go!'

We troop back in. 'Okay,' I announce. 'We accept. On one condition.'

'Which is?' asks Wilmers, looking at my happy face with some curiosity.

'We have a huge celebration party. And Don can pay for it all.'

Wilmers' mouth twitches. He turns to Don. 'Don?'

In the pause that follows, I understand something new about Don.

Wilmers waits, eyebrows raised. 'Well, Don, is that acceptable?'

Don's Adam's apple bobs up and down. I suddenly remember

when he first shaved his moustache off, years ago, when we were together. He looked just like this, vulnerable and defenceless. He swallows again and in a low voice says, 'Erm. Okay. A deal.'

I feel almost sorry for him.

Almost.

> *You can have anything you want,*
> *You can have anything you please*
> *(Fraser)*

The money's on its way. We've done it, we got there. It feels very strange and very wonderful.

Till a small glitch appears, one I hadn't anticipated.

Keith calls. 'You saw the piece in *The Observer*?'

'Hi, Keith. Yes, I did. The piece by Janet Watts? She's a friend of mine. I only gave her our prepared statement. I suppose that's allowed?'

Keith sounds a bit stressed. 'This is quite tricky, you know. You've got to be careful.'

'You mean I shouldn't have spoken to her at all?'

He pauses. 'If you want to protect your tax position, you ought to keep your mouths shut from now on.'

'Keith,' I protest, 'it seems so harsh. For years nobody wanted to know. Now they all do—and I want to tell them!'

'It's a condition, you know that.'

He's right, of course.

'What's the worst that can happen, then? Do you mind explaining again?'

Keith is blunt. He's always blunt. 'You agreed it. All of you.'

'Just run it past me. I was too relieved about everything else to take it on board.'

I hear him sigh. He explains it all once again. The agreement the lawyers made to protect our money, protect Thames's reputation. This time it starts to sink in. It's not pleasant. I call GB.

'Darling, did you get all this?'

'Oh, who cares, as long as we keep as much dosh as possible from the damned tax man?'

'I care,' I say. 'Janet Watts wants to do an exclusive article on us and the case and I have to turn her down.'

'Who she?'

'You remember, my journalist friend from Oxford, the one who did the piece in *The Observer*?'

'Oh, that. I only get *The Sunday Times*. Picture of us and them, wasn't it?'

'That's right. She's dying for me to give her the lowdown on the whole thing.'

'And? Sorry, Annie, just a minute!'—*(shouting)*—'Charley! stop that! I've told you once.'

'The thing is GB, it's not written down anywhere.'

'What isn't?'

'It's a sort of gentleman's agreement the lawyers made. They've said seventy-five percent of our award is tax free as it'll be called loss of enhancement of career.'

'What's wrong with that?'

'They'll go back on it if we talk to the press.'

'I hate the bloody press,' says Gaye with vehemence. 'One of them called on me at seven am last Sunday. I'm not having it.'

'Just as long as you don't ever, *ever* give them my number again.'

'I had to, Annie, he was driving me mad.'

'It's a rule. No actor ever gives out another actor's private number. You know that!'

'Oh come on, Annie. I had to do something. You're turning into a paranoid schizophrenic, ha ha!'

'Ha very bloody ha! Thanks a bunch, you old bag.'

'See you Sunday, Bird's Egg. You bring the pudding and tell Johnny to bring some wine.'

She's no help. No point contacting Di. I take some comfort

from the other condition we asked for, the one that *was* written down. From now on, if any episode or part of *Rock Follies* is shown anywhere in the world, they have to add a line at the end saying: '*Based on an idea by Gaye Brown, Annabel Leventon and Diane Langton*'. Not that we'll ever get to see it. Thames will never expose the story that way. It's lovely to know, though. *Based on an idea by...* Lovely.

A cheque for £50,000 arrives. Johnny takes a photocopy of it and we frame it. It's the first tranche.

'I've bought a house, Annie!' GB announces. 'Balham, gateway to the south. Tantallon Road. Come and see.'

I put the money in the bank and ask them to invest it for me on a weekly basis till I work out what to do. My bank manager's faith in me has paid off. When I was a drama student, I opened an account with Williams Deacons, Belgravia.

'I'll introduce you to Mr Skillern, the bank manager,' my aunt said. 'I've banked with them for years, he'll look after you.'

She was right. Mr Skillern looked after me for nearly twenty years. Once a year he took me out to lunch, as if I were a major shareholder. A proper lunch in a nice restaurant.

'Mr Skillern, this is so good of you,' I say every time. 'I only give you headaches.'

'You stay in the black, my dear. How can that be a headache?'

'Yes, but there's never more than a few pounds in there. I'm a lousy client.'

One day, he folds his napkin and replies, 'My dear Miss Leventon, I don't think you understand. I have faith in you. This is in the nature of an investment. One day, when you are extremely successful, you will repay me by putting the money into your account here.'

I remember beaming. It was ridiculous, of course, to think I'd ever earn money like that. But it was so touching, I wanted to believe.

Now his faith in me has paid off. Of course I don't hesitate. Skillern's retired, Williams Deacon's was swallowed up by Williams and Glynn's and will shortly become The Royal Bank of Scotland. Straight into his branch goes my money. They put it on bid deposit, whatever that means, earning 15% some weeks. Now I see how the rich get richer: I do nothing and my money goes on growing.

We're rich, or will be very soon. Rich enough to buy a house, just as Wilmers wanted. All my life I've lived in rented accommodation. Johnny's tiny house in Chelsea was his grandfather's shop. We borrowed the money from Mr Skillern to convert the shop into a live-in kitchen. Johnny still runs his newspaper delivery service from the cellar. There's a trap door in the middle of the floor to chuck the newspaper bundles in at three am. Someone fell down it one day. Not ideal, really.

To my amazement, Don asks me to record a jingle, on a barge in Little Venice converted into a recording studio by someone called Richard Branson. In the control room there are magazines for when you're hanging around waiting for the next bit, like at the dentists. The magazines are similar, too.

'Got something to show you,' says Don. He opens a copy of *Country Life* at a well-thumbed page. 'Look.'

He points to a photo. A beautiful country cottage. 'Elgar's studio. I'm buying it.'

I'm dumbfounded. He's moving out of London? It's almost on the coast, beyond Petworth.

'Well, that'll be a change from W14,' I venture.

Is he moving there with Jane?

'Keeping West Ken Mansions, obviously,' he says, closing *Country Life* and putting it back on the coffee table. 'This'll be where I do my composing. Like Elgar.'

I don't know what to say.

Two weeks before the Rock Bottom party, I have a test. They

squirt ink up inside me to see if it can get through my fallopian tubes, which should be nice and open after my operation last year. That's what the surgery was supposed to achieve.

'Go and see my gynaecologist,' said Lynda La Plante, who knows about these things. 'Get it checked out.'

Both tubes are blocked. I can't ever, ever get pregnant.

'I'm the last woman of my generation to have a baby, Annie!' Gaye crowed when we visited her and the new baby at Queen Charlotte's, the week I left The Royal Free Hospital after tubal surgery. I was about to be thirty-nine, only a year younger than Gaye. Now she's a mother and has a house as well.

Di already has a house and her little boy Jaymie is nearly grown up. He was a toddler when we were doing *Hair!*

I might as well buy a house, then. And a new car, if I'm not going to have a baby. Instead, I get a job, the title role in *The Duchess of Malfi*, starting in October.

GB, impossible to refuse as always, persuades Elena to give us L'Escargot Restaurant in Greek Street for the party. We invite everyone who's ever shown support. For the first time ever, we don't have to think about budget.

I want to invite David Hirst.

'No way,' says Keith.

'Invite Gorgeous Gordon instead,' suggests GB. 'They can't do you for fraternising with the clerk, can they? It'd make his day.'

I don't think I'll do that. My husband Johnny has been the most loyal, unquestioning support throughout the trial. He knew nothing about Rock Bottom when he met me. The last four years must have been a bit of a shock. He's been unwavering. I shouldn't have potential squeezes there, even if they're pure fantasy. Not so easy: Oscar Beuselinck, John Wilmers, Nick Strauss, Keith Schilling, they're my team. I love them all. Especially Keith. Without him we would never have gone to trial. It had foundered so many times in the five years till he showed up. The dogged strength and purpose with which he seized a moribund case and pummelled it into being; nagged me and provoked me and encouraged me and believed me and simply wouldn't let it go. That's what gave me a new impetus to attack it again, through the heartache of trying to get pregnant, the hormone treatment that made me suicidal, the tubal surgery that didn't work. It would have been so much easier to let the case go and concentrate on being happily married. With Keith on the team, I managed to do Rock Bottom as well. He should be guest of honour.

Finding a date for the party was as fraught as any decision the four of us ever made. It was like trying to organise a rehearsal: it can't be before September as Di won't be free and the lawyers are all on their hols in August; it could be on September 23rd, Don's birthday, but he's got plans. Someone wants the end of September. I press for September 22nd, I want to catch the full moon. Amazingly, it works for everyone. We have an Indian summer right through September. The 22nd is one of those perfect, perfect evenings, still hot well into the night, a cloudless sky and Soho heaving. It's the first bit of London I got to know, filthy in every way, sleazy, lively, fascinating. L'Escargot in Greek Street is at the heart of it. We agree to show up early to greet our guests. And do I dress up! We sent out printed invitations, for goodness' sake. The only other time I did that was for my wedding. I intend to look my best. I certainly feel it.

I show up at six-thirty, without Johnny, who's not well. Gaye's on her own, too. Don has Jane, of course, and Di will come with Derek. The four of us plan to line up inside the door, just like a wedding, so we can greet and thank at the same time. It's so hot Elena has thrown open the beautiful front windows on the ground floor. At seven-fifteen, we're ready and waiting. Except Di.

'Where the fuck is she?'

'It doesn't matter, Annie. You know Di. She'll get here when she gets here.'

'We're the hosts. She has to be here.'

'Ha ha. No such thing with Di. Quick, stand by, here comes someone. Steady the buffs!'

Forty minutes later, the room is full of friends. Champagne flows, the chat is deafening. All of a sudden, people stream towards the front of the room as if by common consent. It's as if a liner is tilting and the passengers are sliding to starboard. We follow them as they crowd the doorway and hang out of the big open windows, laughing and cheering. When I get near the front, I see a powder-blue Rolls Royce trying and failing to park outside. It's too big for a normal parking bay. The passenger door opens and a dignified figure emerges. A bigger cheer. She waves regally and totters towards us.

So that's what she's done with her money. It's Di.

19

Fallout

Life rolls on down off the mountainside of the High Court and the lawyers and the judge and the judgement and the press reports and the cheques promised and paid in and the thanks and the farewells. Rolling towards a new life, a life based on dawning self-respect, acceptance and sudden financial security. And the knowledge we've achieved something huge, tangible and unprecedented.

We need time away from each other, we've got battle fatigue. Luckily I'm in rehearsals. *The Duchess of Malfi* is another mountain to climb, a very beautiful one, but I miss the lawyers, I miss the daily anxiety and hope and thinking and fretting.

GB calls. 'Darling, you have to stop your nonsense. We're all set up now, except you. You have all that money sitting in the bank and you're still rattling around in that dreadful old Morris Traveller. For goodness' sake buy yourself something decent. What's the matter with you?'

I'm in shock, I think, because it's all over. The good, the bad and the demanding. Rock Bottom doesn't need me anymore. It's grown up and left home. Yes, I'm in shock. And I'm bereft. Money can't fill that gap. Nor can it give me back my thirties, or my solo career or, for all of us, our one chance of superstardom. No amount of money can ever make up for that.

During the tour of *Duchess of Malfi*, I feel I'm putting on weight.

'You're not, dear, you're definitely not,' says my dresser.

But it hurts when she pulls the corset tight.

In between performances on matinee days, I'm so tired I have to lie down on the dressing-room floor. I'm bone weary, done in, despite a two-week holiday in Greece before rehearsals began. It's reaction, I know: no baby ever and the case finished. Apart from our tax position, which isn't finalised. That won't keep the adrenalin flowing. As the run goes on, I have to lie down on the floor in between scenes, in full costume, if only for five minutes. I love playing the Duchess, she's intelligent, charming, kind, brave, cultured, trapped. She's not giving me any trouble.

Smudge, my dog, doesn't agree. How come I called my dog Smudge, without realising it's Gaye's cat's name? In rehearsals, Smudge went mad when I was being strangled. On tour, she whimpers when she hears my death scene over the tannoy, she wants me out of there. But I love it. The beauty of the language, the heartbreak, the Duchess's serenity under torture, all those things make it so worthwhile. But when I'm not on stage, my eyelids won't stay open. I wonder whether I should see a doctor, but the touring schedule of two weeks in Oxford, then Taunton, then Bury St Edmunds doesn't give me much opportunity.

The week the tour's over, I collapse in terrible pain. It's a miscarriage.

'Prepare for six weeks of hell,' my doctor warns me. 'The hormones have gone into reverse, they're upset. You're going to have some black moods. But they won't last.'

He is so right. Over Christmas, for the first time in my life I think about ending things. In January, magically, I'm over it. Over the fatigue, too, which had been caused by the pregnancy. I'd misread the signs. I'd assumed they were a reaction to the bad news about my tubes being permanently blocked. They'd been so definite about it, I'd believed them. Now hope flares again, but briefly. I'm nearly forty-two, it's so late, the chances of it happening again so remote. We start to talk about adoption. Not that we can do that in England any more, private adoption has just been banned. We missed it by a whisker. Social Services turn us down. The child would notice how old we are at the school gates and it would upset him/her. In the face of this total bullshit, I get angry again and write all round the world. We'll go anywhere, I can afford it, thanks to Rock Bottom.

Johnny and I fall in love with a house in Primrose Hill, the first place I knew in London, where my grandmother lived when I was a little girl. The house is over-priced in the recession, Primrose Hill is far from fashionable. I spend a large part of my settlement money to pay the asking price.

In spring, Wilmers invites me, Johnny and Smudge over to their country cottage for the day. I tell him about the house.

'That's what I always wanted for you three,' he says, pleased. 'A decent roof over your heads with no mortgage. After tax.'

We laugh about Di's Rolls Royce.

'But she's all right. She already has a house.'

During a walk in the fields, with Smudge chasing blackbirds and charging after rabbits and June Wilmers engaging Johnny in conversation, John has a quiet word.

'You and Don? Whatever happened? I never understood. Both of you in meetings all the time, often with Jane, you never spoke to him, or he to you.'

'He dumped me after we lost Rock Bottom. Went off with Jane. She was a friend of mine. Or so I thought.'

Wilmers looks hard at me. 'How were you able to sit there with him, week after week? Sit next to him in court without killing him? *And* her?'

'I didn't see I had any choice. We had to keep meeting if the court case was to proceed.'

He shakes his head. 'Extraordinary.'

We tell them about us trying to adopt a baby. He and June are encouraging.

'I think that's very brave,' says June.

'I want to hear the minute you're successful,' says John. 'Which you will be. Keep us posted.'

I find a couple of possible routes to adopting outside the UK. The States are too expensive, you get sent from state to state, the lawyers make a fortune. Bolivia is possible, till it turns out to be a baby-trafficking route. I turn it down. Then a contact in Brazil. Johnny and I get on a plane to Rio de Janeiro. When we return, some months later, there are three of us, one of us very small and in a Moses basket. He sleeps almost the entire twelve hours of the flight back. Harry Leonardo.

I drop a note to John Wilmers saying I'd like to introduce Harry to him, giving him a short version of the Brazil adventure. June rings.

'Annabel, I have bad news. John's in hospital with advanced leukaemia. He's undergoing a course of chemotherapy. I read him your note. He smiled and gripped my hand. He can't speak, but I know he's very, very happy for you.'

A week later, she calls to say he's dead.

Keith calls. 'I think you should know.'

'What?'

'Gaye's going round town telling everyone you've adopted a Nazi baby.'

I'd kept the Brazil trip a secret, except for my sister, who helped me decide what to take in case we were successful, which was by no means definite. The thought of coming home with a bundle of unused nappies and baby clothes and baby milk and bottles and sterilisers and an empty Moses basket stopped me telling anyone else. Gaye must have been hurt. It takes nearly eight months before she's willing to meet him. Then we're fine again.

Letters start coming in about our tax position. How much we'll have to pay and when by and what we can do, if anything, to improve the position. None of us wants to part with more of our money than we can help. The lawyers suggest we declare ourselves a partnership. The document we'd already drawn up to say just that isn't legal. Or not legal enough for the tax man. To put it right, all of us to make a formal joint declaration now. If we get taxed as a partnership, not as individuals, it'll save us all thousands. At least that's what I grasp. We have to request them in writing to apply for it. All of us. Di doesn't answer any of their letters, or our phone calls, or our letters begging her to call so we can explain. She's gone AWOL, as only Di can. We know she's around, she's doing a show at the Donmar Warehouse. I worked there when GB was with the Royal Shakespeare Company. She took it for a Sunday night to celebrate her birthday, asking me to join her and also stage it. I had a ball dreaming up stunts, inviting friends (including Joanna Lumley, Chris Biggins, Jack Tinker and Matthew Kelly) to eat dinner at a table on stage (this is a small theatre), with food served from Joe Allen's restaurant, waiters crossing the stage with food during the show.

At the end of Gaye's set, I jumped out of a huge birthday cake singing Paul Simon's *Still Crazy After All These Years* slightly altered to *Still Thirty After All These Years* and smacked a real chocolate cream cake full in her face. Then I did my set. She came back on and did the same thing to me and I walked off singing my song from *Hair!—Easy to Be Hard*—covered in cake. We ended by doing a really stupid double act, calling ourselves The Uggly Sisters, wearing identical green lurex dresses and matching Jackie Kennedy wigs, belting out *Sisters* and *When You Walk through A Storm*. So we know the Donmar rather well. Di is going to be there for three weeks.

'Only thing to do, Annie. She won't answer the phone, she won't reply to the lawyers.'

'She never replies to lawyers.'

'Darling, shut up, we know that. The only way to make her understand is by seeing her in person, explain it ourselves.'

Gaye and I understood it well enough not to let it go, it was too important. First Thames stole our idea, then they screwed us over the settlement, buying one of us off with a huge sum, now the taxman's having his go. We said all along we were a group, Gaye, Di, Don and me, equal parts of a whole. A four-way partnership. Keith and Oscar were now telling us how we could all save money from the taxman. I never really understood the details, any more than Gaye did. But retaining more of our money we certainly got. It seemed like a good option. It just needed us all to agree, sign a piece of paper and the lawyers could apply for it. That meant Di as well. She'd played ostrich for years over Legal Aid, she was doing the same thing now. We had to have her on board.

'Did you write yet?'

'Yes, of course.'

'Any answer?'

'Don't be silly.'

'I left three messages on her answerphone. I said lunch, tea, supper after the show—made it really cheerful, too. Nothing. I think she's avoiding us.'

'Of course she's avoiding us.'

Then Gaye's brainwave. 'Got it, Bird's Egg. We'll go round after the show and take her for a meal. Take her to Joe Allen. She couldn't say no to that. Explain everything. Get her to sign. Done deal. You know what I'm saying?'

I knew. Once we were together again, it'd be sorted. A great idea, one of Gaye's best. Catch her after the show one night and drag her off for dinner. Brilliant!

Off we went to surprise Di at the Donmar. Unfortunately, Di surprised us rather more. It backfired badly. In fact, it was catastrophic. Gaye collapsed in loud sobs, I was so shocked I burst into uncomprehending laughter and a Di I didn't know stormed out to the ladies' loo across the hall, swearing hard, slamming the door and, by the sound of it, kicking the toilet.

Afterwards, we stand on the corner of St Martin's Lane at Seven Dials, Gaye still blowing her nose.

'What happened in there?'

'I don't know.'

'You know her best.'

'I don't.'

'What the hell did she say in there?'

'I don't know, Annie. I don't want to talk about it. Let it go. Not our problem.'

'Whaddya mean, not our problem? Of course, it's—'

'Let it go, Annie. Move on.'

'But we can't just—'

'Shut up, Annie. It's over with Di. I've had it with that girl. *Finito.* I'm off to catch my train.'

When Gaye slams a door, it stays slammed. I don't remember us ever mentioning it again. The shock of Di's rage stopped my brain. Could I even remember why we went to the Donmar in the first place? She was a fox in a trap, snarling and scratching. She cursed and yelled and stamped till the stage manager appeared. 'I'm afraid I'm going to ask you ladies to leave,' she said. 'The audience can hear you all the way down the street.'

Gaye, sobbing noisily into a Kleenex, got up and stumbled out. I followed her. It wasn't us, *we* weren't shouting. We were friendly and cheerful throughout, weren't we? Loud, obviously, we're always loud. Di was burying her head in the sand and it was affecting us all. We *had* to see her. We didn't do anything wrong except show up. When the volcano erupted, I didn't see it coming. Di, who never shouted, never got caught up in Gaye's exaggerated dramas over lovers, harmonies or the price of olive oil. Di, who could handle any tricky situation with the assurance of a lifetime's practice, *Di* cracked. The volcano spewed out fury, melted the dressing-room furniture, blew out the windows, seared my brain. And I stood there and laughed.

The way she screamed in our faces, the fury, the passion, were so shocking, so unexpected, that although I laughed, I was devastated. I'd never seen Di like that, I had no idea why she was angry with us, I didn't understand where it came from or why.

All I knew was if it were wartime, I'd be shot for cowardice. That kind of violence I can't deal with, so I don't. I can't remember anything she said. Something about money, maybe. Something about being betrayed? Possibly. GB was as shocked as me, but she collapsed at once. I took longer.

We both end up wounded.

The silence is deafening. I should pick up the phone, but I can't. I could write to her and I don't. I'm no good with naked in-your-face fury, I shut down. Gaye and I are all right, I can call her any time. But I can't make contact with Di. I tell myself that after such a major upheaval over so many years, we all need recovery time. The only thing to do is give in, pay whatever tax we owe as individuals and get on with our lives. As John Wilmers always said, we've all got a house, we're secure.

So that's what I do. I get on with my life. I give in to Gaye and buy a new car and Johnny and I move to our house in Primrose Hill with the baby and we get divorced and I have to sell the Primrose Hill house and move out of London and life goes on and so does my acting: a few feature films—*Mussolini* with George C. Scott, *Defence of The Realm*, *Wimbledon*; several television series; *Jeffrey Bernard Is Unwell* in the West End with the divine Peter O'Toole, *Honk! The Ugly Duckling*, a musical at the National (all three of us do different musicals at the National at different times), a one-woman show I devise using some of Don's and my songs; cabaret, teaching, coaching, directing, singing. A bit of writing.

Gaye rents out rooms in her Balham house to lodgers who all become her friends forever, Charley's nannies ditto, continues to have stormy affairs that never end well, does three years in *42nd Street* in the West End, plus *The Ratepayers' Iolanthe* playing Margaret Thatcher, *Relative Values* and loads of other films, sells her Balham house, moves to Muswell Hill, her boy Charley grows up and leaves home, she sells up and moves to Normandy.

And Di? I don't know. Once when Gaye and I are singing

Bosom Buddies together at a charity Sunday night show at the Palladium, sharing a dressing-room with Judi Dench, Virginia McKenna and Sian Phillips, I go to the Green Room to get some coffee and bump straight into Di. She's in the show as well, only neither of us knew. We hug wordlessly with tears in our eyes and she's gone. I know she's in shows: *The Rink, Follies*. We each do television shows—*Bergerac, Boon, Minder*, but not in the same episodes. The only show I catch her in is *I'm Getting My Act Together*, in which she's brilliant. I don't go backstage afterwards.

That's all I know about her. A complete and total blanket of silence for twenty years. Di's eliminated me not only from her past but her present. And I have done the same, I've given up on her, she's lost to me. It's worse than bereavement in a way, because she's there, still in the same business, still working, as if Rock Bottom never existed, as if *I* never existed. How can I accept this complete rift without knowing what caused it? It's so painful, I bury it, my usual pattern.

Meanwhile, my fortunes fluctuate. Harry's a teenager, money's tight. After a disastrous two years out of London, where I'm cut off from everything familiar, satisfying and creative, I spend what's left of my Rock Bottom money buying back in North London, where I belong. House prices went up 40% while I was away, so the best I can afford is a tiny ex-council maisonette on the Horton Gardens Housing Estate, next to the Finchley Road. I have a lovely garden and just room for a lodger as well as bedrooms for Harry and me. It's not Primrose Hill, but I'm just relieved to be back in London. And so grateful to darling John Wilmers for making sure I had enough money to bring up a child and keep a roof over our heads. I can now work without travelling an extra four to five hours a day. I can shop at Waitrose on the Finchley Road like I used to. I can settle down again after the turbulence of divorce, moving house and leaving London. I'm back where I belong. Life returns slowly to normal.

Till one day, out of the blue, on my way back from the Residents'
Association Committee meeting for the Horton Gardens Estate
in Swiss Cottage, I get a phone call. *That* phone call. And life
turns upside down again.

'Annie? Annie?'

It's Di-Di.

20

Phone Call

Kilburn, London 2004

Two days. I have two days. Di's little house was always immaculate, mine never is. I run round like a demented whirlwind to receive guests. Di must have a proper domestic routine: furniture polish, yellow dusters, carpet beaters, folded clothes in neat piles in chests of drawers, probably colour-coded. The smell of lavender and beeswax fills her house, you smell it as you walk in. When her boy Jaymie was small, maybe six or seven, she stood in our kitchen in West Kensington, bent over the rickety ironing-board. On the chair next to her was a pile of small tee-shirts, pressed and folded.

'What on earth are you doing, Di?' I asked.

She paused and looked up, pushing strands of curly dark hair off her flushed face.

'Jaymie's off to his grandma's for a few days.'

'Yes, but—'

She was ironing his little socks and underpants, for goodness' sake.

'There's no need to look like that, Annie. I can't help it. I gotta have everything nice, that's all.'

'Nice? It's beautiful! But what the point of—'

She blushed. 'I know it's stupid.'

I laughed. 'Not stupid, darling. Just I can't imagine why. The minute he puts them on they'll be ruined.'

She grinned. 'But they'll all be lovely for him when he opens his little case, see? And his grandma'll know I'm doin' my job.'

I was silenced. I'd never ironed underwear, even for myself. The haphazard housewife, that's me. Like my mother, who never noticed dog hairs, dirt or dust. Now I notice—finally. But not as part of my daily life. Even in this tiny maisonette, there don't seem to be enough hours in the day for much housework. Di's standards are much, much higher. I have two days.

While I was sweeping and tidying and putting away and shopping for champagne and blinis, olives and crackers, my mind was free to roam. Oh, it did. It roamed all right. Flitted like a frightened bat: twenty years since…thirty years since… *help!* I rubbed furniture polish and apprehension into the gate-leg folding table that serves as my dining-table and work desk, a frenzy of fear into the floorboards. I mopped down the front step and wiped the dusty drip-marks off the green window-box, dead-headed the geraniums, weeded the flowerbed, mowed the lawn. And wondered.

Wondered which Di is coming. The one I've known and loved since September, 1968? Or her twin, who arrived without warning like an avenging angel that night in 1984? I should have expected it, of course, she's the Gemini of the group. Gaye, Annie, Di: *Pisces, Aries, Gemini.* I've always loved Geminis. They come right out to meet you. For shy people, they're a gift, a solace. They light up the space you stand in, you're warmed by their presence, their beam of generosity. That's how I'd always thought of her. Her other side, the twin, was revealed, I thought, by her need for sudden, unscripted disappearance. 'Oh you know Di,' we'd say when she failed to show up, or call, or do a recording, 'She's gone walkabout.' The minute she *did* show, we forgave. Her presence so envelops you, you forget the blank spaces in between.

In Di's case, Gemini must mean triplets, not twins. Because what appeared backstage at the Donmar Warehouse in 1984 was neither the divine Di or the unreliable Di, it was a Di I could never have dreamed up, a Di I would never get over. I didn't want that Di in my life. Not now. Not ever.

The Di I loved was always ready with a chuckle and a grin, immersed in the music, always straight from the heart. Two o'clock in the morning, perched on the bar at The Casserole, short skirt, legs crossed, perfect ballet poise, roaring out *Blueberry Hill*. Taking the hand of the big drunk who'd jumped on me from behind and saying sweetly to him, 'Yer just lookin fer the way out, arncher? This way, love.' He followed her like a lamb. Di in November on the North End Road, high heels, peep-toes, cleavage down to her navel, complaining about being whistled at. Di was Di.

After that row, after Gaye's tears were dry and long forgotten, and my laughter had died away, Gaye was healed and I stayed stricken. On a whim, the spin of a sixpence, the crack of a starting pistol only she could hear, Di had revealed another side, proved she was a true Gemini and created an unspoken, unbreachable chasm between us. Now, twenty years later, unprompted, she's asking to see me. I have no idea why, any more than I knew why she'd flown into demented rage in 1984. I'm terrified. And I can't wait. Expect the unexpected, it's Di-Di.

Purdey barks and I blink, jerked back into the present and my little maisonette. What on earth am I doing? In one hand I have a duster, in the other, my gold, once jewel-encrusted, knee-high Rock Bottom boots. Purdey yelps again, scrabbling at the French windows. Outside, two squirrels chase each other up and down the apple tree, leaping and scrambling. I slide the door open for Purdey to squeeze out and bound for the tree, leaving me staring at the boots.

Not many jewels left. I can see where they once were, though. Brown glue-marks on the gold, in regular blobs around the top, down the outside and on the curve of the toe cap. I remember exactly when I got them, in the shoe shop smack in the middle of the North End Road market in 1974. Huge platform soles, from there up shaped just right for my skinny legs, fitting close over the calf and up to the knee. Platforms are surprisingly easy to wear and much less painful than stilettos, the only problem is falling off and breaking an ankle. Not that I cared about that. Not when Rock Bottom was involved.

There is one jewel left, right at the top of the left boot, bright green glass. I spit on the duster and shine it up. Not good enough, not for Di-Di. I take the boots to the kitchen, dampen a sponge, cover the tiny breakfast table with newspaper and give them the attention they deserve. Wherever I've lived, whatever's been packed away in cardboard boxes, stuck in storage or a loft or a lock-up cupboard, the boots are on display, testimony that I was once in a rock group, the first—and only—three-woman rock group in England. Di, Gaye and me. Of everything I've ever done, I'm proudest of Rock Bottom.

Proud of the boots, too. The cheapest in the market, £4 cash, nasty tan leather. I got gold spray, silver and gold glitter dust, I picked out from my sewing box all the shiny buttons, sequins, fake marcasite and coloured glass, cutting bits off cushions and jackets waiting to be altered. I sprayed the boots gold, poisoning myself with the fumes. I shook glitter over the toe caps before the gold had dried. I glued my best baubles all over the damn things and had the best time doing it. When I walked out on stage that first time in 1974 and then every other time, I felt like a million dollars, the roar from the audience lifting me off the floor. We became female giants stalking over our territory, glorying in our power.

Never felt anything like it, before or since. I never will again. My group, my wonderful Rock Bottom. It was Gaye's idea to ask Di. All I wanted was to form the group. We formed it without even meeting: Gaye knew Di, I knew Gaye, Di knew me. We'd never been all together in one room. The band had no name. It didn't exist. I dreamt it up, I dragged it into being, I loved it, fought over it and lost it.

Now I put champagne in the fridge, best glasses ready on a tray, and run round dusting, polishing, grabbing flowers from the garden for the spare room, every now and then stopping to hug Purdey and grin. My gold Rock Bottom boots gleam from my hard work. Shiny enough for Di, or anyway the best I can do. I keep thinking of her phone call: 'Annie? Annie? It's Di. Di Langton.' Me bursting into tears.

After I'd put the phone down, I poured myself a drink, still in shock. And wept some more. Not only did she ring me, she wanted to see me, to explain. After twenty years. She's coming to stay. Harry's gone to university, so there's room. She'll be here in two days. To my amazement, this isn't scar tissue, the wound is alive and bleeding. It all comes back, fresh as spring, the whole mess of the group that never was, that might have been, my dream of thirty years ago, three friends having the time of our lives singing together, changing the world for ourselves and other women, all shapes and sizes, not perfect and groomed and packaged, but open and real and funny and raw. The biggest adventure I could imagine. We so nearly got there.

Suddenly thirty years doesn't seem such a long time after all, not if Di's speaking to me.

When the phone rings again the next morning, hope slumps to the floor. Of course I know who it'll be, no doubt at all. True to form, she'll have changed her mind, she'll have a job to go to, she can't come after all. I wonder why I bother to answer it. Habit, I suppose.

I go through the dreary routine and pick up the phone.

'Hello?'

Pause. Crackle. Interference.

'Annie?'

Louder: 'Annie?'

It's not Di, it's Gaye, calling from France.

'Annie, I'm coming to London. I'm up for something big.'

'That's great, GB. What is it?'

Gaye won't say. 'Just in case it comes to nothing, darling, not going to tempt fate.'

She doesn't trust me, she thinks I might put myself up for it.

'How long are you here for?'

'Just a night or so. Could you put me up?'

Both of them asking to stay? Christ!

'Of course, you can come, Harry's away. When will it be?'

'Thursday.'

Thursday? That's when Di's coming.

I don't know how they feel about each other. Still less do I know how all three of us will be together. It makes me nervous. Very nervous, actually. I tell Gaye about Di.

She shrieks with laughter. 'What could be better? I'll bring champagne. You do dinner, darling.'

Di will have no chance to explain anything to me. My little maisonette is shrinking fast as I imagine us all staying under one roof for the first time ever. Anything could happen. It certainly did last time we met.

That was in 1984. Twenty years ago. Shit!

'Annie, stop worrying, it'll be fine. If Di has Things To Say, I'll be gone in the morning. You'll have all the time in the world. We'll have a great night, you'll see.'

I do see. It could be terrific. Couldn't it?

'And forget cooking dinner, we'll go out. You think of somewhere nice. It'll be like old times. We'll invite Straker. And Rankin. And anyone else you like. Ta-ta. See you Thursday. I've got news, too, but it can wait.'

So I plan The Reunion.

It'll either be a total disaster or the best thing that's ever happened.

21

Reunion

I meet her at the door, heart thudding, tea-towel twisted in my hand. It's a small step down to pavement level. It feels like a chasm. I stand in the doorway, the latch hard and cold against my trembling fingers, the sunlight glancing off the windows opposite a searchlight in my eyes. The thick smell of geranium hangs in the air.

I almost can't look. Or speak. It's twenty years. I lay in bed counting them most of last night. 1984, I think, I *know*. It was summer time then, too. The heat rose off the lights and the audience in the tiny Donmar Warehouse. No air-conditioning in theatres then. Thin walls, thinner than I'd ever thought walls could be, after the show. GB and I slipped in at the curtain-call, schoolgirls flouting the regulations, sat on the stairs watching the performers grin and duck their heads and bow knees in stage humility. Di does it to perfection. There's something about the way she points her front toe, foot placed just so in front of the other one, something about the curve of her ankle, graceful, balanced, something only years of training can give. Something about her face, lifted to the applause, drinking it in, beaming back. It made us proud.

Now here she is at my front door, in the same perfect ballet position, with an armful of flowers, neat little overnight case, vast cleavage, black eyeliner, hair bleach-blonde again as it was in *Hair!* Short as ever, and a lot wider. Stout, even.

And a look of mute terror on her face.

In the silence, a train rattles by on its way to Finchley Road Station.

'Di-Di?' in a gasp.

'Annie?' in a croak.

The space between us vanishes. Arms round necks, mascara down cheeks, laughing, patting, screeching relief. Flowers squashed, case dropped, tea-towel dabbing eyes. Purdey leaps round and round in an agony of excitement, trying to find a way in to all this love. There's no room, even for a dog. Twenty years of waiting and wondering and dread gone, wiped away forever. Abracadabra.

'Oh Annie, I'm so relieved. I thought you mightn't want to see me.'

'Not want to—? You idiot, I've been waiting twenty years for this. I thought I'd never see you again.'

After clasping each other and re-clasping and hugging and patting and exclaiming over each other's haircuts, I go to the fridge and bring out the Dom Perignon.

'Not too early, is it? Not for this!'

'Oh, Annie, that's what I came to tell you. Well, one of the things. I don't drink no more.'

I stare at her, foil half off the bottle. 'What?'

Di looks down.

'And another thing.'

It's no good rushing Di. Or pushing or leading or pleading. She has to do things her way. I put the champagne back in the fridge and boil the kettle while she makes little pleats in her skirt and gazes out of the window.

'Nice place you got here, Annie,' she ventures. 'Your garden's a treat.'

'My pride and joy,' I reply, getting a tray and cups and saucers and milk and the biscuit tin. 'It's the first time I've ever had a hobby. Shall we have tea outside? It's too hot in here.'

'Oh!' she exclaims. 'I haven't got that one!'

She's looking at a Rock Bottom photo, framed and on the wall. It's not just the gold boots on display wherever I live, it's the photos, too. And Stephen's cartoon.

'I'll make you a copy,' I promise her.

'Oh!' she says again, catching sight of my Rock Bottom boots, glowing to the right of the fireplace, as clean as I could make them, still with the shadows of the sequins and buttons and bits of glass jewellery, the piece of bottle-green glass still in place.

'Oh!' she says. 'I love them boots.'

'Me, too.'

We stand for a second side by side, looking at them. She squeezes my hand.

'Let's go out, then.'

The garden is in riot. I've got roses and honeysuckle up the wire dividing fence on one side, the apple tree in front of us with clematis climbing right through it and the border by the south-facing wall blazing with drifts of love-in-a-mist, evening primrose, blue and white solanum, tomato plants, sweet peas and anything else I could cram in that likes sun.

We sit and drink our tea. I wait.

'The thing is, Annie.' Di hesitates and looks down at her tea cup. A blackbird sings in the little tree behind her.

'The thing is, I've had a rough time with work recently. I haven't had any for over a year.'

I'm shocked. Di is the one person who is never, ever, out of work.

'I know, Annie, I know. I bin so lucky till now. I'm very frightened. I dunno what to do.'

She sips her tea.

'What does your agent say?'

'Her? She does nothing. We don't speak.'

'Oh, Di. That's no good. Weren't you with Barry Burnett?'

'Not any more. I was so stupid, Annie, I dumped him.

Thought I could do better. I hurt him so much, I know. Shouldn't have done it, but I did. I done a lot of things—'

I top up her tea and wait some more. This can't be easy for her.

'The thing is,' she says, 'the thing is, being out of work all this time, I got to think a bit. And...and...I realised some things.'

'Did you?' I say cautiously.

'Yes. I did. Not very nice things, if you know what I mean. Anyway, I...I'm sitting in the garden by the pool, trying to paint me toenails, though I've put on so much weight I can't reach... and that sets me off. I start crying and crying and thinking of all the things I done wrong. The people I hurt. Then I mop myself up a bit and have a cup of tea and then I pick up the phone and ring you, don't I? Right away before I lose my nerve.'

Pause.

'That's why I rung, Annie. I want to say sorry. Try to put things right.'

My friendly robin is on the lawn a few feet away, his head cocked on one side, looking for crumbs. Below us, the Metropolitan line rumbles through to Finchley Road and Harrow. I pour more tea and wait.

'That row we had.'

'Yes?'

'I know I went berserk. I couldn't help it, I was so rattled when you two showed up. I'd had a terrible show and it was so hot in there, Annie. I had all these flipping letters I should've opened. I knew it was wrong not to. So I felt really guilty.'

Another pause. She takes a deep breath.

'And I was angry because you got more money than me. That's God's truth. Angry and hurt. And I took it out on you. It wasn't your fault, I can see it now, I never could understand those bloody letters so I never read them. You're clever, Annie, you'd have understood what the lawyer meant. And it made me mad. I felt stupid, see? And I lashed out.'

Pause.

'And I'm so, so sorry.'

Tears are pouring down my face again. I put my cup down, wipe a few away and take her hand. We sit in silence, while the shadows lengthen on the lawn, Purdey at our feet, head on my sandal.

Drrrring! goes the doorbell. Purdey barks and runs in.

I look at my watch. 'Fuck! That'll be GB.'

'What? You never said, Annie. Fuck! I got mascara everywhere, so've you. Oh well. It's only Gaye.'

'Only Gaye??'

At this, we burst out laughing.

'Coming!' I yell and together we go to greet Rock Bottom Number Three, the other force of nature.

'Di! Annie! What larks, Pip! Shut up, Purdey. Take this, would you, darling? And stick this in the fridge. Where the fuck do I put the car round here? Oh, great. Sorted, then. Where's the champagne? Christ, Annie, the place is looking good, what's going on? When I first saw it, Di, I despaired. The kitchen was covered in Sixties orange and brown daisy tiles—hideous beyond belief—the hallway was dark—and the wallpaper! You've done miracles, given what it is. Still got that ridiculous kitsch fireplace, I see. At least you got rid of that appalling chandelier. What? In the garden? Let's have a look. Oh, that's funny. Really comic. In the apple tree. You're barking. You know it's hot enough to fry eggs on the pavement today? What? Oh yes, here they are. Only two glasses? You're getting more Scottish by the minute, Annie. Who's the teetotaller here? Certainly not me. Jesus, Di, not you, is it? Obviously not. Must be you, Annie. Another one bites the dust, eh? Oh. Never mind. On antibiotics, are you? I never take any notice of that myself. Get another glass, Annie, it's not every day we get together, girls, is it? Let's go into the garden, I have to take the weight off my feet.'

She collapses on the garden bench, shrugs her shoes off, puts her feet up on the wooden table and looks around. 'Oh my goodness, darling, this is a total transformation. No, not the chandelier, idiot, the whole thing. It's divine. I could almost live here myself. How brilliant you've been. Who would've thought you could make anything out of this poky little—cheers, girls! Together again! To friendship!'

We clink my best champagne glasses, Di's one full of sparkling water.

'To friendship!'

It's the best thing. The best thing that's ever happened. We slide into the old relationship like a hand into a silk glove. Louder than that, closer than that, funnier than that. We sit in my garden drinking, shrieking, giggling. Friends arrive: Straker, Liz White from the *Hair!* company, Mel Smith who is Straker's director and my neighbour with whom we've all worked over the years. More champagne. We all go off to The Ripe Tomato, a restaurant run by our friend Ethel, also once in *Hair!* Our collective energy could run the National Grid. At three in the morning, we shoo the stragglers away and stagger up my thin staircase, clutching the bannisters, groaning with laughter.

'This is ridiculous, Annie. Just like old times. We might as well do the show right here.'

'Come on, girls, this is amazing. Just like we always were. Let's start again. Let's just do it.'

'We'll write a sequel. *The Band That Never Was.* We'll do our own TV series and show 'em all.'

'All the blokes do it.'

'Do what?'

'Re-form. Go out on the road when they want to. Why shouldn't we?'

Why not indeed?

The End

(for now)

Acknowledgements

I have had as much support writing this book as we had getting the group off the ground in the first place, especially from:

GB and Di-Di, for their extraordinary recall of vital moments;

Susan Elderkin, the best creative writing teacher and mentor anyone could have; and her Pennard House group, who carry on the good work;

Judy Rich, in whose front room I acquired the habit of writing;

Susan Pleat, for giving up her own writing time to look at my efforts;

Claire Fennell, whose editing skills made this book a whole lot more readable;

Keith Schilling and Nick Strauss for their generosity, kindness and expert advice;

Brian Winston, who, as a hugely respected professor of film, found time to edit the book for me;

David Fowler of Farthings Publishing, who courteously pushed me towards publication;

Robert Lipson and Trish Bertram for their endless support with social media, music and technical stuff.

Finally and especially: David Aukin and Nancy Meckler, whose unending support, kindness, counsel, humour, wisdom and analytical skills helped me rework a rough draft into a complete script.

Annabel Leventon

Won a scholarship to Oxford and then to LAMDA. Nominated as Actress of the Year for her first leading role in London in the original production of rock musical *Hair!*, she has since played many times in the West End, including *Jeffrey Bernard Is Unwell* (with Peter O'Toole), *The Dresser* (directed by Sir Peter Hall) and *Noel and Gertie*. She played Sir Andrew Aguecheek for the Royal Shakespeare Company, a dyke chicken for The National Theatre and many roles in television and film, including *M. Butterfly* (directed by David Cronenberg) *Le Mur de l'Atlantique* and *The Rocky Horror Picture Show*. She regularly performs cabaret at Brasserie Zedel and The Pheasantry. She has devised and written several shows for theatre, directed several others and co-produced and co-written a film, *Camille and Ben*. This is her first book.